The Creative Curriculum® for Preschool, Sixth Edition

Volume 3: Literacy

Cate Heroman, Candy Jones, Heather Baker

 TeachingStrategies® · Bethesda, MD

Teaching Strategies, LLC
Bethesda, Maryland

www.TeachingStrategies.com

978-1-60617-700-6

Library of Congress Control Number: 2016934946

Printed and bound in China
2024   2023   2022   2021   2020
13   12   11   10   9   8   7   6   5

Contents

How to Use This Book. vi

Chapter 1.   Components of Literacy 1

Literacy as a Source of Enjoyment 4
What Does Research Say?   6
The Teacher's Role in Promoting Literacy as a Source of Enjoyment   7

Vocabulary and Language 9
What Does Research Say?   10
The Teacher's Role in Promoting Vocabulary and
Language Development   11

Phonological Awareness 13
What Does Research Say?   16
The Teacher's Role in Promoting Phonological Awareness   17

Knowledge of Print 19
What Does Research Say?   21
The Teacher's Role in Promoting Knowledge of Print   22

Letters and Words 25
What Does Research Say?   26
The Teacher's Role in Promoting Knowledge of Letters and Words   27

Comprehension 29
What Does Research Say?   31
The Teacher's Role in Promoting Comprehension   32

Books and Other Texts 34
What Does Research Say?   36
The Teacher's Role in Promoting Understandings About Books
and Other Texts   37

Chapter 2.   Planning Your Literacy Program 38

Objectives for Language and Literacy Learning 41

Creating a Literacy-Rich Environment 43

Literacy Throughout the Day 45

Meeting the Needs of All Children 49

Supporting English-Language Learners   49

Supporting Advanced Language and Literacy Learners   58

Supporting Children With Disabilities   59

Guide to Implementation 61

Chapter 3. Teaching Strategies 64

Talking, Singing, and Playing With Language 66

How to Begin   67

Supporting Children's Oral Language Learning   69

Reading Aloud 75

How to Begin   76

Effective Ways to Read Aloud   78

Storytelling 88

How to Begin   89

Telling Stories With Children   91

Story Retelling 97

How to Begin   97

Supporting Children's Story Retelling   99

Writing 103

How to Begin   104

Supporting Children's Writing   107

Meaningful Play 112

How to Begin   113

Supporting Children's Play   114

Studies: Using Literacy to Learn 118

Beginning the Study   118

Investigating the Topic   121

Concluding the Study   123

Chapter 4. Literacy Learning in Interest Areas and Outdoors 124

The Library Area as the Hub of Literacy Learning 126

Creating an Effective Library Area   126

Observing and Responding to Children   128

Interacting With Children in the Library Area   130

Special Challenges in the Library Area   133

Literacy in the Block Area 135
Using Blocks to Teach Literacy Skills   137
Observing Children's Understanding   138

Literacy in the Dramatic Play Area 139
Using Dramatic Play to Teach Literacy Skills   143
Observing Children's Understanding   144

Literacy in the Toys and Games Area 145
Using Toys and Games to Teach Literacy Skills   146
Observing Children's Understanding   147

Literacy in the Art Area 148
Using Art Materials to Teach Literacy Skills   150
Observing Children's Understanding   152

Literacy in the Discovery Area 153
Using Discovery Materials to Teach Literacy Skills   155
Observing Children's Understanding   157

Literacy in the Sand and Water Area 158
Using Sand and Water to Teach Literacy Skills   160
Observing Children's Understanding   161

Literacy in the Music and Movement Area 161
Using Music and Movement to Teach Literacy Skills   164
Observing Children's Understanding   166

Literacy in the Cooking Area 166
Using Cooking to Teach Literacy Skills   170
Observing Children's Understanding   171

Literacy in the Technology Area 172
Using Technology to Teach Literacy Skills   174
Observing Children's Understanding   176

Literacy Outdoors 177
Using the Outdoors to Teach Literacy Skills   180
Observing Children's Understanding   181

References 182

Index 196

How to Use This Book

The Creative Curriculum® for Preschool, Volume 3: Literacy is a critical part of Teaching Strategies' language and literacy program. This volume expands on the information provided in *The Creative Curriculum® for Preschool, Volume 1: The Foundation*, showing how and why oral language and literacy can and should be part of children's everyday experiences and activities. It discusses early literacy learning and explains when and how to teach directly the skills and knowledge children need to become successful readers and writers.

Chapter 1, The Components of Literacy, discusses the essential skills, knowledge, and understandings that preschool children need in order to become competent and confident readers and writers. It reviews the research about each component and explains what teachers can do to help children progress. The seven components are 1) literacy as a source of enjoyment, 2) vocabulary and language, 3) phonological awareness, 4) knowledge of print, 5) letters and words, 6) comprehension, and 7) books and other texts. Readers who want to learn even more than what this book presents can use the research citations as a starting point for further study.

Chapter 2, Planning Your Literacy Program, helps you get started. To plan, you have to know exactly what children already know and what you want them to learn. This chapter therefore begins with an at-a-glance chart of the 38 curricular objectives and calls your particular attention to the 10 objectives that address language, literacy, and English language acquisition. They will guide your observation and planning, so you will see references to these objectives throughout the book. Because the physical environment has a powerful effect on children's learning, we explain how to create a literacy-rich classroom that includes a wide range of materials that encourage children to engage in oral language experiences, reading, and writing. We also show how every event of the day, from children's arrival to their departure, is an opportunity to promote oral language and literacy skills. Because some children have special needs, this chapter offers specific strategies for children who are English-language learners, children with disabilities, children with advanced abilities or experience, and children who have not yet had rich language and literacy experiences. The chapter concludes with a step-by-step guide for planning your literacy program.

Chapter 3, Teaching Strategies, introduces seven aspects of teaching early literacy: talking, singing, and playing with language; reading aloud; storytelling; story retelling; writing; supporting children's literacy learning through play; and using studies to promote literacy. As you read about them, reflect on your current teaching practices. While most of these strategies are probably familiar to you, think about how you are using them. Consider how you can use them throughout the day in a more intentional way.

Chapter 4, Literacy Learning in Interest Areas, invites you to reconsider your interest areas as the context for literacy learning. The chapter begins with a discussion of the Library area, which is the hub of literacy learning in *The Creative Curriculum*® classroom. The discussions of the remaining nine interest areas and the outdoors are formatted in the same way. The first section of each discussion looks at everyday experiences that typically occur in the area and points out their relationship to literacy learning. As you evaluate your interest areas, use the suggestions from this chapter to include literacy-related materials and books. The discussions also include suggestions about how to scaffold children's learning as they engage in everyday experiences in the area. A final section helps you observe children's understanding while working in the area.

The Creative Curriculum® *for Preschool, Volume 3: Literacy* can be used in a variety of ways. Teachers can use it to broaden their understanding of literacy and learn appropriate strategies to support children's literacy learning. It can also serve as the content for focused professional development efforts, either in study groups or learning teams, or as part of ongoing training. Teachers could learn about a specific component and accompanying strategies and then practice them in the classroom. These classroom experiences can be discussed at later sessions with colleagues. In addition, teacher mentors can model particular strategies, demonstrate how the major components of literacy are addressed, and then coach teachers in their use of the techniques explained in this book.

The Components of Literacy

Literacy as a Source of Enjoyment 4
What Does Research Say?
The Teacher's Role in Promoting Literacy as
    a Source of Enjoyment

Vocabulary and Language 9
What Does Research Say?
The Teacher's Role in Promoting
    Vocabulary and Language Development

Phonological Awareness 13
What Does Research Say?
The Teacher's Role in Promoting
    Phonological Awareness

Knowledge of Print 19
What Does Research Say?
The Teacher's Role in Promoting Knowledge
    of Print

Letters and Words 25
What Does Research Say?
The Teacher's Role in Promoting Knowledge
    of Letters and Words

Comprehension 29
What Does Research Say?
The Teacher's Role in Promoting Comprehension

Books and Other Texts 34
What Does Research Say?
The Teacher's Role in Promoting Understandings About
    Books and Other Texts

The Components of Literacy

As an early childhood teacher, you know the importance of language and literacy learning. You know that literacy learning depends upon more than teaching the ABCs, introducing children to environmental print, setting up a Library area, or clapping out the syllables of a word. Language and literacy are tools for thinking and communicating. When teachers plan meaningful ways for children to use language and literacy as tools, children are motivated to become readers and writers, and they learn about the features, forms, and functions of written and spoken language.

Young children seek to be part of a social group and to communicate with the important people in their lives, first orally and later through print. While young children might not use sophisticated communication strategies, they are definitely eager to share urgent thoughts, ideas, needs, and feelings. Their desire to communicate and participate in the classroom community motivates young children to persist in the often challenging tasks of early literacy. Because literacy learning is based on continuous interactions with knowledgeable adults, teachers who use *The Creative Curriculum®* integrate oral and written language experiences into their overall, comprehensive programs.

This approach recognizes that play is an essential part of preschool children's learning. The skills children learn through purposeful, productive, high-level play—skills in verbalization, vocabulary, language comprehension, problem solving, observation, empathy, imagination, assuming another's perspective, using symbols, and learning to cooperate with others—are foundational skills for all cognitive development (Olfman, 2003). *The Creative Curriculum®* explains how to maximize children's learning during play by thoughtfully observing children, reflecting on what children are doing, and planning ways to guide and extend learning. This process is also used to plan appropriate direct instruction.

In order to create a high-quality literacy program, teachers must understand the components of literacy. The components described in this chapter and in the research literature are the basis for the intentional teaching strategies described later. An understanding of the components is necessary in order for teachers to observe children effectively and to assess and evaluate their development and learning. Then the teacher can decide which strategies and activities best support the literacy development of a particular child or group of children. These are the seven components of literacy: literacy as a source of enjoyment, vocabulary and language, phonological awareness, knowledge of print, letters and words, comprehension, and books and other texts.

Literacy as a Source of Enjoyment

When children enjoy having books read to them and when they are excited about what they are hearing and learning, children are motivated to learn to read and, later, read to learn. Children's vocabularies increase as they are introduced to new words in meaningful contexts, and then it is easier for the children to read those words when they encounter them in print. Children practice reading more often when they find it enjoyable and useful. By reading a lot, children increase their fluency, or the ease and accuracy with which they recognize words and comprehend the text.

Most preschool children do not read yet. A central goal is to introduce young children to the power and pleasure of literacy. A love of reading can begin long before children start formal schooling. When a family member holds a child and reads aloud, the child begins to experience reading as a pleasurable activity. Those experiences later inspire the child to persist through the often difficult stages of literacy learning. Not all children have had these enjoyable experiences, so it is essential to provide positive literacy experiences in the preschool classroom.

A child who enjoys literacy activities will probably participate during interactive read-aloud times, notice print in the environment, ask questions about the meaning of print (e.g., *What does that say?*), and spend time reading once he or she is able. Teachers consider a variety of ways to motivate children and help them experience the power and pleasure of literacy learning. Keep the following questions in mind as you think about how you help children experience literacy as a source of enjoyment:

Positive Role Models

- Do children see adults enjoying reading and writing?
- Do teachers show enthusiasm during read-aloud times and talk about why they enjoy the books?
- Do children see adults reading and writing to accomplish meaningful tasks?
- Do children hear adults communicating effectively?
- Do adults interact periodically with children in meaningful ways in the Library area during choice time?
- Do teachers encourage families to enjoy reading and writing together?

Creating an Attractive and Inviting Library Area

- Is the area attractive, with comfortable furniture that helps children relax as they look at books?
- Is the area furnished with cozy, homelike touches such as plants, rugs, pillows, pictures, stuffed animals, and dolls?
- Is attention drawn to special books by displaying them with their covers facing out?
- Is there high-quality literature of interest to children?
- Are story retelling props located near the related book? Are books and recordings stored together?
- Are books in good condition and rotated periodically?

Linking Literacy With Play

- Do teachers observe children and offer materials and real-life reasons to use literacy in their play?
- Are literacy materials provided in interest areas to inspire children's play?
- Do teachers encourage children to talk about their play?

Offering Choices

- Are children able to choose the reading and writing materials they want?
- Are sufficient literacy materials available from which children may choose?
- Are children able to choose peers with whom to work?

Challenging Yet Achievable Literacy Experiences

- Are children's literacy efforts successful?
- Are the literacy activities age-appropriate?
- Are the literacy experiences and activities appropriate for each child's interests and abilities?
- Do teachers observe children's literacy abilities and scaffold their learning by gently challenging them?

When adults observe and interact with children and provide stimulating opportunities for language and literacy learning, children begin to experience literacy as a source of enjoyment. They are motivated to engage in language and literacy experiences.

What Does Research Say?

Use of literature

Literature use increased dramatically when teachers incorporated enjoyable literature activities into the daily program, when library centers were created in classrooms, and when recreational reading was scheduled on a daily basis (Morrow & Weinstein, 1982, 1986).

Literature-based programs positively affect children's attitudes toward reading (Gambrell, 2011).

Children want to read more often when they have a choice about what they read, have the opportunity to interact with others to discuss what they have read, and feel successful about reading (Gambrell, Palmer, & Coding, 1993).

Kindergarteners who demonstrated a strong interest in books scored significantly higher on standardized reading readiness tests and were rated higher on work habits, general school performance, and social and emotional development than those whose book interest was lower (Morrow, 1983).

Children who have never experienced the pleasure of literacy are likely to be unenthusiastic about learning to read and write (Snow, Barnes, Chandler, Goodman, & Hemphill, 1991).

Role of adults

Children tend to go to the book corner when teachers are there intermittently, not when they were never there or when they were always there (Rawson & Goetz, 1983).

Children benefit when teachers provide children with daily opportunities to experience literature pleasurably, to discuss stories, to relate literature activities with content, and to share the books they read or look at (Galda & Cullinan, 1991; Huck, 1976; Stewig & Sebesta, 1978).

Adults support children's literacy by reading books to their children and demonstrating through their own actions how reading is useful and enjoyable (Fernandez-Fem & Williams, 2013).

Reading to children at school or at home leads them to associate reading with pleasure and provides them with models of reading (Morrow, 2001).

Good feelings gained in story readings transfer to the act of reading, itself (Hiebert, 1981; Taylor, 1983).

When materials only and materials coupled with adult scaffolding were compared, children engaged in significantly more literacy-related play when adults were present and involved (Pickett, 1998).

Children are more likely to be fluent readers and enjoy reading more if parents have fun reading to them and if they show children that reading books is a source of enjoyment (Snow, Burns, & Griffin, 1998).

Reading with a young child develops literacy skills and a love of books long before the child has the ability to read on her own. How and how much adults read to a child during the early years has a significant impact on the child's school readiness and ultimate life trajectory (Suskind, 2015).

Environment

Before entering school, children who have access to books choose to look at them independently. They appear to value literacy as a source of entertainment (Baker, Scher, & Mackler, 1997).

Literacy-enriched play centers increase, often dramatically, the amount of literacy-related activities in which children engage during play (Neuman & Roskos, 1990; Vukelich, 1990; Noble & Foster, 1993).

Appropriately supportive and inviting classroom literacy settings engage children as readers and motivate them to use prior knowledge, employ cognitive strategies, and interact socially as members of the literate community (Baker, Afflerbach, & Reinking, 2012).

The Teacher's Role in Promoting Literacy as a Source of Enjoyment

Teachers play a crucial role in encouraging children's positive attitudes toward reading and writing. What you do and say help promote a lifelong habit of reading and writing for pleasure and for giving and receiving information. Here are important strategies for supporting children's experience of literacy as a source of enjoyment:

Talk about enjoyable purposes of literacy. When you read a story to children, talk about why you chose the book and why you enjoy it. Talk about getting good news from a friend in a letter or an e-mail message. Share a greeting card you received and explain why it is special to you.

Make story time pleasurable. Demonstrate your enthusiasm and excitement about reading. Create a warm, nurturing atmosphere for reading aloud so that the children look forward to participating. Select high-quality literature that the children will want to hear. Invite visitors—family members, directors, community volunteers—to read stories to children individually or in groups. Read books that you enjoy. Your love of the stories will show in your facial expressions and your voice.

Capture children's interest before beginning to read aloud. Set the stage for a story by connecting it with an experience familiar to the children. For example, you might introduce a story by asking, "Have you ever thought about what you could do with a magic pebble? In our story today, Sylvester, the donkey, finds one." Use props, sounds, fingerplays, games, or personal recollections as ways of motivating children to listen and respond to the story.

Invite children to choose books to look at independently and request for story time. Encourage children to talk about their favorite books and share their recommendations with others. Keep sticky notes and pencils in the Library area so children can identify their favorite books by writing their names on the notes and placing them on the covers.

Include books and use reading strategies that invite active participation during story time. Involving children in read-aloud times motivates them, promotes their oral language skills, and supports their comprehension.

Make your Library area attractive and inviting. Draw children to this area by displaying interesting books with their covers facing out and spotlighting special books with props for retelling. Use homelike touches, such as rugs, rocking chairs, plants, pillows, framed pictures, and beanbag chairs, to make the area one that the children want to visit and where they can relax as they read. Rotate the books periodically to add fresh reading material and maintain interest. Include books related to the topic your class is studying, as well as others of special interest to the children.

Add books that children made to the Library area. Children can dictate the text to you or write independently. A photo album with captions written beneath the pictures is also a nice addition to the area.

During choice time, go to the Library area periodically. Children enjoy interacting with their teachers by discussing what they are reading or doing. Your presence in the Library area will attract children to it. However, if some children enjoy reading alone, your presence may deter them. The best solution is to go to the Library area periodically during choice time, but do not remain there the entire time.

Create opportunities for children to work together during literacy experiences. Children are motivated by working together. Children can work cooperatively as they retell stories, write and illustrate books, clap rhymes, use literacy-related computer programs and apps and games for the tablet, and create and play with signs and other literacy props.

Work with families to make literacy experiences at home pleasurable. Emphasize to families the importance of reading and talking about books with their children every day. Through newsletters, conversations, family workshops, and conferences, show families how to make literacy activities fun rather than something children are forced to do. Suggest that families take their children to the library and obtain a library card. Offer opportunities for children to take books home from the Library area. Encourage families to keep story time warm, nurturing, and enjoyable.

Your Teaching Practice

Think about your own reading experiences. Do you read for pleasure? Do you explore a variety of genres? Remember that you play an important role in fostering children's love of literacy. Be mindful of how you talk about and introduce literacy experiences in the classroom. Think about how you can convey enthusiasm for reading as you interact with children throughout the day.

Vocabulary and Language

Oral language is the foundation of literacy. Literacy learning begins with listening and speaking. Infants listen to familiar voices, and then they learn to babble and later speak. Through speech, children learn to organize their thoughts and ideas. They construct their own understanding of the rules of language as they interact with adults and others in meaningful exchanges. They gradually learn the rules for ordering sounds and using language in standard forms. As they acquire literacy skills, children transition from oral language to written language. Written language—both reading and writing—requires a well-developed vocabulary and a good understanding of the rules and structure of language. Literacy learning also requires the insight that written language is different from spoken language.

Language is a system of words with rules for their use in listening, speaking, reading, and writing. Language can be divided into two areas: *receptive language* and *expressive language*. *Receptive language* refers to the language that a person takes in, the language one hears and reads. *Expressive language* is the language that a person speaks and writes. Children acquire language by moving through predictable stages, but the pace differs from child to child.

There are four kinds of vocabulary:

1. listening vocabulary—the words we understand when we hear them

2. speaking vocabulary—the words we use to express ourselves orally

3. reading vocabulary—the words we understand when we read them

4. writing vocabulary—the words we use to express ourselves in writing

When children are learning to read, their listening and speaking vocabularies help them make sense of written words. Later, their experience with reading and writing helps them to expand all of their vocabularies.

Children learn new words and learn about the structure of language in four basic ways:

- talking with peers and adults throughout the day in informal and guided conversations

- songs, rhymes, fingerplays, and movement activities

- hearing new words to describe what they experience firsthand

- listening to print read aloud and talking about new words

These important experiences can encourage the rapid language development of children who come to preschool with limited language skills. When teachers guide conversations and use particular words to describe children's experiences, they intentionally teach the vocabulary and language rules that children need in order to think and communicate more effectively.

If you have children whose primary language is not English, recognize that a strong base in a first language promotes school achievement in a second language (Snow, Burns, & Griffin, 1998). English-language learners are more likely to become readers and writers of English if they understand the vocabulary and concepts in their primary language first. The long-term goal is for children to be able to understand, speak, read, and write in both their home, or first, languages and English. You therefore want to support children's first languages as you help them acquire proficiency in English.

What Does Research Say?

Vocabulary development

Children learn the meaning of most words indirectly, through everyday experiences with oral and written language. In addition, there are times when teaching children the meaning of words directly can be effective (National Reading Panel, 2000).

Conversations matter when children are young. Talking with children provides them with experiences that are important to both their cognitive and their social–emotional learning (Hart & Risley, 1995).

When children are engaged in tasks in which they are learning vocabulary, they have larger vocabulary gains (Dickinson & Smith, 1994; Sénéchal, 1997; Drevno et al., 1994; Daniels, 1994, 1996).

The context in which new words are learned is critical. New vocabulary should be words that the child will find useful in many different contexts (McKeown, Beck, Omanson, & Pople, 1985; Kameenui, Carnine, & Freschi, 1982; Dole, Sloan, & Trathen, 1995).

Research has demonstrated a clear link between adults' oral storytelling activities and children's later language skills, vocabulary, and readiness for school. For example, 3- and 4-year-old children of parents who received training in oral storytelling showed significant improvement in their decontextualized vocabulary (Suskind, 2015).

Children with larger vocabularies have more developed phonological sensitivity (Wagner et al., 1993, 1997). This can be noticed early in the preschool years (Burgess & Lonigan, 1998; Chaney, 1992; Lonigan, Burgess, Anthony, & Barker, 1998; Lonigan, Burgess, & Anthony, 2000).

Children benefit from teacher–child conversations that include varied vocabulary and that are about topics that challenge children's thinking (Dickinson & Tabors, 2001).

Reading development

The majority of reading problems could be prevented by, among other things, increasing children's oral language skills (Snow, Burns, & Griffin, 1998).

There is a positive correlation between individual differences in oral language skills and later differences in reading skills (Bishop & Adams, 1990; Butler, Marsh, Sheppard, & Sheppard, 1985; Pikulski & Tobin, 1989; Scarborough, 1989; Share, Jorm, MacLean, & Mathews, 1984).

Vocabulary is critical in oral reading instruction (National Institute of Child Health and Human Development, 2000b).

Reading aloud

Storybook readings help teach children meanings of unfamiliar words (Robbins & Ehri, 1994).

The frequency of a target word in a story influenced the occurrence of the word in the child's retellings, and read-aloud events seemed to help children learn new words by incidental learning (Leung, 1992).

Teacher talk associated with storybook reading has an impact on the amount of child-initiated analytic talk important for vocabulary gains (Dickinson & Smith, 1994).

Repeated readings of a story to prekindergarten children enhanced vocabulary gains. Children learned more from answering questions during readings than they did when simply listening to the narrative (Sénéchal, 1997).

The Teacher's Role in Promoting Vocabulary and Language Development

The best way to help children increase their vocabularies and learn other language skills is to provide opportunities for them to hear different forms of language. You do this by modeling language, having extended conversations, and reading aloud. While most children easily learn the language they hear, some children do not. For these children, more direct teaching is necessary. Here are important strategies for supporting children's vocabulary and oral language development:

Serve as a good language model. When talking with children, use complete sentences. Expand children's language by building on what they say. Use the children's words and add more of your own. For example, if a child says, "Go outside," respond by saying, "Would you like to go outside today? We'll go outside right after we finish cleaning up."

Give children interesting firsthand experiences to talk about. Provide experiences that spark children's curiosity and wonder. Encourage children to use their senses to explore and to talk about what they are thinking and doing. To inspire children to talk, make changes in the environment, bring in natural items, and share your own experiences. These give children important background knowledge for later learning.

Repeat and reinforce new words. When a new word has been introduced to the children, use it in different contexts throughout the day. For example, after reading aloud the story *The Enormous Turnip*, talk about having an enormous appetite or how enormous a tree seems.

Observe, wait, and listen. Pay close attention to what a child is trying to tell or show you. Ask questions. Be patient and wait for the child to respond. Listen attentively to what the child says so you can answer and model language appropriately.

Talk with children frequently. Listen to what children say and then respond appropriately. Encourage children to carry on lengthier conversations, striving for at least five exchanges in each conversation. Clarify the meaning of words and encourage higher-level thinking as you talk together.

Encourage conversations that go beyond the here-and-now. Discuss things that happened yesterday and last week and that might happen in the future. Invite children to use their imaginations and think. Talk with children and pretend to be in another situation or another time. For example, ask a child, "If you could be any animal, what would you be? What would you do?" Challenge children's thinking.

Use open-ended questions and prompts. Open-ended questions are those that can be answered in a number of different ways. They can't be answered with a simple *yes* or *no*. Prompts such as "I wonder what would happen if…" encourage children to think and to express their ideas.

Read to children daily and talk about the story before, during, and after reading. Discussions while reading aloud not only help children practice their language skills and increase their vocabularies, but they also aid comprehension. Make sure you read aloud two or more times a day to individuals, small groups, and/or the whole class.

Enjoy songs, rhymes, and fingerplays together throughout the day. By doing so, children learn new words, hear different forms of language, and develop an awareness of the rhymes, rhythms, and other patterns of language.

Play language games and provide language materials. During small- and large-group activities, play games that focus on language. For example, a game of "20 Questions" helps children learn to ask questions and to reason.

Offer models so children can hear their first languages. If you are not fluent in all of the languages spoken in your classroom, try to find people who are proficient in them. This could be your assistant, family members, resource persons, or volunteers. Encourage these individuals to converse, play, read, and sing with the children. Communicate with families about topics of study and activities, and encourage them to discuss these topics with their children in their first languages.

Share informational books that relate to the children's particular interests. Such books introduce children to new ideas and information and extend children's vocabulary and language about topics that go beyond the here and now.

Your Teaching Practice

Think about the following questions as you consider your interactions with children:

- Do you prefer a quiet classroom environment most of the time?
- Do you provide opportunities for children to share ideas uninterrupted?
- Do you ask follow-up questions to encourage conversation?

It is important to remember that opportunities for language development can happen at all times of the day, whether during quiet conversation or lively group discussion. How do you make sure that all children feel supported to share ideas?

Phonological Awareness

Phonological awareness (sometimes referred to as phonological sensitivity) is hearing and understanding the different sounds and patterns of spoken language. It includes the different ways oral language can be broken down into individual parts, for instance, separate sounds and syllables. For some children, hearing these different parts of spoken language can be difficult because it requires them to attend to the sounds of speech separately from meaning.

Phonological awareness develops as a progression, from simple skills (e.g., listening) to very complex skills (e.g., manipulating individual sounds in words). Each phonological awareness skill involves varying levels of difficulty.

Phonological awareness begins with **listening** to sounds in the environment. These beginning listening skills help children later attend to the separate sounds in words. The next skills are noticing and discriminating **rhyme** and **alliteration**. For preschool children, rhyming requires recognizing the sounds in word endings. Alliteration involves hearing similar initial sounds, such as in *big beautiful buttons*.

As children begin to understand how language works, they become aware that language is made up of words that are grouped together. After becoming aware of the beginning and ending sounds in words, children can be helped to hear the separate **syllables** in words. In preschool, children can clap the words of a sentence or tap rhythm sticks to mark the syllables in their names.

Another way to explore sounds, syllables, and words is by examining **onset** and **rime**. *Onset* refers to the part of a syllable before the first vowel. It is a consonant, consonant blend, or digraph. *Rime* is the rest of the syllable, that is, the first vowel and everything after it. For example, in the one-syllable word *ball*, *b* is the onset, and *-all* is the rime. Preschool children can be taught to play with onset and rhyme while reciting the "Jack Sprat" nursery rhyme or similar verses. When older children learn about word families (e.g., *ball, call, fall, tall*), they are paying attention to onset and rime.

At the more complex end of the continuum of phonological awareness, the focus is on the smallest unit of sound, the **phoneme**. When preschool children play with words, they usually play with phonemes. For example, if you sing, "Dow, dow, dow your boat, gently down the stream," the children will probably say, "No! That's not right! It's *row*." In this playful way, they are paying attention to phonemes.

As children's phonological awareness skills advance, they learn to manipulate phonemes in many different ways. They blend and segment phonemes, or substitute one phoneme for another. These manipulation skills found at the most complex end of the progression are called **phonemic awareness**. Research shows that these advanced skills are one of the most powerful predictors of success in learning to read.

The following chart will help you understand the difference between beginning phonological awareness skills and more advanced skills. Notice that, for listening, most of the behaviors are at the beginning level. At the level of phonemes, most of the skills are more advanced.

	Beginning Phonological Awareness Skills	More Advanced Phonological Awareness Skills
Listening	Attends to sounds in the environment Discriminates sounds that are the same and different Remembers sounds Discriminates one sound from many	
Rhyming	Joins in and repeats rhyming songs, fingerplays, and poems Fills in the missing rhyming word of a song, fingerplay, or story	Decides whether two words rhyme Distinguishes rhymes from non-rhyming choices Generates rhyming words in isolation from context
Alliteration	Participates in songs, stories, and rhymes with alliterative text Notices the similar initial sounds of words that begin the same way Identifies the beginning sound of familiar words	Generates a group of words that begin the same way
Sentences and Words	Claps separate words in a sentence Listens for a particular word or phrase and segments compound words	Blends and segments compound words
Syllables	Claps syllables of own name Claps syllables of familiar words	Identifies the syllables in two- and three-syllable words Blends syllables to form words Deletes syllables
Onset and Rime	Recites rhymes, songs, or fingerplays that focus on onset and rime Begins to separate initial sound from rest of word	Separates initial sound from rest of word Blends onset and rime to make words
Phoneme	Plays with the sounds of words	Matches sounds Counts phonemes Identifies sounds in words (beginning, ending, medial) Blends phonemes Segments words into separate phonemes Deletes phonemes Substitutes phonemes

Phonological awareness skills are promoted by songs, stories, and rhymes. Children also develop understandings about sounds, letters, and words as they attempt to write. You will notice this in their play. When attempting to write a shopping list, a child may initially write a single letter to stand for an entire word (e.g., *M* for *milk*). Later he or she will begin to add more letters (e.g., *MK* for *milk*). You may hear the child say the word slowly to listen to the sounds while writing.

Children with language delays may have difficulty in isolating, distinguishing, or processing language sounds. Of course this affects their language development. Phonological awareness skills are particularly difficult for these children, so they may need different activities or more repetition of activities than other children need.

English-language learners have to distinguish phonemes in English that may not be part of their first languages. This may mean a child has difficulty hearing and/or pronouncing the sounds of English. English-language learners may need more repetition of the songs, rhymes, and fingerplays you use in the classroom. Repetition gives them opportunities to develop greater understanding of the meaning of the words as well as to learn the sounds.

Phonological awareness lays the groundwork for **phonics**. After children have a good understanding of the sounds of language, they begin to connect printed symbols with their corresponding sounds, for example, *M* with /m/. Be aware that phonics is not the same as phonological awareness, which involves only auditory skills and not sound–symbol correspondence.

What Does Research Say?

Skill development

Phonological awareness plays a crucial role in learning to read. Development of this ability typically begins by about age 3 and improves gradually over many years (Snow, Burns, & Griffin, 1998).

Young children's phonological sensitivity is a strong predictor of later reading, writing, and spelling ability (National Early Literacy Panel, 2008).

There is a developmental progression from phonological awareness of "large" units of speech (such as rhymes, words, and syllables) to the "small" units of speech (e.g., phonemes) (Goswami & Bryant, 1990).

Phonological awareness skills are less likely to develop through incidental exposure (Sulzby & Teale, 1991).

Phonological awareness can be facilitated, and that facilitation can lead to reading improvement (Alexander, Anderson, Heilman, Voeller, & Torgesen, 1991).

Rhyming

Rhyming is one of the first skills to develop in phonological awareness (Snyder & Downey, 1997).

Young children become sensitive to the sound of rhyming words at an early age (Apel, 1997; Ball, 1993; Braunger, Lewis, & Hagans, 1997).

Young children are typically able to detect words that rhyme, even when other phonological skills have not developed (Whitehurst & Lonigan, 1998).

Children develop a sense of the sound structure of language by saying rhymes, singing, and reciting fingerplays (Jenkins & Bowen, 1994).

Rhyming and alliteration are significantly related to later reading success (Snowling & Stackhouse, 1996; MacLean, Bryant, & Bradley, 1987; Bradley & Bryant, 1978, 1993).

Rhyming may be an initial step toward phonemic awareness (MacLean, Bryant, & Bradley, 1987).

Alliteration

Children typically begin to develop alliteration skills at about age 3 (Apel, 1997; Ball, 1993; Moats, 1998, MacLean, Bryant, & Bradley, 1987).

Alliteration requires children to pay attention to parts of words that are smaller than a syllable (Ball, 1993).

Segmentation and blending of words, syllables, onset and rime

Young children are first able to represent and manipulate more holistic units of speech (e.g., syllables) before they become able to segment phonemes (Fowler, 1991).

Onset and rime awareness develops earlier than phonemic awareness and also correlate to later reading ability. (Bradley & Bryant, 1983; MacLean, Bryant, & Bradley, 1987).

Onset and rime awareness may be the key to unlocking phonemic awareness (Adams, 1990).

What Does Research Say?, continued

Phonemes

Few children acquire phonemic awareness spontaneously (Adams, Treiman, & Pressley, 1998).

Phonemic awareness is the most potent predictor of success in learning to read. It is more highly related to reading than tests of general intelligence, reading readiness, and listening comprehension (Stanovich, 1986, 1994).

Phonemic awareness is central in learning to read and spell (Ehri, 1984).

Preschool, kindergarten, and primary-grade teachers should provide linguistically rich classroom environments where children play with sounds (Adams, 1990; Griffith & Olson, 1992; Mattingly, 1984; Yopp, 1992).

The Teacher's Role in Promoting Phonological Awareness

Children differ in their need for instruction in developing phonological awareness. Teachers therefore need to use a range of strategies with individual children, small groups, and large groups. Remember that phonological awareness activities should be playful and engaging as well as intentional. Here are important strategies for promoting children's phonological awareness:

Know each child's level of phonological awareness and provide appropriate experiences. You may have some children who have already progressed beyond the very earliest stages of phonological awareness. They may demonstrate their skills during everyday activities and be ready for more advanced activities. However, you may have some children who have not been introduced to language play. They may need more direct teaching. As with all skills, it is important to know each child's level of development and to support his or her learning appropriately.

Use songs, stories, and rhymes that play with language. Preschool teachers have always included songs, stories, and rhymes in their daily activities. Now research confirms the importance of these language forms in promoting phonological awareness. Think about the phonological awareness skills you can encourage by using particular songs, stories, and rhymes. Informally but intentionally, draw children's attention to the sounds of language.

Encourage children's curiosity about and experimentation with language. When you model curiosity about language, it can be contagious! Demonstrate your enjoyment of words, and children will soon follow. Invite children to make up new verses to songs and rhymes.

Include phonological awareness activities in your daily schedule. There are many opportunities to promote phonological awareness throughout the day. Consider saying a chant during cleanup, dismissing children to go outside by the first sound in their names, reading a book at story time, tapping syllables with rhythm sticks during large-group time, and playing a game with sounds during small-group activities.

Explain to families the importance of sharing songs, stories, and rhymes with their children. Suggest that they sing songs from their childhoods and other familiar songs and rhymes that help build phonological awareness. Songs such as "This Old Man," "Skinamarinky Dinky Dink," "Polly Wolly Doddle," "Baby Bumblebee," and "Michael Finnegan" are examples of old favorites. There are also many "oldies but goodies" that families remember and enjoy singing together. Encourage families of children who are English-language learners to sing and to recite chants and rhymes in their first languages.

Your Teaching Practice

Think about how you typically incorporate these types of language experiences in your classroom each day. Do you enjoy learning new songs and rhymes to share with children? Do you prefer to return to old favorites? Consider partnering with another teacher to share ideas so that children are continually engaged in a variety of learning experiences related to phonological awareness.

Knowledge of Print

Knowledge of print refers to the concepts related to how print is organized and used to convey meaning. To make sense of written language, children need to understand how sounds, words, and sentences are represented in writing. They need to know that thoughts and feelings are expressed in particular ways.

Children's development of print knowledge varies according to their interests and experience with language. Children begin to understand that print carries meaning but that written language is different from oral language. They develop an understanding that print serves a number of purposes in our society (**functions of print**). They also learn that print has distinct features and forms (**forms of print**), and that print is organized in a particular way (**print conventions**). An important goal during the preschool years is therefore to introduce children to a variety of texts.

Functions of Print

Print has many purposes, and messages can be conveyed through many different forms of print. In the world around us, we read signs to find out where to go and what to do. We depend on print to show us where things are located, and we fill out forms to provide information to others. We read messages, menus, instructions, and labels. In the classroom, print serves similar functions:

- to identify individuals and to show ownership (e.g., names on cubbies, sign-up sheets, personal signatures, and authors' and illustrators' names)
- to help children and adults recall information and make choices (e.g., answer a question and choose a drink for snack)
- to encourage interactions with others (e.g., thank-you notes, greeting cards, and message boards)
- to give directions or tell someone what to do (e.g., recipes and instructions for handwashing)
- to communicate information (e.g., class address book and observation logs)
- to express ideas and feelings (e.g., dictation and journal writing)

Most young children are very aware of environmental print, that is, the print that they see in their everyday surroundings. Especially if children are not aware, teachers should call attention to this print, talk about it, and explain what it means. Children are often familiar with logos of businesses they visit frequently, such as restaurants and stores, as well as print on products they use often, such as toothpaste, snacks, and cereal. You can also help children read environmental print by designing learning activities that involve it.

Forms of Print

As children become more aware of print, they begin to notice that print has different forms. They learn that letters and words have distinct features and different configurations, names, and sounds. They realize that a list is formatted differently from a letter to a friend. They see that an envelope is addressed in a particular way and that a sign is written in another. By planning experiences that involve different forms of written communication and offering children opportunities to read and write on their own as they play, teachers promote children's understanding of the forms of print. The different forms of print that preschool children use include

- lists
- signs and labels
- newspapers, magazines, and pamphlets
- menus
- sign-in sheets
- letters and envelopes
- greeting cards
- books

- directories and address books
- instructions
- charts and schedules
- recipes
- notes and messages
- e-mail
- journals
- captions
- calendars and appointment books

Conventions of Print

Rules govern the way in which print works. Readers must understand these important concepts:

- Print is a form of language. Each spoken word can be written down and read, and each written word can be spoken aloud.

- Printed words function differently from illustrations. Pictures support the words and can be used to predict and confirm the text.

- Books are read from the front cover to the back, page by page, in English and many other languages.

- Print is read from left to right and top to bottom, in English and many other languages.

- Letters are written in two forms, uppercase and lowercase.

- Letters represent sounds, letters are grouped together to form words, and words can be organized into sentences.

- Spaces are used between words.

- Punctuation serves a purpose.

Children learn the conventions of print by using environmental print, participating in interactive read-aloud times, and seeing and hearing adults model reading and writing. Teachers call attention to these conventions every day as they work with individual children and with small and large groups. For example, as children participate in read-aloud times, teachers demonstrate that printed words function differently from pictures and that readers attend particularly to words to find meaning. Teachers call attention to the way print is organized on the page, that is, words are typically ordered from top to bottom and left to right on a page, and the text continues on the next page when it is turned. In addition to discussing the story, teachers talk about the title and the author's and illustrator's names.

When children see adults model writing, they see firsthand where to start writing on a page, how print is ordered from left to right, and how to return to the left side of the page after reading a line of writing. They listen to the teacher talk about using an uppercase (capital) letter to begin a sentence or a name and that a period signals the end of a sentence.

What Does Research Say?

Development of print awareness
Children's knowledge of print concepts is an important predictor of later literacy achievement
(Clay, 1979; McCormick & Mason, 1986, Wells, 1985).

Young children's concepts about print are a moderate predictor of later reading, writing, and spelling ability (National Early Literacy Panel, 2008).

Children as young as 3 years know that print carries a message (McGee, Richgels, Charlsworth, 1986).

Children learn the uses of written language before they learn the forms (Gundlach, McLane, Scott, & McNamee, 1985; Taylor, 1983).

Prior to entering kindergarten, many children begin to construct meaning from print (Downing, 1986).

Before entering kindergarten, children learn print conventions, including directionality, the concept of a word, and punctuation (Clay, 1993).

Children learn about print from a variety of sources, and, in the process, they come to realize that although print differs from speech, it carries messages just like speech (Morrow & Smith, 1990).

Knowledge of print conventions is children's understanding of the way text works (Johnston, 2002; Whitehurst & Lonigan, 1998).

Knowledge of print conventions is an integral part of the process of learning to read (Dickinson & Tabors, 1991; Mason, 1992).

Big books help children develop understandings about books, print, and the meaning of the text (Holdaway, 1979).

What Does Research Say?, continued

Role of adults

Knowledge of print concepts develops through direct contact with books and explicit modeling by skilled readers, as well as through exposure to environmental print. These experiences are lacking in some homes (Adams, 1990).

Reading to children contributes to their awareness of the functions, form, and conventions of print (Mason, 1980).

When adults supported children's learning in a print-rich environment, children were found to learn significantly more words in context than their peers who experienced a print-enriched environment without adult interactions (Vukelich, 1994).

Environment

Print exposure has substantial effects on the development of reading skills at older ages when children are already reading (Allen, Cipielewski, & Stanovich, 1992; Anderson & Freebody, 1981; Cunningham & Stanovich, 1991, 1998; Echols, West, Stanovich, & Zehr, 1996; Nagy, Anderson, & Herman, 1987).

Four-year-olds awareness of environmental print (e.g., signs and logos) may be indicative of a print-rich home environment, a factor associated with early literacy development (Dickinson & DeTemple, 1998).

A central goal during the preschool years is to enhance children's exposure to and concepts about print (Clay, 1979, 1991; Holdaway, 1979; Teale, 1984; Stanovich & West, 1989).

The Teacher's Role in Promoting Knowledge of Print

Print concepts are learned gradually over an extended period of time. By drawing children's attention to the features of print while sharing books and by supporting children's efforts to use print in functional ways during everyday activities, teachers help children become readers and writers. Here are important strategies for promoting children's knowledge of print:

Create a print-rich environment. Include print that is meaningful, functional, and interesting. Add common signs, such as *Exit, Stop, Open*, and *Closed*, as well as logos from familiar products or businesses. Write labels, signs, and charts, and ask children to sign attendance sheets and waiting lists. Use charts to take attendance and identify jobs on a daily basis. Draw children's attention to letters and words as appropriate. It is important, however, not to clutter the environment with too much print.

Display print at the children's eye level. Position yourself at the children's eye level in the classroom. Can you see the signs, charts, information, and other print in the room?

Use story and informational books and planned writing experiences to teach about print. Children need materials to support their literacy development. Intentionally plan to read books aloud to large groups, small groups, and individuals. Also provide books for children's independent use. Place both fiction and nonfiction books in various interest areas so children can find the information they need and discover purposes for print. Stock the interest areas with writing materials so children can express themselves by drawing and writing.

Model literate behavior. Intentionally model reading and writing in meaningful, purposeful ways. Talk about what you are doing and why you are doing it. Write classroom materials (posters, charts, schedules, recipes, labels, etc.) in the children's presence rather than when children are not around. Describe the process as children watch you write.

Make a point to distinguish between children's writing and drawing. When you are talking to children about drawing and writing, use the words *drawing* and *writing* in your comments. For example, you might say, "You drew a red dress when you drew your mom's picture. I see that you wrote her name over here."

Draw children's attention to the conventions of print. As you record a child's dictation, talk about where you are starting to write, why you are beginning a sentence with an uppercase letter, and what the punctuation mark means at the end of the sentence. When you read a book or a chart, move your finger under the words to help children learn directionality.

Talk about the uses of print. Draw children's attention to the many ways print is used around them. Refer to the newspaper to check the day's weather forecast. Read the lunch menu aloud. Talk about the note that a father sent about a classmate who is not feeling well.

Point out concepts about books each time you read to children. Talk about where the writing starts on the page and which way to proceed when reading. Draw children's attention to the print on the page so they learn that readers attend particularly to the words, not the pictures.

Invite children to help you make signs and labels in the classroom. By doing so, children will learn that print has a purpose. For instance, offer Ben markers and paper to create a "Do not touch" sign for his block creation. Ask Juwan help you make a feeding schedule for the class pet.

Structure times during the week when children use writing to anticipate a future experience. They might write or draw about something they are looking forward to doing, such as going to a party.

Encourage children to write words that are important to them. The most important words to preschool children name important people and relate to important experiences. These include their own names and the names of family members, playmates, and pets. Encourage the children to write these words as they create drawings, messages, or greeting cards. As they do, they will be making a connection between spoken and written words.

Observe children throughout the day and consider ways of supporting their play with print. Think of ways to encourage reading and writing as children play. Offer paper and markers for making signs, writing tickets, or creating appointment books. Add books, newspapers, and magazines to pretend waiting rooms and home settings. Think of the many ways that print is part of your life and then offer reading and writing materials to children as they enact real-life situations.

Your Teaching Practice

When planning your day, think about how writing and print experiences fit into your plans. Do you usually prepare written materials in advance? Do you look for opportunities to engage children with print? Keep in mind that it may require a bit more time in your schedule, but making time for these experiences helps children see firsthand how writing and print occur naturally throughout the day.

Letters and Words

Knowledge of letters and words is an important component of literacy, and it involves more than reciting the ABC song or recognizing individual letters. Readers must understand that a letter represents one or more sounds. A more complex level of understanding requires knowing that these symbols can be grouped together to form words and that words have meanings. The idea that written spellings correspond to spoken words is called the **alphabetic principle**. Children's understanding of the alphabetic principle is a predictor of future reading success.

Children demonstrate their understanding of the concept of a word when they match each spoken word to a printed word. You might notice children pretending to read and touching each word on the page as they recite a narrative. These children understand the concept of a word, and they realize that readers attend particularly to printed words rather than pictures.

Teachers help children learn specific skills related to letters and words. Children learn to

- recognize and name letters
- recognize beginning letters in familiar words, especially in their own names
- relate some letters to the sounds they represent
- match spoken words with written words, one-to-one

Most children learn to recite the alphabet at a young age by singing the ABC song. Then they learn the shapes of the letters made familiar by the song. In other words, they recognize the letters of the alphabet. Learning letter names helps children learn some of the sounds that letters represent. For example, if a child knows the name of the letter *e*, he also knows the long sound of *e*. Once children gain confidence in their ability to recognize letters, they begin to attend to their sounds. Then they group the letters together to write words, ordering the letters in the way they think the sounds are ordered.

Children often recognize the letters in their own names first, because these are the letters of the words that are most important to them. Including activities with children's own names is an excellent way to make letters and words meaningful. After children learn the letters in their own names, they often learn the letters of other words that are significant to them, such as the names of family members and pets. Reinforce children's learning about letters in meaningful ways with activities such as:

- *Mighty Minutes* 09, "Writing in the Air"
- *Mighty Minutes* 92, "Name Cheer"
- *Mighty Minutes* 104, "Alphabet Stew"
- *Mighty Minutes* 152, "Letter Quest"

As children write, teachers can observe their understanding of letters and words. In their early writing attempts, children often use a single letter to represent a word, such as *S* for *soup*. This demonstrates their understanding of beginning sounds. Other children may write letters that represent beginning and ending sounds, such as *LV* for *love*. As their phonological awareness becomes more refined, they hear more sounds in words, and their invented spellings become more accurate and conventional. You will also notice their use of spaces between letters, groups of letters, and words, signifying an understanding of the concept of a word.

If you are teaching English-language learners, be aware that some letters in their first languages may represent the same sounds in English and other letters may not. For example, while vowels look the same in Spanish (*a, e, i, o, u*), they are named differently and correspond to different sounds. Knowing this, teachers help children learn to say and understand words in English before expecting them to be able to distinguish the sounds accurately or use invented spelling (Peregoy & Boyle, 2000).

What Does Research Say?

Alphabet

A pre-reader's alphabet knowledge is one of the single best predictors of eventual reading achievement (Adams, 1990; Stevenson & Newman, 1986).

Young children's alphabet knowledge is a strong predictor of later reading, writing, and spelling ability (National Early Literacy Panel, 2008).

The ability to name letters is a predictor of early reading success (Chall, 1967; Torgesen, 1998).

Letter names provide relevant information about the sounds they represent, and beginning readers appear to use this information in reading and writing (Ehri & Wilce, 1986; Read, 1971; Treiman, 1993).

Children's own names are highly motivating for learning letter names (Share & Jaffe-Gur, 1999; Bloodgood, 1999).

Preschool children's letter knowledge is a unique predictor of growth in phonological sensitivity across one year (Burgess & Lonigan, 1998).

Exposure to alphabet books may increase children's letter knowledge and phonological processing skills (Baker, Fernandez-Fein, Scher, & Williams, 1998; Murray, Stahl, & Ivey, 1996).

Children who can instantly and effortlessly recognize the letters of the alphabet are able to focus their attention on the other literacy tasks (Hall & Moats, 1999).

Alphabet books that use alliteration help increase phonemic awareness (Murray, Stahl, & Ivey, 1998).

The shapes of letters are learned by distinguishing one character from another by its spatial features (Gibson & Levin, 1975).

Letter–sound relationships

Familiarity with the letters of the alphabet and awareness of the speech sounds, or phonemes, to which they correspond are strong predictors of the ease or difficulty with which a child learns to read (Adams, 1990)

A beginning reader who has difficulty recognizing and distinguishing the individual letters of the alphabet will have difficulty learning the sounds those letters represent (Bond & Dykstra, 1967; Chall, 1967; Mason, 1980).

Before children learn to decode words in and out of context, they become able to use some letter–sound information to recognize, remember, and spell words. This is possible even if they are not taught the letter sounds, because the names of the alphabet letters provide clues to the phonemic representations in words (Mason & Allen, 1986).

The Teacher's Role in Promoting Knowledge of Letters and Words

Children gain knowledge of the alphabet when teachers plan meaningful activities and experiences that include letter recognition. These activities range from reading alphabet books; manipulating magnetic letters; playing alphabet matching games; singing the alphabet song; helping children learn to recognize the letters in their names; and writing, or attempting to write, letters and words. Here are important strategies for promoting children's knowledge of letters and words:

Focus on letters and words as part of meaningful activities. Talk about letters, sounds, and words as you take dictation and read it back, compose messages, and help children write during their daily activities. The alphabet is a system of symbols. Taken alone, each letter is of limited value. When letters are used in combination with other letters, words are created. For this reason, teaching the alphabet through "Letter of the Week" activities confuses some children about the purpose of letters in relation to written words. Such contrived activities are not the best use of classroom time.

See *Intentional Teaching Card* LL01, "Shared Writing," for guidance on taking dictation during group times.

Display the alphabet. Post the alphabet at the children's eye level. Make it more meaningful by displaying each letter with a child's name that begins with that letter. Provide smaller alphabet strips or cards in the Library area so a child can place a strip nearby and refer to it easily while writing.

Add alphabet books in the Library area and other interest areas. Some alphabet books with story lines are ideal for group reading, such as *Chicka Chicka Boom Boom* (Bill Martin, Jr.) and *The Alphabet Tree* (Leo Lionni). Other alphabet books are great for sharing one-on-one, but they are not ideal for group reading because there are no story lines. As you and the child explore an alphabet book together, talk about the letters, their shapes, and the names of pictured objects that begin with the letter. When selecting alphabet books, make sure that the pictures begin with a single letter sound, rather than a blend. Saying "*S* is for *ship*" might confuse a child who is beginning to make the sound-symbol connection for *S*. Similarly, seeing "*C* is for *circle*" might also cause confusion, because most children learn the hard *c* sound (as in *cold*) first. In addition, choose books that use upper- and lowercase letters. Make sure books have simple illustrations that children will recognize and that each pictured object has only one common name (not, for example, dog/puppy). English-language learners benefit greatly from books that focus on a single word and picture per page.

Sing the alphabet song. Singing the alphabet song helps familiarize children with the names and order of the letters. Sing it slowly enough so that the letter names do not run together. For example, pronounce *l, m, n, o* separately and not as one word, *elemeno*. For variety, sing it to a different tune, change the tempo, or start and stop at different parts of the song. Have a large alphabet chart handy so you can point to the letters as you sing them.

Teach about shapes. Learning about shapes not only involves mathematical concepts, but it is also important for letter recognition. Written letters are combinations of straight lines, curved lines, slanted lines, circles, dots, and angles. As you help children learn to recognize and write letters, describe their shapes (e.g., *Olivia, your name starts with an O. It looks like a circle, doesn't it?*).

Encourage sensory exploration of the alphabet. Children obtain and interpret information more readily when several of their senses are stimulated. They make important connections and understand concepts more easily when the learning experience includes sight, sound, and touch. By seeing and feeling letters, they not only learn the names of letters, but they also learn their features and how each letter is formed. Offer children a variety of ways to explore the alphabet: by using sandpaper, salt trays, clay, magnetic letters, and felt letters and by forming letters with their bodies.

- LL07, "Letters, Letters, Letters"
- LL15, "Textured Letters"
- LL17, "Walk a Letter"

Encourage children to write while they play. Through their play, children explore writing for different purposes. As they write, observe their knowledge and use of the alphabet.

Help children create a personal word collection. On cards, write words that are important to each child, such as the names of people and pets. Talk about the words as you write them. Store the word cards in a special box or envelope or on a ring. Children can refer to their personal word collections when creating greeting cards and writing captions for drawings.

Promote letter–sound association and phonological awareness when helping children learn about the alphabet. As you look at alphabet books and guide children's writing, talk about the sounds of letters and words. For example, you might say, "This sentence has lots of words that begin with the /m/ sound: *merry, music, melody*, and *Max*. Can you think of someone in our class whose name begins the same way?"

For Dual-Language Learners

Display the children's first-language alphabets. Alphabet books, alphabet strips, and word cards in their first languages promote children's first-language literacy. If a child's first language uses symbols other than letters, provide cards and books with the symbols of common words.

Your Teaching Practice

Think back to your own childhood experiences related to letters and words. Did you enjoy writing when you were young? Did you avoid it? How do you feel about it now? Take a moment to think about how you convey your feelings about writing when working with children.

Comprehension

Comprehension, the process of making meaning, is the goal of reading instruction. It involves connecting what you read and hear with your experience. Your background knowledge helps you understand the meaning of language. You connect the language you read and hear with personal experiences, information you have already learned, and concepts you understand. The more the language of a text relates to your prior knowledge, the more you are able to make sense of what is being read. Each reader brings a broad range of background information to any text. Rather than merely calling words, the reader constructs understanding.

Although most preschool children are not yet reading, comprehension is still important to them. They try to comprehend stories being read and told, oral directions and information, conversations, and subject area content (e.g., scientific, mathematical, and musical concepts). Listening comprehension skills are crucial when children begin to read.

Through language-rich activities, such as read-aloud times, conversations, and engaging in firsthand experiences, children develop comprehension skills in an integrated, meaningful way. Comprehension is enhanced when the content of an experience is interesting, relevant, and worth learning. Children who are learning to read must

- expand general background knowledge
- increase vocabulary
- understand the grammar, or structure, of the language
- make connections
  - construct, compare, and combine ideas
  - notice similarities and differences in information
  - recall and apply prior knowledge to new situations
- listen to and understand speech
- question, predict, hypothesize, and use language to process information
- judge the importance of particular information
- be motivated to learn

When preschool children attempt to make connections between stories they hear, conversations, and personal experiences, they use many of the same cognitive processes that older children and adults use when they read. Some researchers argue that this ability to make connections to text strongly predicts future reading comprehension, even more than the other basic literacy skills (Van den Broek, 2001).

Encouraging children to find meaning should be the primary goal of all literacy activities. Comprehension skills begin to develop long before children learn to decode print. It begins with building knowledge about the world and about language in order to understand and communicate.

Background Knowledge

Good readers have background knowledge that helps them understand written language. As they develop stronger reading skills, reading then helps them increase their knowledge. A major goal in preschool is to provide many firsthand experiences that help children construct understandings about the world. Meaningful experiences are crucial to children's development and learning, and talking about them promotes both language and cognitive development. Encouraging children to reflect on their experiences, ask questions, make predictions, hypothesize, and experiment helps them construct understandings about the world and about language.

As children engage in many varied experiences, they learn new words. They hear words, such as *squishy, damp, vehicle, experiment,* and *patterns,* in meaningful contexts. They not only hear the words, they experience the meaning of the words, using all of their senses to take in information and construct understandings. Later, as they encounter the words in print, they will be able to use those understandings to comprehend the text. The more you help children develop understandings through experience, the more likely they are to use their understandings in new contexts.

Comprehension of a story depends a great deal on the child's background knowledge. When selecting stories to read aloud, consider these questions:

- Do the children have the background knowledge needed to understand the story?
- Will the topic of the story interest the children?
- How complex is the language of the story?
- How many new words are introduced in the text?
- Is the book the right length for the children?

You can assess children's listening comprehension in many ways. You can pay attention to their questions and observe how they focus their attention, apply the information they hear, and incorporate what was heard in their play. You will know whether children are comprehending a story if, while listening, they

- describe the details of the story so far
- recognize the sequence of events
- predict outcomes
- make associations
- relate the story to personal experiences

Follow-up activities will also help you determine whether a child has comprehended a story. When you observe children using props as they retell a story, note the complexity of the story details and sequence that they remember.

What Does Research Say?

Active experiences aid comprehension

Children who engage in frequent activities with books have larger, more literate vocabularies and learn to read better than children who have few book experiences (Dickinson & Tabors, 1991; Wells, 1986).

Dramatic play is related to comprehension in powerful, yet complex, ways. Metaplay is a significant factor in increasing story comprehension (Christie, 1983; Pellegrini & Galda, 1982; Saltz, Dixon, & Johnson, 1997; Silvern, Williamson, & Waters, 1983).

Story retelling helps children develop a sense of story structure and understandings about language that contribute to their comprehension of text (Morrow, 1985).

Reading aloud

When adults discuss story content, ask open-ended questions about story events, explain the meaning of unfamiliar words, and point out features of print as they read to children, they promote language development, competent comprehension, knowledge of story structure, and awareness of the units of written language (Berk, 2012).

Children who hear stories in small-group settings show stronger comprehension skills than children to whom stories are read individually or in large-group settings. Similarly, children's comprehension seems to be better when stories are read to them individually than when stories are read to them in a large group. Children in the studies asked more questions and made more comments when stories were read to them individually or in small-group settings rather than read to the whole class. These skill differences are attributed to differences in teacher–child interactions in the various settings (Morrow and Gambrell, 2002).

Children's comments and questions increase and become more interpretive and evaluative when they have listened to repeated readings of the same story. Children also elaborated more and offered more interpretations after repeated readings of the same story (Pappas, 1991).

The primary goal of a read-aloud event is the construction of understanding from the interactive process between adult and child (Vygotsky, 1978).

A teacher's reading style has an impact on children's comprehension of stories (Roser & Martinez, 1985).

Familiarity that comes with repeated readings enables children to reenact stories or attempt to read them on their own (Sulzby, 1985).

Background knowledge

Comprehension is essential to future reading success because it enables children to process what they hear and read (Teale & Yokota, 2000).

The reader's background knowledge is important for understanding texts (Anderson & Pearson, 1984; Anderson, Spiro, & Montague, 1977; Bransford & Johnson, 1972).

Vocabulary knowledge is a major correlate of comprehension ability (Davis, 1968).

Children learn real-world knowledge from picture books (Crain-Thoreson & Dale, 1992).

Children identified as "low achievers" in school have limitations in their prior knowledge and understandings rather than any limitations in their ability to learn (Anderson, Spiro, & Montague, 1977).

The Teacher's Role in Promoting Comprehension

Preschool children develop comprehension skills through experiences that promote oral and written language skills, such as discussions, sociodramatic play, retellings, and interactive reading. Reading and re-reading many different types of books aid in building comprehension. Most important is the teacher's role in helping children connect new information and experiences with what they already know. Here are important strategies for promoting children's comprehension:

Building Background Knowledge and Vocabulary

Help children connect new information and ideas to what they already know. Introduce and discuss new words in meaningful contexts. Provide experiences to help them learn what things are and how they work. Find out what children know about a topic and have them develop questions to guide their exploration. Discuss what they learn, helping them to link old and new knowledge. Ask questions such as "How is _____ like _____?"; "Have you ever _____?"; and "What do you know about _____?" Promote their ability to solve problems and figure things out.

Encourage children to ask questions when they do not understand. Many children ask, "Why?" or "How come?" Others do not. Children who do not actively seek to understand are at a disadvantage as learners. You can model requests for clarification and more information. For example, you can say, "I'm not sure I understand," and ask, "What do you mean?"

Extend children's ideas. Give children new information to expand their understandings about the world. When they talk about new words and ideas, listen actively to what they are saying. Respect their ideas and add new information to what they already know.

Promoting Listening Comprehension

Talk with children frequently throughout the day. Use every opportunity to help children learn new information and clarify their thoughts and ideas. Talk about what you see and hear. Wonder aloud. Help children learn the give-and-take of conversations: "I talk while you listen; you talk while I listen."

Use language that is easy for children to understand. As you introduce new words and ideas to children, explain meanings in language they can relate to and understand. This will help them connect new information with prior knowledge.

Help children understand language by rephrasing it when necessary. When a visitor comes or when you are on a study trip, rephrase some of the conversation so children can understand what is being communicated. Rephrasing may also be necessary while reading stories.

Play listening games. Games help children sharpen their listening comprehension skills. They learn to attend to particular sounds and words and focus on important information.

Help children learn to follow and give directions. Play games with rules. Encourage children to create games and explain the directions to others. Use routines (e.g., setting the table and putting materials away) and transitions to practice following directions. This helps sharpen children's listening comprehension skills.

Promoting Story Comprehension

Read aloud to small groups of children. Children who listen to stories in small groups are able to share conversations about the stories. They learn from each other's comments and questions. In addition, a personal experience shared by one child in relation to a story may help other children make personal connections to it.

Prepare children for the reading by taking a "picture walk." Introduce the story by previewing the pictures. Ask the children to predict what the story is about by looking at the cover. Turn the pages slowly and encourage them to talk about what they see.

Be sure to show children the pictures as you read. Talk about the pictures informally as you read the story, to support children's comprehension of the narrative.

Be aware of the learning styles of the children you teach. Some children may get the most out of reading experiences by talking about the story, looking at pictures, or listening as you read. Be sure to offer a variety of experiences so that children can get the most out of reading experiences.

When reading to children, encourage them to ask questions, make predictions, talk about the story, and connect new ideas with what they already know. As you read, talk about the characters, the setting, and the sequence of events. Help the children think about whether their predictions were correct. Ask questions and make comments, such as "Have you ever had a really bad day?"; "Do you think a giant is real or make-believe?"; and "Where do you think Corduroy will find his button?" "This tugboat is much like the one we saw on our field trip."

Facilitate story retellings. Retelling stories requires children to think about what they have heard and to restate it in a way that others can understand. They must remember details of the story, such as the characters, setting, and order of events, and they must use their own language as well as story language. (Chapter 3 of this volume, "Teaching Strategies," discusses story retelling in greater detail.)

Books and Other Texts

When children explore books and other texts, they learn that written language serves many purposes. They realize that written language is a valuable tool for learning about the world and a way to communicate with others.

To increase children's understanding of books and other texts, teachers give children experience with a wide variety of books from different categories, or genres, and help them develop concepts about books and book-handling skills.

Experience With Various Types of Books

Children need extensive experience with many different types, or genres, of books. Each type serves a different purpose and is read differently. The most familiar type of book in preschool classrooms is the **narrative picture book**, or **storybook**. As children learn to read, stories are an important part of their learning. They learn, for example, that to read a narrative book they start at the beginning and read through to the end, although not necessarily in one sitting. Experience with stories and discussions about them builds a solid foundation for literacy. Through storybooks, children learn story elements such as the characters, setting, dialogue, and sequence of events. While they may not know these terms, they talk about these elements during interactive read-aloud times and story retellings. The more children hear and discuss story narratives, the more they learn about how they are organized. Gaining this sense of story is very important to children's comprehension.

Other types of books offer other learning opportunities. **Wordless books** encourage readers to use their imaginations to create their own narratives. **Poetry** is structured differently from prose. **Informational books** are used to learn new concepts and find answers to particular kinds of questions. Some informational books are structured as stories, while others are not always read in their entireties. As children gain an understanding of the purposes of different types of books, they learn basic rules about how each book genre is structured and how it is meant to be read.

When preschool children have experience with different genres of books, they begin to understand that language is structured differently for various purposes. The language of print is usually different from that of conversations and from what is heard on television. Written language is usually more complex and abstract, and it makes different demands on the reader. The language of books usually has more formal grammatical structures and is more descriptive than casual speech. Vocabulary tends to vary more in books than in children's conversations. The language of children's books is also structured to help children attend to the sounds of language in ways that ordinary conversations do not.

With adult guidance, children notice how the language of storybooks differs from that used in informational books and poetry. In addition to narrative picture books, these are some of the various genres of early childhood literature:

- informational, or nonfiction, books (e.g., *The Way Things Work* by David Macaulay and *Me on a Map* by Joan Sweeney)

- concept books (e.g., *What is Black and White?* by Petr Horacek, and *Fish Eyes* and *Eating the Alphabet* by Lois Ehlert)

- wordless books (e.g., *Good Dog, Carl* by Alexandra Day and *Changes, Changes* by Pat Hutchins)

- contemporary fiction (e.g., *Uptown* by Brian Collier and *I Love My Hair* by Natasha Tarpley)

- fantasy (e.g., *Harold and the Purple Crayon* by Crockett Johnson and *Where the Wild Things Are* by Maurice Sendak)

- fairy tales and folktales (e.g., *Anansi the Spider* by Gerald McDermott and *Sleeping Beauty*)

- fables (e.g., *The Hare and the Tortoise* and *The Lion and the Mouse* by Aesop)

- historical fiction (e.g., *Giorgio's Village* by Tomie dePaola and *Tough Boris* by Mem Fox)

- biographies and autobiographies (e.g., *Martin's Big Words: The Life of Dr. Martin Luther King, Jr.* by Doreen Rappaport and *The Art Lesson* by Tomie dePaola)

- poetry (e.g., *Wake Up House! Rooms Full of Poems* by Dee Lillegard, *A Child's Garden of Verses* by Robert Louis Stevenson, and *Mother Goose* by Blanche Fisher Wright)

- songbooks (e.g., *Cumbayah* by Floyd Cooper and *Philadelphia Chickens* by Sandra Boynton and Michael Ford)

Children also learn that there are materials to read in addition to books. They can read magazines, message boards, menus, cookbooks, programs, lists, brochures, charts, signs, digital and online information, journals, letters and cards, circulars, billboards, and instruction books. Each serves a different purpose, is formatted in a different way, and is designed for a particular audience. When children are familiar with a particular form of text, they know how to approach a similar text.

Your Teaching Practice

As you think about how you share books with children, consider the following questions:

- Do you enjoy reading aloud?

- Do you invite children's questions when reading with them?

- Do you prefer to read only illustrated storybooks?

- Do you talk with children about the types of genres you prefer to read?

Thinking about these questions may help you better understand how you can make positive changes to your reading experiences with children.

What Does Research Say?

Reading aloud

When children are read to, they develop knowledge about books and the routines and language used to share them (Durkin, 1966; Ninio & Bruner, 1978; Pappas & Brown, 1987; Sulzby, 1985).

Through storybook reading, children begin to learn about narrative structure (Heath, Branscombe, & Thomas, 1986; Sulzby, 1985).

Reading to children enhances background information and a sense of story structure. It also familiarizes children with the language of books (Cullinan, 1992; Morrow, 1985).

Children with storybook experience learn how to handle a book and are familiar with its front-to-back progression. They also become familiar with story structure (beginning, middle, and end), as well as the concept of authorship (Smith, 1978).

Children who are read to frequently will "read" their favorite books by themselves, by trying to imitate the oral and written language routines of their literate models (Sulzby & Teale, 1987, 1991).

Book-reading interactions provide children an opportunity to understand stories in addition to models of literary language and structures not typically found in daily speech (Cochran-Smith, 1984; Purcell-Gates, 1988).

Children's initial questions and comments during story readings are related to pictures and the meaning of the story. Later they pay more attention to the names of letters, the reading of individual words, or attempts to sound out words (Morrow, 1987; Roser & Martinez, 1985; Yaden, 1985).

Informational texts

Greater attention to informational texts will make children better readers and writers of informational text (Christie, 1984, 1987).

Children are able to respond to and learn from informational texts in sophisticated ways (Hicks, 1995).

Young children can learn about and from informational texts. Exposure to informational texts results in fast-developing knowledge of expository text structure and book language (Duke & Kays, 1998).

Engaging with books

Understanding the structure or characteristics of texts is important to later reading and writing success (Gunn, Simmons, & Kameenui, 1995; Mason & Allen, 1986)

While young children consider each page of a book as a separate unit, older children respond to each page as part of a complete story (Sulzby, 1985).

Fiction or nonfiction stories can spark a child's curiosity about people, places, and things beyond the realm of his experiences; stories with true-to-life portrayals of his home culture and community help him feel good about himself and his heritage (Bardige & Segal, 2005).

The Teacher's Role in Promoting Understandings About Books and Other Texts

First, teachers prepare an environment rich with children's literature from a wide range of genres. They intentionally teach concepts about books and help children understand that information and ideas can be found in many types of text. Here are important strategies for promoting children's understandings about books and other texts:

Use a variety of genres when you read with children. Give children experience with picture books, including folk- and fairy tales; poetry; and informational books. Call attention to the ways ideas are presented in different ways in various types of books. Talk about how various books are the same and different.

Include high-quality children's literature throughout the classroom. Children benefit from experience with the rich language of books, beautiful illustrations, and stories that help them learn concepts and information about the world. In addition to reading books to children, make books available in interest areas where children may handle them.

Use books as sources of information. Show children how to search for information in a book. If a child sees a spider on the playground and wonders whether it is poisonous, refer to an encyclopedia or book about spiders. Together, look in the index to find the relevant page number. Read the information to the child and discuss the picture. If you know that a child is interested in big machines, locate books related to that topic. By matching books to children's interests, teachers can build on children's natural curiosity.

Encourage children to become authors and illustrators and to produce different types of print materials. Suggest that they make books of various genres, such as picture dictionaries and alphabet books, informational "how-to" books, and song books. Encourage them to make up their own versions of stories and add their names as the authors and illustrators.

Provide children with opportunities to use various other texts in their play. Observe children and brainstorm ways of adding literacy materials to extend their play. Offer children many forms of print, such as menus, cookbooks, directories, coupons, empty product containers, manuals, magazines, newspapers, schedules, brochures, catalogs, paper, pencils, markers, and envelopes.

Promote children's general knowledge of the world by helping them use informational books. Place these books throughout the classroom where children can refer to them as they play. Books about fish might be displayed next to the aquarium. A book about bridges or castles might inspire play in the Block area, and a book on drawing will encourage children's exploration in the Art area.

Planning Your
Literacy Program

**Objectives for Language
and Literacy Learning**   **41**

Creating a Literacy-Rich Environment   **43**

Literacy Throughout the Day   **45**

Meeting the Needs of All Children   **49**
Supporting English-Language Learners
Supporting Advanced Language
  and Literacy Learners
Supporting Children With Disabilities

Guide to Implementation   **61**

2

Planning Your Literacy Program

In order to plan a high-quality literacy program, teachers must understand the components of literacy. Planning for literacy learning is active and continuous, and it involves all staff members in finding ways to meet the strengths and needs of each child and the group as a whole.

Before teaching, think about these questions:

- What do I want children to know and be able to do?
- What approaches to learning am I fostering?
- How will I assess children's learning?

While teaching, think about these questions:

- Are children learning what I expected?
- Is unanticipated learning occurring?
- Are things going as planned?

After teaching, ask,

- What worked?
- What needs to be changed?
- What is the evidence?

When planning is careful and tailored to children's strengths and needs, their efforts are more likely to be successful. Without ongoing planning, learning is left to chance.

In order to plan an effective literacy program and address the questions presented on the preceding page, teachers need to know the objectives for children's oral language and literacy learning. As you read the at-a-glance chart that is presented in the next section, note the 10 objectives that are related specifically to oral language, literacy, and English language acquisition.

Because children's oral language and literacy skills affect and are affected by development in other areas, teachers also need to know the objectives for children's development and learning in those other areas. For example, as you observe children in order to gather information about their social–emotional development, you will probably find that their oral language skills have a lot to do with the level of their development in terms of Objective 2, "Establishes and sustains positive relationships."

With the objectives for development and learning in mind, teachers create a stimulating physical environment that promotes oral language and literacy. They also think about how to incorporate oral and written experiences purposefully in all routines and activities throughout the day.

Because today's preschool classrooms are very diverse, teachers must find ways to meet the strengths and needs of all children. They have to explore ways to support English-language learners, children with advanced skills, and children with disabilities. The final section of this chapter, "Guide to Implementation," offers advice for making language and literacy a central part of your program.

Objectives for Language and Literacy Learning

The following chart shows the 38 objectives that are included in *The Creative Curriculum®* *for Preschool* objectives for development and learning. They identify the skills and knowledge that children are expected to develop and learn before entering kindergarten. Objectives 8–10 are related specifically to language. Objectives 15–19 concern literacy, and Objectives 37 and 38 are related to English language acquisition.

Social–Emotional

1. Regulates own emotions and behaviors
2. Establishes and sustains positive relationships
3. Participates cooperatively and constructively in group situations

Physical

4. Demonstrates traveling skills
5. Demonstrates balancing skills
6. Demonstrates gross-motor manipulative skills
7. Demonstrates fine-motor strength and coordination

Language

8. Listens to and understands increasingly complex language
9. Uses language to express thoughts and needs
10. Uses appropriate conversational and other communication skills

Cognitive

11. Demonstrates positive approaches to learning
12. Remembers and connects experiences
13. Uses classification skills
14. Uses symbols and images to represent something not present

Literacy

15. Demonstrates phonological awareness, phonics skills, and word recognition
16. Demonstrates knowledge of the alphabet
17. Demonstrates knowledge of print and its uses
18. Comprehends and responds to books and other texts
19. Demonstrates writing skills

Mathematics

20. Uses number concepts and operations
21. Explores and describes spatial relationships and shapes
22. Compares and measures
23. Demonstrates knowledge of patterns

Science and Technology

24. Uses scientific inquiry skills
25. Demonstrates knowledge of the characteristics of living things
26. Demonstrates knowledge of the physical properties of objects and materials
27. Demonstrates knowledge of Earth's environment
28. Uses tools and other technology to perform tasks

Social Studies

29. Demonstrates knowledge about self
30. Shows basic understanding of people and how they live
31. Explores change related to familiar people or places
32. Demonstrates simple geographic knowledge

The Arts

33. Explores the visual arts
34. Explores musical concepts and expression
35. Explores dance and movement concepts
36. Explores drama through actions and language

English Language Acquisition

37. Demonstrates progress in listening to and understanding English
38. Demonstrates progress in speaking English

This volume of *The Creative Curriculum® for Preschool* focuses on the language and literacy objectives for preschool children. The appendix of this book includes excerpts from *Volume 6: Objectives for Development & Learning* that show the dimensions of each language, literacy, and English language acquisition objective. They also show the typical progression of skill development for each dimension. Each progression shows a rating scale, indicators, and examples. Age-range expectations are presented in *Volume 6*. Understanding each progression is critical to planning an effective oral language and literacy program.

Keep the developmental progression for each objective in mind as you plan for each child and the group. Understand that individual children will be functioning at different developmental levels. You will tailor your strategies as you scaffold children's learning and help them move to the next level of the progression. The assessment information that you collect by using the *GOLD®* assessment system will guide you in determining each child's level and probable next steps.

Also recognize that children do not progress at the same rate. Some children learn new skills and abilities quickly, while others need more time, practice, and experience before they move to the next level.

A deep understanding of children's skill development enables teachers intentionally to plan routines and experiences that advance children's thinking and support their oral language and literacy development. Teachers must provide appropriate experiences and interact skillfully with children throughout the day to support their learning. Expert teaching is critical to making sure that preschool children gain the knowledge, skills, and dispositions to succeed in kindergarten.

Creating a Literacy-Rich Environment

Creating a literacy-rich environment does not mean merely covering the walls with words or placing charts from floor to ceiling. Teachers encourage literacy learning by thoughtfully planning the physical environment and including print that is meaningful to children. Classroom literacy materials must serve a purpose. Meaningful print materials help children communicate messages and ideas, learn new information and concepts, organize and express their thoughts, care for the classroom, and know what to do. A literacy-rich environment conveys the message that reading, writing, listening, and speaking are valuable and enjoyable.

Preschool children need to engage with literacy materials; to use them in their play; and to talk with adults about what they are doing, thinking, and feeling. Teachers must act intentionally to help children use written and spoken language throughout the day.

To create a literacy-rich environment, consider the basic principles that are presented in the following chart.

Creating a Literacy-Rich Environment

Organize space to promote conversations and other language use.

Divide space into interest areas that are intimate and that encourage conversations.

Create spaces for large-group discussions as well as spaces for small-group and individual work.

Encourage social interaction through the arrangement of furnishings (e.g., two chairs at the computer or easels placed side-by-side).

Identify interest areas with print and pictures.

Create cozy, comfortable places to relax and read.

Develop a Library area that is attractive and inviting.

Incorporate print throughout the environment.

Write children's names conventionally (using upper- and lowercase letters) on charts, cards, cubbies, and children's work.

Display a daily schedule that is presented with pictures and words, and refer to it throughout the day.

Display the alphabet and have smaller alphabet cards available for children to handle as they write.

Display dictated signs, labels, chart titles, posters, and other writing that serves a purpose.

Add message boards and class mailboxes for children and families to use.

Post poems, fingerplays, song lyrics, rhymes, and recipes.

Display samples of children's writing.

Include print materials related to a study (experience stories, charts, and labeled displays) and provide related literature.

Remove print when it is no longer useful to the children.

Include literacy materials in all interest areas.

Provide books related to the interest area. Display them so that the covers are visible.

Add relevant posters, brochures, magazines, newspapers, and so on.

Label containers and shelves with pictures and words written conventionally with upper- and lowercase letters.

Provide reading and writing materials and tools for children to use in their play and to imitate adult literacy behaviors (e.g., paper, appointment books, phone books, pencils, and markers).

Provide interesting materials that encourage children to talk, read, and write.

Place sign-up sheets for popular activities and interest areas that can only accommodate a few children at one time.

Literacy Throughout the Day

Many young children enter school already knowing a lot about reading and writing. They know how to handle books; they can recognize familiar signs, labels, and logos; they notice and tap the icons on a tablet screen; they know the purpose of recipes, lists, and letters; and they can recognize and write their names and those of family members. Researchers who study literacy experiences in these children's homes find that literacy is a regular, integral part of the children's daily experiences. The children have many language experiences and access to reading and writing materials. They also have many opportunities to interact with supportive adults who respond to their questions, comments, and efforts and who provide experiences that help them learn to read and write.

Teachers who use *The Creative Curriculum*® nurture children's literacy learning in much the same way. They make talking, listening, reading, and writing an integral part of every event of the day. Teachers have many conversations with children throughout the day. Children have opportunities to use and to see adults use reading and writing in meaningful, functional ways from the time they arrive until they leave at the end of the day. Here are some ways to support children's language and literacy learning in your classroom. They are discussed in greater detail in later chapters.

Arrival

Preparing the Environment

Create an attendance chart for which each child has a name card.

Have children and families sign in each day.

Create job and helper charts. Post any directions children might need for completing a job (e.g., how to care for the class pet).

Post a "question of the day" and have children respond in writing.

Create a message board for children and families to send and receive notes.

Interactions

Have informal conversations with children and family members.

Interact with children to facilitate language learning (e.g., talk with children, ask open-ended questions, play with children, and model literate behavior).

Read the "question of the day" with the children and help them respond.

Group Meeting

Preparing the Environment

Display a daily schedule that is presented with pictures and words, and refer to it throughout the day.

Display a chart with words to the song, story, or rhyme you are using.

Prepare name cards to use during group activities.

Have books and related props ready for story time.

Have blank chart paper and markers ready for interactive writing.

Interactions

Refer to the schedule throughout day.

Sing; read or recite poems, rhymes, and fingerplays; and play language games.

Review the attendance chart together to determine who is at school and who is absent.

Refer to the job chart to review responsibilities for the day.

Have children share news about important events and experiences in their lives.

Guide discussions about study topics.

Write experience stories about study trips and visits from experts (e.g., a firefighter or dentist).

Invite experts to talk with children. Have children prepare questions to ask the expert. Record them on a chart.

Introduce new vocabulary as you present new props, materials, and activities.

Create class rules with the children. Record and post them, and review them when necessary.

Read and talk about a variety of books and other texts. Include a variety of genres and formats.

Choice Time

Preparing the Environment

Create choice boards for interest areas. Children use their name cards to indicate their decisions.

Provide literacy props for children's play.

Provide abundant writing materials for children to document their learning and discoveries.

Create sign-up sheets for favorite activities.

Display intriguing pictures in interest areas to encourage conversation and writing.

Write and post rules or directions for using particular materials and equipment. Review them with the children when necessary.

Post picture and word directions for routine procedures (e.g., washing hands) and call attention to them.

Interactions

Talk and sing with children; ask open-ended questions; play with children; retell stories; model reading and writing; and call attention to letters, words, and other features of print.

Include a variety of books in each interest area. Read them with individuals and small groups of children. Show children how to use books to find information.

Offer to take dictation about children's drawings, paintings, or constructions.

Call attention to signs, labels, and other print in various interest areas. Talk about the functions of each. Involve children in creating new signs or labels for the areas throughout the year.

Small Groups

Preparing the Environment

Prepare print materials for various activities, such as recipe charts, poems, name cards, and blank books.

Keep blank chart paper and markers ready for recording children's ideas.

Have books and props ready for reading aloud, storytelling, and retelling.

Interactions

When appropriate, begin with a fingerplay to help children focus their attention.

Read stories and share informational texts.

Retell or enact familiar stories.

Play language games.

Guide discussions about interesting topics, pictures, and objects.

Write with the children (e.g., charts, letters to people, or lists).

Make simple books about topics of interest to the children.

Invite children to bring and read environmental print from home.

Have children draw or write in journals.

Integrate literacy with other content learning (e.g., label a graph and record observations during a simple experiment).

Snack and Mealtime

Preparing the Environment

Write, review, and post the breakfast, lunch, and snack menus.

Post written procedures for washing hands and cleaning dishes.

Post the picture and word recipe if children are to make their own snacks.

Label the food items that the children will use to prepare their snacks.

Interactions

Read the recipes and ingredient labels with the children.

Have children prepare snack by following picture and word recipes.

Have informal conversations with children.

Transitions

Preparing the Environment	**Interactions**
Prepare name cards to use when dismissing children to interest areas.	Play a variety of language games.
Think about appropriate songs, rhymes, and chants in advance.	Sing, and recite rhymes, chants, or fingerplays, both to signal the beginning of a transition and to facilitate learning while children are waiting.
Plan in advance for any appropriate activities that illustrate literacy concepts such as	

Mighty Minutes 47, "Step Up"

Mighty Minutes 57, "Find the Letter Sound"

Mighty Minutes 77, "Hello Bingo"

Mighty Minutes 83, "Let's Make a Cake"

Outdoor Time

Preparing the Environment	**Interactions**
Create inviting areas for reading and writing.	Have informal conversations with children.
Provide materials for children to record their outdoor discoveries.	Sing, and recite rhymes or chants (e.g., while children are jumping rope or playing hand games).
Provide materials for labeling plants.	
Incorporate signs that the children might see elsewhere in the community (e.g., road signs, exit signs, and warning signs).	

Rest Time

Preparing the Environment	**Interactions**
Offer books and writing materials (e.g., magic slates, magnetic drawing boards, and chalkboards) for children who do not sleep.	Read a soothing story in a calm tone before the children rest.
Play soft music or recordings of environmental sounds (e.g., ocean, wind, and night sounds).	

Departure

Preparing the Environment	**Interactions**
Prepare literacy packs for children to take home and share with their families.	Have the reporter announce the results of the "question of the day" when responses were recorded.
Record "What We Did Today" on an erasable board or a chart outside of the classroom so family members can discuss the day's events with their child.	Talk about the events of the day. Record the highlights on the class calendar, a chart, or in a class journal.
	Sing, and read or recite poems, rhymes, or fingerplays.
	Say something special to each child as you say good-bye.

Meeting the Needs of All Children

Early literacy development is critical for all children, but children come to school with vastly different levels of skill and understandings about language and literacy. Some have not had rich experiences at home; others have developmental delays. Other children are English-language learners or have specific disabilities. Many children have particular needs that require special consideration. There are many ways to modify the environment, materials, and teaching strategies to meet each child's strengths and needs.

The preschool schedule calls for a balance of large-group, small-group, and choice-time activities. However, for some young children, leaving an activity in which they are deeply engaged and moving to another activity is unsettling and difficult. Supporting these children during transitions makes it easier for them to stop what they were doing and approach the new activity with greater ease. Once children have made the transition smoothly, teachers can prepare them for the new activity by using strategies such as these:

- Ask the children to take several deep, relaxing breaths or use a warm-up such as "Open the cupboard, reach in, take out your listening ears, and put them on."

- Create a picture board to remind children how to attend during group time. You can review it with the children before beginning an activity and as often as necessary.

Supporting English-Language Learners

You will probably have children in your classroom who are English-language learners (ELL). These are children whose first languages are not English. Some will be learning English for the first time in the preschool setting, and others will have developed various levels of English proficiency before coming to preschool. Many educators use the term *dual-language learners* (DLL) instead. That term refers to young children who are learning two or more languages at the same time (simultaneous language learning) as well as those learning a second language while still developing basic competency in their first language (sequential language learning) (Ballantyne, Sanderman, & McLaughlin, 2008; OHS, 2009). In *The Creative Curriculum*®, the term *English-language learner* is used to refer to all children who are learning English in school and whose first languages are not English. Most programs use a combination of teacher observation, teacher judgment, and a home- or first-language survey to determine which children are English-language learners.

Current research and the experiences of successful programs show that intentional support for the ongoing development of children's first languages is critical to the long-term success of young children whose first languages are not English. Young English-language learners have a wealth of cultural knowledge and understand a lot about language and how to use it effectively. They simply have not mastered the particulars of English. They are in the process of acquiring another language (English), but they usually already know much about storytelling, social rules of language use, and the vocabulary and grammar of their first languages. In order to make the most of their knowledge while they are progressing toward full English proficiency, English-language learners need particular kinds of classroom support. The high-quality early literacy practices explained throughout this volume benefit all preschool children, but certain strategies are of particular importance to children who are English-language learners. Those instructional and assessment strategies are discussed in greater detail below.

Individual Differences

Early childhood teachers need to know about the developmental sequence of English language acquisition and methods to assess the overall language abilities of young English-language learners. Teachers must also understand the influence of home cultural practices, family values, and how the context of language, learning environments, and social interactions inform and shape reading and writing (Hull & Moje, 2013). Preschool children also vary in their readiness to use their new language to express what they know. There are many important individual differences among young English-language learners: the language(s) they hear and speak at home, the social and economic resources available to their families, the amount and timing of their exposure to English, the timing and circumstances of the family's migration to the United States, the families' cultural practices, the children's temperaments, and so on. Teachers must find out about each family's unique circumstances in order to design individualized approaches that build on each child's strengths and prior knowledge.

Maintaining First Languages and Cultures

Helping children maintain and build their first languages while promoting English fluency is especially important because it enables children to keep their primary cultural identity, continue to stay closely attached to the customs and traditions of their families, and progress toward becoming fully bilingual (Espinosa, 2008). "Children's identities and senses of self are inextricably linked to the language they speak and the culture to which they have been socialized. They are, even at an early age, speakers of their languages and members of their cultures. Language and culture are essential to children's identities. All of the affectionate talk and interpersonal communication of their childhoods and family life are embedded in their languages and cultures" (Genesee, Paradis, & Crago, 2004).

In addition, researchers who measured English-language achievement have shown that teaching early literacy skills to English-language learners in their first languages is more effective in the long run. Immersing young children in English (even though they appear to pick it up quickly) does not lead to higher achievement in English in the long run (Espinosa, 2008). We now know that *all* children can become bilingual when they receive enough support for both languages. Research has shown that some children with disabilities—even language impairment—can also learn more than one language (Gutierrez-Clellen, Wagner, & Simón-Cereijido, 2008; Paradis, Crago, Genesee, & Rice, 2003).

In addition to supporting each child's first language, early childhood teachers can intentionally promote the acquisition of English. However, when introducing children to English in an early childhood program, it is important to implement an *additive* model of English acquisition (supporting both English and the children's first languages) and not a *subtractive* model (substituting English for the first language) (Garcia, 2003). When teachers and other school personnel communicate respect and appreciation for the children's first languages and the families continue to use their first languages, the children value and show positive outcomes in both languages. Children who have the opportunity to learn two languages should be encouraged to maintain both so they can become proficient in their first languages as well as English and enjoy the linguistic and cultural benefits of bilingualism.

Developmental Sequence of English Language Acquisition

The following chart explains the typical developmental sequence of English language acquisition by describing what you might observe children doing at each level (adapted from Tabors, 2008).

Levels of Learning a Second Language	What You Might Observe
First language use	Children continue to use their first language with teachers and other children, even if it is not understood. This period can be as short as a few days, but some children persist for months in trying to get others to understand them.
Nonverbal/ observational period	Children limit (or stop) the use of their first language as they realize that it is not understood by others. Children use nonverbal methods to communicate, such gesturing or pantomiming, usually to get attention, make requests, protest, or joke. This is a period of active language learning for the child. He or she is listening to and learning the features, sounds, and words of the new language (receptive language) but not yet using the new language to express him- or herself. This is an extremely important stage of second-language learning that may last for a few months to a year. Any language assessments conducted during this stage of development may underestimate the child's language capacity.
Telegraphic and formulaic speech	Children begin using one- and two-word phrases in English and begin to name objects. They may use groups of words such as "Stop it," "Fall down," or "Shut up," although they may not always use them appropriately. Formulaic speech refers to the child's repetition of chunks of language that he or she has heard often. They may be unanalyzed groups of words or strings of syllables. For example, Tabors (2008) reports that English-language learners in the preschool she studied frequently used the phrase "Lookit" to engage others in their play. The children repeated the phrase they heard others use to achieve their social goals, even though they probably did not know the literal meaning of the words and were repeating familiar sounds because they were functionally effective.
Productive/fluid use of language	Children begin to use simple English sentences like those they hear in meaningful contexts. They begin to form their own sentences by combining words they have learned. Like all young children, they gradually increase the length of their sentences. Errors are common during this period as children experiment with their new language and learn its rules and structure.

Basing Instructional Strategies on the Child's Level of English Language Acquisition

Levels of English Language Acquisition	Instructional Strategies	Assessment Strategies
First language use	Start slowly. Establish consistent routines, post a daily schedule with words and picture cues, and offer picture cues that explain routines and instructions. Encourage peer interactions and voluntary participation in large- and small-group experiences. Use gestures and physical demonstrations to clarify messages. Offer places in the classroom where the child does not need to talk. Speak slowly and clearly. Give the child time to respond, and accept and support first language use. Learn a few words in the child's first language (with correct pronunciation). Pre-read texts in the child's first language and make connections between the child's first language and English. Provide materials (books, audio recordings, and computer programs and games) that use the child's language and depict the child's culture.	Interview family and staff members who are fluent in the child's first language about the child's first language abilities. Observe the child in multiple settings to determine the child's preferred language and extent of English comprehension.
Nonverbal/ observational period	Continue previous methods. Repeat important messages and highlight English vocabulary. Point out important words in texts, in both the child's first language and English. Offer expanded definitions of new English words. Provide many gestures to support the child's understanding of all instructions and interactions. To help the child respond verbally, ask closed questions and phrase questions to include an answer, (e.g., *Do you want the red block or the blue block?*).	Observe the child to gauge comprehension, e.g., when directions are given, note whether the child follows peers or whether the child can follow directions independently. Use focused language interactions and verbal games to assess the child's understanding of simple instructions, e.g., ask the child to point to the picture of a ball, to put his hands on his head, to get ready to go outside, and so on. Continue to monitor the child's first language skills.

Levels of English Language Acquisition	Instructional Strategies	Assessment Strategies
Telegraphic and formulaic speech	Continue earlier strategies. Extend the child's language. For example, when a child says, "I want more," respond, "You want more carrot sticks," while holding up the carrots. Then say more, such as "I like carrots, too. They taste good!" Speak in simple sentences. Accept language mixing as a normal part of second-language learning. Restate the child's utterances in conventional English.	Continue to use earlier assessment methods and possibly combine them with a more formal measure of English language proficiency. Check the child's understanding frequently during instruction and transitions, e.g., while reading *The Very Hungry Caterpillar*, ask the child, "How many strawberries did he eat?"
Productive/fluid use of language	Continue previous strategies while you also raise expectations for English-language usage. Start to increase language demands on the child, e.g., ask the child to say what he or she wants instead of just pointing to an object. Ask more open-ended questions and give the child sufficient time to respond in English. Ask the child to repeat book narratives and tell personal stories in English. Continue to accept language mixing and grammatical errors as the child begins to use more complex language. Help the child make personally meaningful books in both English and his or her first language.	Carefully collect information about the child's acquisition of English through observation and focused language interactions. Continue to use previous assessment methods and perhaps a formal measure of English proficiency as well as the *GOLD*® assessment system. Document the information.

Here are some general strategies for promoting children's English language acquisition:

Cultural supports

- Learn about the cultures, rules, and values of the families in your program and how each family's expectations and practices might differ from the program's expectations and practices.

- Communicate respect for and acceptance of each family's values.

- Integrate children's home cultures and family practices into everyday routines and learning experiences.

- Invite family and other community members to demonstrate skills and practices, and to talk about such topics as clothing, history, and important experiences.

- Display photos of each family. Write captions in the child's first language to explain who the people are and what they are doing.

- Incorporate children's first languages in daily classroom activities through greetings, songs, stories, poetry, rhymes, and counting.

Social–emotional supports

- Establish and follow regular routines so children feel comfortable and confident that they know what to do and when.

- Make sure English-language learners are included in small-group activities and participate in mixed playgroups.

- Use language and other social interactions intentionally to establish warm and nurturing relationships.

- Help English-language learners feel included as valued members of the classroom community.

Environmental supports

- Provide comfortable places where English-language learners can get away from the pressures of communicating and observe activities and interactions until they are ready to join.

- Carefully label materials, learning areas, and wall posters in each family's language. Color coding each language consistently helps children distinguish among the different languages.

- Offer literacy materials that correspond to children's family experiences and their cultural and linguistic backgrounds.

- Provide spaces where teachers, other adults, and children can interact individually and in small groups.

Oral language supports

- Combine nonverbal communication (e.g., gesturing, physical demonstration, and facial expression) with your speech.

- Keep your language and directions short and simple. Emphasize and repeat important words.

- Repeat common phrases slowly and articulate the sounds clearly.

- Learn some important words or phrases in the children's first languages, such as common greetings, family names, safety words, phrases that provide comfort, and terms of politeness. Be sure to pronounce the words correctly because young children need good language models for all of the languages they hear. Enlist the aid of a family member to translate these words and phrases and to write them phonetically in English so that you can remember how to say them. Post the list in the classroom for all adults to use.

- Describe what a child is doing. (*Carlos is building a tall tower with blocks.*)

- Use self-talk to describe your actions. (*I'm putting my coat on because it is cold outside.*)

- Read predictable books that encourage children to join in by saying rhymes, refrains, and important phrases.

- Use books with simple illustrations that provide visual cues about the meaning of the narrative.

- Repeat songs and rhymes with motions so children feel more comfortable about participating and practicing expressive language.

- Adjust communication and instructional strategies according to the children's levels of English-language acquisition.

- Encourage children who speak English to talk and play with English-language learners.

- Introduce books and important concepts in the first languages of the children before you present and read the books aloud in English. (Multilingual staff members or volunteers can help if you do not speak the children's languages.)

- Ask closed questions that children can answer by pointing to pictures or by saying one word. Throughout this book we recommend asking children open-ended questions, but some open-ended questions are too difficult for beginning English-language learners. As children develop more English-language skills, you can begin to introduce open-ended questions and support children's ability to answer by gesturing and by modeling language.

- Teach English vocabulary intentionally. Define the words verbally and by using pictures, objects, gestures, and demonstrations. Associate English words with words in the children's first languages.

- Schedule frequent small-group and individual learning experiences, including time for reading together and for having informal conversations.

- Extend what the child says. Model correct grammar and intentionally engage children in conversational turn-taking.

- Value bilingualism for all children. Teach English-speaking children some words and phrases in the other first language(s) of the children in your class.

Literacy supports

- Include environmental print, books, magazines, and other texts in the languages spoken by the children in the class.

- Connect literacy activities and book reading to the children's homes and family practices.

- Provide appropriate computer programs and tablet games and apps in other languages as well as in English.

- Build on the literacy knowledge each child brings. English-language learners may already love storybooks, know rhymes and stories in their first languages, and understand many print conventions of their first languages.

- Conduct read-alouds in small groups with culturally appropriate books. Whenever possible, introduce the book in the children's first languages first. Highlight important concepts and vocabulary in the children's first languages and English. Include family members in these activities.

- Engage children in dictating personally meaningful stories and making books. Read them back in the child's first language and English if they are written in both languages.

- Read alphabet books that are written in various languages.

- Sing, recite poems that emphasize rhymes, and do fingerplays daily. Activities that encourage children to manipulate English sounds promote phonological awareness.

- Identify and emphasize English sounds that are not common in the child's first language. For instance, Spanish words rarely end with the /ed/ sounds, so emphasize the sounds for Spanish speakers when you add them to form the past tense of many English verbs (e.g., *wanted*).

Family partnership supports

- Recognize that multilingualism is a gift that families can give to their children and how important it is for families to promote their children's oral language and literacy skills in their first languages. Assure families that their first languages, cultures, and practices are valued in your program.

- Let families know about the children's studies and other learning activities. Encourage them to talk at home about study topics in their first languages. That will support the children's understanding of concepts and their acquisition of related vocabulary in more than one language. Provide books, vocabulary lists, and family activity suggestions.

- Communicate in each family's preferred language when working with families who have limited English-language proficiency. This may mean having an interpreter who is fluent in the child's first language. If you and a family do not share a common language, arrange for the services of an interpreter for family meetings and conferences. It is best to avoid asking a child to interpret. Some families do not consider that to be a child's responsibility. Furthermore, you and the family might use language that the child is not able to interpret accurately. You might also want to discuss concerns about which you do not want the child to become anxious. A bilingual member of another family could be helpful in assisting with interpretation, but be sure to follow confidentiality guidelines in these circumstances. Another great source for interpreters could be local community centers, churches, and social service agencies that work with families from diverse language backgrounds.

- Send books home in advance for family members to read and talk about with their children in their first language. If a particular book is not available in their first language, send the English version home and ask the family to discuss the pictures in their first language. This will help the child understand the book when you read it in English.

- Family members should always be encouraged to read storybooks in their first languages. Even if they are not able to read their first languages, most families can tell stories orally, narrate wordless picture books, say rhymes, and sing.

- Invite families to contribute empty food containers labeled in their first languages, calendars, and menus to be used as play props.

These strategies help to create a supportive classroom environment for English-language learners. A carefully designed environment sets the stage for the interactions that help children begin to understand and use their new language while also maintaining the languages of their families.

Supporting Advanced Language and Literacy Learners

In *The Creative Curriculum®* classroom, teachers strive to meet the strengths and needs of every child, including those who have skills, knowledge, or abilities that are more advanced than those of their peers. A child who is already reading needs to learn new skills, as does the child who is just beginning to explore print. One of the teacher's main challenges is to match classroom experiences to each child's previous experiences. All children must be challenged appropriately in the early years so that they do not lose their motivation to learn.

It is important to look at the whole child and remember that a child's skills may be advanced in one area but not another. For example, a child who has exceptional verbal skills may lag in motor development. You may encounter a preschool child who reads fluently but who can barely write his name. Knowing each child's unique combination of skills will be a critical factor in helping him progress in all areas.

As for all children in your class, it is important really to know the child who has advanced language and literacy skills and to provide experiences that are challenging and meaningful. Here are a few tips to remember:

- Include a selection of books appropriate to the child's reading level. Make sure the books are also appropriate for the child's level of social–emotional development.

- Continue reading aloud to the child. Interact before, during, and after each reading.

- Provide materials that spark the child's curiosity and creativity and that promote critical thinking skills.

- Offer books to help the child learn more about a topic that interests him, even if the topic does not interest most children in your class.

- Use more complex language and higher-level questions and prompts when you talk with the child.

- Avoid language activities that do not encourage the child to build on skills and concepts that he or she has already mastered.

- Communicate with the child's family often, to share information about what he or she is doing at home and at the program.

As you work with preschool children who have unusually high abilities or a great deal of experience with language, keep in mind that no single approach will be appropriate for all. Learn what excites each child's curiosity and imagination. Finally, consider ways to encourage each child to use literacy as a way to explore many interests, feelings, and his or her own imagination.

Supporting Children With Disabilities

The Creative Curriculum® encourages children's active involvement in literacy and play, but certain kinds of disabilities make this challenging for many children. They need their teachers' and families' intentional support in order to participate in language and literacy experiences, such as handling books, engaging in conversations, or writing with pencils and paper. In *The Creative Curriculum®* classroom, the teacher's role is to determine how to support each child's full participation in the program. Here are strategies to consider:

Environmental supports

- Offer alternative seating options, such as sitting on an adult's lap or next to an adult.
- Use tape or carpet squares to help children identify the boundaries of personal space.
- Provide appropriate assistive devices so all children can use the computer and the tablet. Select programs, games, and apps that provide auditory as well as visual feedback.
- Place books and other literacy materials where all children—including children in wheelchairs—can reach them and put them away.
- Equip electronic devices, such as audio recorders and CD players, with switches that all children can use independently.

Routine supports

- Preview books or activities with children who need help with transitions or new experiences.
- Break tasks and activities into smaller parts and provide verbal and visual cues as necessary.
- Encourage children to participate to the degree that they are able to do so.
- Use consistent, predictable routines to help children feel comfortable and secure. To encourage adaptability and flexibility, introduce changes gradually.
- Create picture boards with simple directions or reminders about how to behave during group activities and how to complete daily tasks.

Tactile, visual, and auditory supports

- Attach a piece of textured material to a child's name card so that he or she can identify it by touch. Alternatively, let the child choose a unique shape for his card, e.g., a circle if other children's cards are rectangles.
- Modify books by adding textures or raised outlines to illustrations.
- Encourage the child to handle related props when you introduce and reinforce book vocabulary.
- Provide audio recordings to accompany commercial or teacher-made books.
- Include children's books with large print.

Language supports

- Articulate clearly and adjust the speed at which you speak.

- Repeat important directions.

- Make photo albums of various classroom activities to assist children in making choices.

- Use pictures or objects to represent important concepts. Check often for understanding.

- Select books with repetitive language. Record the refrains and important phrases on the child's communication device.

Physical and sensory supports

- Make sure that all children are comfortably positioned and able to reach the materials.

- Select books with clear, simple pictures and familiar concepts.

- Provide objects for children to hold and manipulate as you read a story.

- Place large dots made from hot glue in the upper right-hand corner of the page. This will separate the pages, making them easier for children to turn.

- When making class books, use thick paper such as cover stock or cardboard to make pages that are easier to turn.

- Use hook-and-loop fasteners or magnetic strips, rather than clothespins, to attach cards on attendance and job charts.

- Provide a variety of writing tools, including markers, crayons, and pencils of various thicknesses. Place a piece of rubber tubing over some pencils and markers to make them easier to grasp.

- Include books that enable children to use several senses, for example, books with textures, pop-up books, and scratch-and-sniff books.

Guide to Implementation

In *The Creative Curriculum®* classroom, teachers promote language and literacy learning intentionally. Their understanding of how literacy develops enables them to observe and interact with children and to evaluate their learning. It also enables teachers to plan thoughtfully, choosing strategies that help children progress. The following list of tasks will help you think about how to offer a high-quality language and literacy program.

Build your knowledge about early literacy development and best practices.

1. Become familiar with the components of literacy.

2. Understand literacy development and what you can do to help children progress.

3. Broaden your knowledge of early literacy and current research on oral language, reading and writing, and English-language learning. Read professional journals, take classes, and participate in learning teams or study groups focused on early literacy.

Establish an environment that promotes oral language and literacy learning.

1. Create a classroom Library area and make certain that you have included space and materials for reading, writing, listening, storytelling, and talking about books.

2. Include print throughout the classroom to label objects, provide information, and explain classroom practices.

3. Display books throughout the classroom from a wide range of genres: predictable, story, concept, informational, alphabet, number, rhyming, song, and poetry books.

4. Talk continually with children about what they are doing, thinking, and feeling.

5. Look for opportunities to encourage oral language and literacy in interest areas, studies, group activities, and daily routines.

6. Display the alphabet where children can refer to it easily.

Plan for literacy learning every day.

1. Large-group experiences
   - Phonological awareness songs, fingerplays, and rhymes
   - Study discussions and planning
   - Oral language activities

2. Small-group experiences
   - Phonological awareness songs, fingerplays, and rhymes
   - Reading aloud and story retelling
   - Shared writing experiences
   - Oral language activities

3. Interest areas

   – Literacy props and materials

   – Other materials that build general knowledge

4. Routines and Transitions

   – Songs, rhymes, and fingerplays

   – Children's name cards

   – Language games

Track children's progress.

1. Prepare for ongoing literacy assessment.

   – Become familiar with *The Creative Curriculum®* objectives for development and learning. Focus on the objectives for language, literacy, and English language acquisition as you observe children.

   – Create a management system for recording observations and collecting other documentation.

2. Observe and document children's literacy abilities. Collect samples of their work.

   – If you use *GOLD®*, use features like the *GOLD® Documentation* app, the On-the-Spot Observation Recording Tool, and the *Assessment Opportunity Cards*™ to assist in collecting documentation.

3. Evaluate children's literacy learning by using the curricular objectives.

   – If you use *GOLD®*, tag literacy objectives and dimensions, and assign preliminary levels when adding documentation to link children's skills, knowledge, and abilities to where they are demonstrated along the literacy progressions.

   – If you use *GOLD®*, assign preliminary levels using the Assess feature that is part of *Intentional Teaching Experiences*.

4. Use the information you learn from assessment to plan for individuals, small groups, and the whole class.

   – If you use *GOLD®*, use the Class Profile Report to review each child's most up-to-date Literacy information for each objective and dimension.

   – If you use *GOLD®*, use the Class Profile Report to purposefully search for language and literacy *Intentional Teaching Experiences* based on the most up-to-date information regarding children's skills, knowledge and abilities.

Inform and involve families.

1. Encourage families to listen to, and talk and read with their children. Stress the importance of reading aloud daily and having conversations about what each family member does during the day.

2. Let families know what language and literacy skills you hope children will learn and how that learning will be supported.

3. Use daily contacts with families to share information about children's literacy learning.

4. Plan family literacy sessions.

   – Establish regular times and places for family literacy sessions.

   – Identify topics for the year and plan ways to share information during the sessions.

   – Find ways for families to participate.

   – Encourage family literacy activities.

   – Review other family resources and include manageable amounts of useful information in your sessions.

5. Keep families informed about their children's progress.

   – Emphasize children's strengths.

   – Plan next steps for promoting literacy skills at home and at school.

Teaching Strategies

Talking, Singing, and Playing With Language
66

How to Begin
Supporting Children's Oral
   Language Learning

Reading Aloud
75

How to Begin
Effective Ways to Read Aloud

Storytelling
88

How to Begin
Telling Stories With Children

Story Retelling
97

How to Begin
Supporting Children's Story Retelling

Writing
103

How to Begin
Supporting Children's Writing

Meaningful Play
112

How to Begin
Supporting Children's Play

Studies: Using Literacy to Learn
118

Beginning the Study
Investigating the Topic
Concluding the Study

Teaching Strategies

With their understanding of the components of literacy, teachers plan ways and choose strategies to support children's development and learning. This chapter discusses six essential aspects of teaching literacy in the preschool classroom: talking, singing, and playing with language; reading aloud; storytelling; story retelling; writing; and conducting long-term studies.

Each part of the discussion explains a way of offering coherent, skills-based instruction that meets children's needs and interests. Sometimes teachers plan activities for particular times of the day. For example, many teachers plan to read aloud regularly at the end of the day. At other times, teachers extend children's learning by interacting with them spontaneously in interest areas. For example, teachers often facilitate children's conversations in the Dramatic Play area in ways that introduce more complex language and new vocabulary.

Talking, Singing, and Playing With Language

Oral language is the basis for children's development of reading and writing skills. Children need many opportunities to talk, sing, and engage in playful and serious oral language experiences. Oral language activities support many components of literacy.

Teachers demonstrate that **literacy is a source of enjoyment** by creating an environment where children can take risks safely as they experiment with language and by showing their delight in children's efforts.

Teachers promote **vocabulary and oral language development** when they engage children in discussions and more casual conversations, sing, and recite rhymes. As children gain experience with many forms of language, they hear new words, learn their meanings, and develop understandings about the ways language is structured to convey meaning. Many aspects of oral language are used to read and write (e.g., choosing the appropriate words and grammar, understanding the language of others, sustaining a conversation, and discussing events in sequence).

Children strengthen their **phonological awareness** during oral language activities. When they hear texts with repetitive language; listen to many chants, rhymes, and songs; and learn to detect the patterns of language, they become more aware of the similarities and differences in the individual sounds of words. This is a step toward understanding the sound structure of language and a step toward learning to read.

Teachers promote **knowledge of print** through activities that help children understand that print is meaningful. They create experience charts with children that help them understand that people talk, write, and read about personal experiences. Teachers help children learn about print by writing familiar songs, poems, rhymes, and fingerplays on charts and pointing to the words as they are read, sung, or recited.

Once children have learned a song or rhyme, the teacher can model how the spoken words are matched to the printed words in a **book or other text**. Teachers can invite children to develop new verses and then create their own books. Placing these books in the Library area and other interest areas enables children to handle books and practice reading skills.

Listening **comprehension** develops before children learn to read. Interacting with children, challenging them to talk about their thoughts and feelings, and asking open-ended questions to encourage their efforts are ways teachers help children build listening comprehension skills.

How to Begin

Children need opportunities to experiment with language, to explore language sounds, patterns, and meanings. They also test the uses of language in different settings: social situations, problem-solving situations, and everyday routines and activities. In *The Creative Curriculum®* classroom, talking, singing, reciting rhymes, and playing with language are integrated with each other and with other activities throughout the program day. Children have meaningful reasons to communicate, and they feel free to experiment with language. Teachers

- plan oral language experiences
- create an environment that encourages language use and experimentation

Planning Oral Language Experiences

A day that is filled with enjoyable and interesting experiences encourages children to talk with others and to experiment with language. Here are three ways that teachers intentionally promote children's oral language development:

Offer firsthand experiences. In order to comprehend what they read, children must acquire knowledge—including understandings about concepts—and develop their vocabularies. For this reason, teachers should offer children many firsthand experiences in which they are introduced to new and interesting topics and rich vocabulary, actively explore concepts and materials, and talk about their ideas and feelings.

Have conversations. Conversations involve extended back-and-forth exchanges. Research shows that children who have frequent opportunities to participate in meaningful conversations with responsive adults acquire vocabulary, other language skills, and knowledge about the world, all of which contribute to early reading success. In contrast, language that is used to control children, give directions, or elicit information from children without encouraging complex thought contributes little to their literacy development (e.g., *Stop that!*; *Put this in your cubby*; *Eat your lunch before it gets cold*; *What color is this?*).

Conversations should occur throughout the day. Some conversations are casual, such as those that typically occur during meals or when children arrive. Others are more guided, such as those that take place when an expert is invited to speak with the children about a particular topic or when you lead discussions before, during, and after reading a book aloud. Through verbal exchanges with you individually, with a small group, and with the whole class, children learn to communicate effectively. They learn to follow conversational rules (e.g., taking turns, listening attentively, and staying on the topic); develop knowledge about the world; and gain confidence in their ability to use language.

Use songs, rhymes, and other language-play activities. Singing songs and reciting rhymes, fingerplays, chants, or tongue twisters enable children to explore language in a playful, enjoyable way. The patterns in these language forms encourage children to experiment with language. They refer to familiar people, animals, and objects, but new words are also introduced. Large-group meetings are perfect settings for singing and for reciting rhymes, while small groups are more appropriate for other types of oral language activities and games.

Teachers can slow down the rate of singing and speaking for children with certain kinds of language delays and for English-language learners. Sometimes it is helpful to make a recording of classroom favorites at a slower speed. Children can use these recordings to learn songs, short poems, and fingerplays.

Use activities that encourage singing and reciting rhymes such as:

- *Mighty Minutes* 100, "La, La, La"
- *Mighty Minutes* 165, "A Chat With a Cat"
- *Mighty Minutes* 178, "Happy Moths"
- *Mighty Minutes* 194, "Wind-Up Robots"

Creating an Environment That Promotes Oral Language Development

Children talk when the environment is filled with interesting materials to explore, when they have a need to communicate, and when ample time and opportunity are provided. Here are ways to create an environment that encourages children to listen and speak:

- Create interest areas that encourage conversations and cooperative play among children.

- Provide interesting props and materials that invite children to explore, experiment, learn new words, and use extended language. (For suggestions, see chapter 4 of this volume and see *The Creative Curriculum® for Preschool, Volume 2: Interest Areas*.)

- Provide a variety of hands-on experiences that introduce children to new concepts, words, and forms of language.

- Encourage children's dramatic play because it encourages their exploration of roles, conversation, and the expression of ideas and feelings. Provide adequate time and materials for children to play freely and become fully engaged.

- Interact with children during choice time to encourage them to talk about their ideas and feelings. Use open-ended questions and prompts to encourage children to expand on their ideas and experiment with language.

- Encourage children to settle conflicts by talking.

- Provide texts and story-related props that invite children to explore book language.

Supporting Children's Oral Language Learning

Because each child is unique and because children have varied backgrounds, they differ in the age and rate at which they learn particular language skills. Researchers who studied these differences have concluded that the amount of language children experience influences vocabulary and other aspects of oral language development dramatically. The implication for early childhood programs is that teachers should offer many opportunities for children to participate in varied language experiences that introduce new words, concepts, and linguistic structures. In addition, children need the direct support of teachers and other trusted adults who listen, allow them to experiment with the uses and forms of language, and respond.

Read the following example to see how the teachers in one classroom skillfully use conversation, song, and a game to promote children's oral language and literacy learning. Note that the boxes on the right explain what the teachers are doing and noticing.

The children in Ms. Tory's and Mr. Alvarez's preschool class arrive at varied times. They routinely put their things away, check to see if they have a job for the day, and then work in interest areas until it is time for the morning meeting. Ms. Tory and Mr. Alvarez move freely around the room, greeting children and family members and interacting with children.

Derek and Dallas enter the classroom, talking and laughing. They head toward the cubby area to hang up their jackets and backpacks.

Dallas:	*Not again, Derek!* (He laughs.) *That's my cubby. Here's yours.* (He points to Derek's cubby.)
Ms. Tory:	(She stoops down and smiles at Derek.) *I think Dallas is right. Your name does have a capital* D, *like Dallas's name. See?* (She points to the *D*s in both names.) *But your name is spelled capital* D-e-r-e-k, *and* Dallas *is spelled capital* D-a-l-l-a-s. (She points to each letter.) *Also remember that your picture is here to help you and to let others know that this is your cubby.*

Draws attention to letters of the alphabet

Calls attention to the similarities and differences in written words

(Then she smiles at Tasheen, who reluctantly enters the classroom with her dad, and stoops to speak to Tasheen as she unpacks her backpack.) *Welcome back. We missed having you at school these past few days. We have lots to share with you, and I bet you have lots to share with us!*

Speaks with a child at the child's eye level

Tasheen:	(Smiles at Ms. Tory but doesn't speak.)	Recognizes a smile as the child's way of communicating
Ms. Tory:	*I heard that you are now a big sister. Your mom and dad are very lucky to have you to help them with the new baby!*	

Tasheen:	(Takes a picture from her backpack and shows it to Ms. Tory.)	Recognizes that the child is using a photo to convey a message
Ms. Tory:	*Ahhh, I see you brought a picture of you and the new baby to share with us. What are you going to tell us about the new baby?*	Asks an open-ended question to prompt a conversation

---

Tasheen:	*He's a boy, and his name is Jeremiah.*	Makes a relevant comment and asks a question to keep the conversation going
Ms. Tory:	*He looks like he's smiling. Is he a happy baby?*	
Tasheen:	*Sometimes he cries a lot, and it is really loud.*	

Ms. Tory:	*Babies do cry a lot sometimes. I wonder why.*	Wonders aloud to prompt conversation
Tasheen:	*Dad said they can't talk, so they cry to let us know they need something.* (She and her dad smile at one another.) *Sometimes he cries because he's hungry or when he needs his diaper changed. Sometimes he just wants us to hold him.*	

Ms. Tory:	*He's not crying here. He must like it when you hold him like that.* (Points to the picture, and Tasheen smiles.)	Signals that she is listening by making a relevant comment
	I know you have lots more to tell us about Jeremiah. What do you need to do in order to share your picture?	Asks a question to guide behavior
Tasheen:	*Put it in the "share chair."* (Ms. Tory nods. Tasheen hugs her dad goodbye and skips off with her picture.)	

When all the children have arrived, Ms. Tory and Mr. Alvarez move through the room to tell the children they have 5 more minutes to play before gathering on the rug for morning meeting.

Soft music begins to play, and the children begin putting their materials and belongings away. A few family members are still in the classroom, and they offer to help the children clean up. Mr. Alvarez overhears a conversation between Juwan and a parent.

Juwan:	*All the farm animals go in this tub. See the picture and words? That says, "Farm animals."* (Points to the picture and each word.)	Notices the child's understanding of some print
	Then you put it on the shelf, right here. (Points to an identical picture and word label on the shelf.) *See? It says the same thing: "Farm animals."*	Hears the child give oral directions
Parent:	*You read the words and looked at the pictures to know where to put the animals.*	
Juwan:	*I know.* (Goes to the rug.)	

Ms. Tory:	(Sits facing the children; refers to the picture/word schedule posted on the wall behind her; points to a word and reads.) *Arrival.*	Calls attention to a purpose of print Orients children to print
	Let's see if everyone has arrived. (Looks at the attendance chart.) *Someone is not with us today. Who is it?*	Asks a question to prompt children's thinking
Children:	(Some look around while others look at the name card on the attendance chart.)	Allows children time to investigate
Zack:	*Malik.*	
Ms. Tory:	*That's right, Zack. Malik is not here today.* (Sweeps her hand under Malik's name.). *I don't see Malik, and her name card is still on the side that reads, "See Who Is at Home"* (Points to each word on the attendance chart.) *I hope Malik will be back with us tomorrow.*	Shows children the correspondence between spoken and written words Demonstrates left-to-right directionality

Ms. Tory:	(Begins singing "Clap a Friend's Name With Me," which she taught the children the day before.)	Promotes phonological awareness by using a song and movement that call children's attention to syllables
Children and Ms. Tory:	(Sing to the tune of "Mary Had a Little Lamb.")	

Clap a friend's name with me,
name with me,
name with me.
Clap a friend's name with me.
Let's try Crystal.
Crys·tal.

(They clap each syllable in Crystal's name. Then they continue to sing, substituting different children's names and clapping the syllables in each.)

Ms. Tory:	*I wrote the song on a chart so we can use it as we sing. I put a piece of hook-and-loop fastener tape in the space where one of your names will go. I think I will put Ben's name in first.* (Puts Ben's name card in the space; then sings the song for the children, this time pointing to each word as she sings.)	Demonstrates left-to-right directionality Helps children understand the concept of a word Encourages the children's enjoyment of literacy
Various children:	*Sing about me! Do my name!*	
Ms. Tory:	*Let's play a game to see whether you can guess whom we will sing about next.* (Shows the children a brightly colored gift bag with their name cards inside. Explains that she will slowly pull a card out, revealing and naming one letter at a time, and they are to guess whose name it is.) *Are you ready?* J.	Introduces a game that helps children build alphabet knowledge
Janelle and Juwan:	*Mine!* (They raise their hands.)	Recognizes that children are demonstrating letter knowledge
Ms. Tory:	*Your names start with* J, *but remember to wait for the next letter.* (She continues.) O-n-e-t-t-a.	Acknowledges what children know and challenges their thinking
Jonetta:	*Mine!*	
Ms. Tory:	(She places Jonetta's name card in the space and invites the children to sing the song as she points to each word. They repeat the process, inserting another child's name card and singing the song.)	Demonstrates the way to do the activity

Zack:	*Will you put the chart and name cards in the Music and Movement area so we can sing it at choice time?*	
Ms. Tory:	*We can do that, Zack! Why don't you go with Mr. Alvarez to find a good place to put the chart and name cards.* (Zack takes the bag of name cards and goes with Mr. Alvarez eagerly.)	Supports a child's suggestion that will extend learning opportunities
Ms. Tory:	*Our meeting is almost over. Who can tell what we will do next?* (Refers to the daily schedule, pointing to the words *Choice time.*)	Calls children's attention to a purpose of print Gives the children a reason to read
Children:	(Read in unison.) *Choice time.*	
Ms. Tory:	*To begin choice time, we will play a listening game. You will need to listen for words that have the same beginning sound as your name. If they do, you may choose an area to play. Listen carefully.*	
	If your name begins like big, ball, *and* bump, *I want you to buzz like a bumblebee to an area.* (Ben hesitates at first; then he buzzes away.)	Promotes phonological awareness by drawing children's attention to initial sounds
	Listen again. If your name begins like the words tiny, tipsy, *and* toothbrush, *I want you to tiptoe to an interest area.* (Continues until all of the children are dismissed.)	

Chapter 4 of this volume offers more examples of ways teachers interact with children to support language learning.

Tips to Share With Families

- Have conversations about what you are doing together and what you notice. Offer interesting observations that invite your child to respond.

- Encourage friends and other family members to use your child's first language during family activities.

- Sing, march, dance, and make up songs in the language you are most comfortable speaking.

- Teach your child songs that you sang growing up. (Don't worry if you can't carry a tune.)

- Teach your child nursery rhymes.

- Make up silly rhymes and sayings.

- Make up rhymes involving your child's name.

- Talk about what you are doing so your child learns the language that describes everyday experiences.

- Use words that are new to your child when you talk with him or her.

- Describe what you experience and ask questions that encourage your child to talk with you.

- Try to keep conversations going back and forth at least five times. Asking your child for more information is often a good way to keep a conversation going.

- Accept your child's way of speaking while you model conversational skills and standard language.

- Look for your child's nonverbal attempts to communicate. Model language that your child might use to express ideas and feelings.

- When you ask your child a question, give him or her plenty of time to think about what you are asking and to respond.

Reading Aloud

While many activities contribute to children's literacy development, none is more powerful than reading aloud. Research indicates the value of reading aloud to support skills related to each of the components of literacy.

For most children, being read to is an emotionally satisfying experience. The intimacy and warmth children associate with sharing books with adults helps to promote **literacy as a source of enjoyment**. This association leads children to explore books, practice reading abilities, and later read successfully for their own information and pleasure.

Reading aloud is a primary way to enrich children's **vocabulary and oral language**. As children listen to storybooks, informational books, and poetry, they hear words that are new, interesting, and less common than words they hear in ordinary conversations. Reading to children also introduces book language, which is usually more formal, complex, and abstract than language heard in everyday conversations.

The language in many children's books focuses attention on the sounds of words, thereby promoting **phonological awareness**. Reading stories with rhyme and alliteration help children become sensitive to the similarities and differences among the individual sounds in words. Some books that contain repeated and varied language patterns highlight and segment the sounds of words, and they encourage children to experiment with language.

Reading aloud helps children gain **knowledge of print**. Children learn that print conveys meaning. They develop understandings about the correspondence and differences between spoken and written language, and they learn about directionality (that English and many other languages are read from left to right and top to bottom) when they see the teacher sweeping her fingers under the text as she reads. They observe book-handling skills, such as how to hold a book upright and turn the pages in order.

Reading aloud helps children understand that **letters** can be grouped together to form **words** and that words have meaning. Alphabet books typically introduce a letter along with pictures of objects with names that start with that letter. This helps children recognize and name the letters of the alphabet and introduces them to letter–sound associations. Illustrated concept books also contribute to children's understanding of individual words, because each page usually pictures an object that is identified by a single printed word.

The language of **books and other texts** is different from the language of children's usual conversations. By hearing books read aloud, children learn how to listen to and understand the language of stories and informational texts. They develop a sense of story, that stories have a setting, characters, a theme, a plot, and a resolution. When they hear books read aloud by adults who read fluently, change their voices for different speakers, and use inflection to aid comprehension, children develop understandings about how ideas and feelings are communicated through written language.

Interactions among adults and children before, during, and after a text is read aloud help children develop comprehension skills. When teachers invite children to make predictions, prompt them to supply words or phrases, ask and answer questions, offer information, and relate the text to real-life experiences, they help children process the meaning of the language they are hearing.

How to Begin

Read aloud several times daily to meet the needs of all children, including those who are English-language learners and those who have had few previous experiences with books.

Successful story reading and book sharing involve more than selecting a book from the shelf and reading it aloud. Like other activities and experiences offered to preschool children, reading aloud requires planning. Teachers must

- plan for small groups and individuals, as well as for the large group
- establish regular times for reading aloud
- judge the appropriate amount of time
- create a physical space in which children are comfortable

Choosing Good Books

Know your children's interests, cultural and family backgrounds, and life experiences so you can select books that will be meaningful to the children. As you choose, keep in mind the characteristics of a book that is good to read aloud:

- The topic is already or likely to be of interest to the children.
- It is a good match for the children's developmental levels (e.g., for young preschool children, the book has lots of rhymes and repetition; for older preschool children, the story has suspense, plot twists, dialogue, and engaging characters).
- It relates to the children's experiences.
- A familiar—and favorite—author wrote it.
- The story and illustrations are relevant to children's families and cultures.
- The story and illustrations introduce new family and cultural experiences.
- It is already or likely to become a favorite that children like hearing again and again.
- New information and ideas are presented through text and pictures.

For further guidance on the types of books to choose for your classroom, see *The Creative Curriculum® for Preschool, Volume 2: Interest Areas*. As you determine the appropriateness of a book, consider these questions:

- How long will it take to read? Can the children pay attention for that much time?
- Will any concepts or ideas be unfamiliar to the children? How can you explain them?
- Do the illustrations have surprises or tiny details to point out to the children?
- How can you make sound effects (e.g., animal noises or sirens) and gestures part of the reading?
- How can you vary your voice to dramatize the different characters?
- What props (e.g., hats or musical instruments) would enhance the reading?
- How can you encourage the children to participate? Can they say rhymes, join in as you read the refrain, predict what will happen next, and answer questions?

Planning for Groups and Individuals

In most preschool classrooms, teachers tend to share books with large groups of children rather than with small groups or with individuals. Although sharing books with the whole class is often an appropriate activity, large-group interaction must be limited so that it does not interrupt the flow of the narrative. To give them more opportunities to respond, children should be offered regular opportunities to listen to stories and informational books in small groups and individually with an adult. Children's literacy learning and motivation to read are affected more by the interaction that occurs between adults and children during the reading than by the actual narrative.

Research suggests that children who hear stories in small-group settings show stronger comprehension skills than children to whom stories are read individually or in large-group settings. Similarly, children's comprehension seems to be better when stories are read to them individually than when stories are read to them in a large group. Children in the studies asked more questions and made more comments when stories were read to them individually or in small-group settings rather than read to the whole class. These skill differences are attributed to differences in teacher–child interactions in the various settings (Morrow and Gambrell, 2002).

Establishing Regular Times to Read Aloud

Young children thrive when they have consistent daily routines, so establish regular times for reading with them. Teachers who use *The Creative Curriculum®* read to children at least twice a day. You might choose to start or end the day with a book, and you might read to children after choice time or before nap time. Of course you can still look for other opportunities to read, such as during snack time or outdoors, while maintaining your regularly scheduled reading times.

Many teachers find it helpful to plan ways to signal periods for reading aloud. These might include singing a particular song, reciting a rhyme, or wearing a special hat or apron to signal to children that read-aloud time is about to begin. Once children have gathered, teachers help children get ready to listen and respond by reviewing expectations for behavior during the reading. Reading is interactive and usually ends with a fingerplay, movement activity, or a discussion that helps children make personal connections to the story.

Judging How Much Time to Allow

Especially at the beginning of the year, not all of the children in your class will be equally ready for group reading. Consider how long particular books take to read and whether the children can pay attention for that much time. Some children will have had few previous experiences with books and are not accustomed to listening to books read aloud, while others may become restless or distracted even if they are experienced. You can plan for these children by scheduling short read-aloud times and by using books that have bold illustrations and simple, predictable, repetitive text. Other strategies include minimizing distractions during this time, asking an assistant or volunteer to sit close to these children to help them focus on the book, or making plans to share books with these children in smaller groups or individually in the Library area. As children become accustomed to reading routines, you will be able to share books that are longer and have richer, more complex text.

Creating Special Places for Reading

If reading is to be an enjoyable experience for children, you will need to create a place where they can sit comfortably and be near enough to you to hear the book and see the pictures clearly. The Library area is the ideal location for reading aloud if it is an attractive area equipped with soft furnishings, beautiful picture books, and props that invite lively interactions with books. If the Library area is not large enough to accommodate all of the children, use the space where you typically hold group meetings and reserve the Library area for small-group reading or sharing a book with one child. Wherever you choose, remember that the space should be one that children come to recognize as a special place for sharing books.

Effective Ways to Read Aloud

Reading aloud well is not a skill that comes easily for all teachers, but it can be developed over time. Try these strategies:

Practice reading the book before you read it aloud to children so that you become very familiar with the language, characters, and plot. Write questions and reminders on sticky notes and stick them on the appropriate pages so you will know how and when to prompt the children's thinking.

Start the reading by giving children a reason to listen to the book. The first step in reading aloud is to get the children's attention and help them focus on the book. You might read the title and the names of the author and illustrator, discuss the cover and what the book might be about, and suggest things for which the children can look and listen.

Here are more suggestions for introducing a book:

- Explain how the story is related to familiar feelings or a recent experience.
- Share an object that is an important part of the story.
- Relate a new book to a familiar one.
- Explain how the book is related to what the children are studying.

While reading, use strategies that hold the children's attention and that provide information about books and print. Start to read as soon as the children are seated comfortably and you have their attention. Here are some tips for reading aloud:

- Hold the book to one side so the children can see the pictures.
- Use your voice and facial expressions to make the characters and their experiences come alive.
- Change or define words to help the children understand the story.
- Stop to talk about the pictures, answer questions, discuss what might happen next, and think about what the characters might be feeling.
- Answer the children's questions if they are related directly to the book. Save other questions and comments for later.

- Run your finger under the text.
- Pause at the end of sentences.
- Invite children to join in with repeated and predictable words, phrases, rhymes, and refrains.
- Discuss interesting words and ask what the children think they mean.
- Call the children's attention to words that rhyme or have sounds like those in other words the children know.

After reading, discuss various aspects of the story and invite children to participate in follow-up activities.

Here are a few suggestions:

- Ask the children to react to or share their opinions about the story.
- Briefly summarize the story (characters, setting, theme or problem, plot, and resolution).
- Continue to help the children make connections between the story events or characters and their own lives.
- Discuss or clarify new words in the story.
- Encourage the children to respond to the story by drawing, writing, constructing, or retelling.
- Explain that the book will be placed in the Library area or another interest area and encourage the children to explore it more.

Your Teaching Practice

Think about your reading style when sharing books with children. Do you read quickly? Slowly? Loudly? Softly? Do you prefer that children wait until you finish reading before adding their own ideas? If you are unsure, consider recording a read-aloud session and viewing it to determine ways you may wish to change your approach to reading.

Ms. Tory is a preschool teacher who is skilled at sharing books with her class. In the example that follows you will see how she shares *Jennie's Hat* by Ezra Jack Keats. The comments on the right explain how Ms. Tory uses the read-aloud strategies and prompts suggested in the "Interactive Story Reading" chart found in chapter 4 of this volume.

	It is choice time, and the children are engaged in various activities throughout the room. Ms. Tory picks up the xylophone and begins to play it softly. Looking up from their play, the children see Ms. Tory making her way toward the rocking chair in the Library area. The children put away their materials and then, one by one, eagerly join Ms. Tory where she sits with a large round gold box in her lap. Mr. Alvarez helps children who are still cleaning up, and then they join the other children on the rug. Ms. Tory makes sure everyone is comfortable and comments on how well the children cleaned up. Mr. Alvarez joins the group, and Ms. Tory begins story time.	Helps the children transition to story time by using the xylophone as a signal Makes sure that everyone is comfortable and relaxed before beginning story time
Ms. Tory:	*Today I have a story for you about a girl who gets a gift that disappoints her a little. Does anyone know what I mean by* disappointed?	Introduces new vocabulary before reading the story
Dallas:	*Sad.*	
Setsuko:	*Yeah, sad because you think you're going to get something and then you don't get it.*	
Ms. Tory:	*Have you ever been disappointed?* (Children offer examples of disappointments.) *Show me how your face looks when you are disappointed.*	Helps children connect the story with previous experiences
Ms. Tory:	*The gift the girl was waiting for was something you wear on your head. Can anyone guess what it was?*	Encourages predictions Provides a way for children to participate
Various children:	*A scarf! A cap! A hat! A visor! A football helmet!*	
Ms. Tory:	*Those are all things someone might wear on his or her head. Why would someone need or want to wear something on her head?*	Asks an open-ended question Promotes logical thinking
Sonya:	*My grandma wears a scarf on her head so her hair won't blow everywhere.*	

Leo:	*My dad wears a cap to keep the sun out of his eyes.*	
Crystal:	*Yeah, my mom wears a visor to keep the sun out, too.*	
Dallas:	*And football players wear helmets so their heads won't get hurt when they get tackled! You have to wear a helmet if you play football. It's a rule!*	
Ms. Tory:	*Those things help to protect us from sun, getting hurt, or getting our hair all messed up.*	Acknowledges the children's contributions to the discussion

	(Ms. Tory holds up the box and asks the children to think to themselves about which of the items they mentioned is most likely to be in the box. She asks them to listen while she gently shakes the box.)	Plans a way to capture the children's interest and gathers all necessary props (a hat and hatbox)

Ms. Tory:	*Do you think this could be a football helmet?*	Encourages reasoning skills
Setsuko:	*No. The box isn't big enough.*	
Dallas:	*And we would hear a clunking sound.*	
Ms. Tory:	*How about a scarf?*	
Sonya:	*No. A scarf doesn't need a box. My grandma keeps her scarves folded in a drawer in her dresser.*	
Ms. Tory:	(Slowly cracks open the lid of the box to reveal a small section of the brim of a straw hat.)	
Leo:	*I think it's a cap, because I saw that piece that hangs over your face.*	
Ms. Tory:	*The part of a cap that extends over your forehead is a visor. The kind of visor that Crystal's mom wears has a band to keep the front piece on her head. Let's take a look at what's in the box. It is for someone's head, but it's a little different from a cap.* (Takes the hat out of the box and places it on her head.) *It's not a football helmet, a scarf, or a cap. It's a hat. The part that Leo noticed is called the brim.* (Runs her finger around the brim.) *It has a brim instead of a visor.*	Introduces new vocabulary Helps children verify their predictions

Ms. Tory:	*The title of this book is* Jennie's Hat. *The author is* Ezra Jack Keats. *(Holds up the book and runs her finger under the words as she reads. Points to the cover picture of a girl with a basket on her head and leads a discussion about who the girl might be and why she has a basket on her head. Shows the first several pages of the story and asks the children to describe what they see and predict what will happen. Returns to the beginning of the book and reads the first few pages about Jennie's disappointment with her new hat.)*	Uses book language such as the terms *title* and *author*

Demonstrates that print is read from left to right

Draws children's attention to the illustration to help them make predictions and discuss their ideas

Takes children on a picture walk through the book to demonstrate how pictures are clues that can help them predict and confirm what the story is about |
| Tyrone: | *She didn't like her hat!* | Notices that children listen attentively to see whether their predictions are correct |
| Ms. Tory: | *Jennie was disappointed with her hat. Have you ever cried because you were disappointed?* | Helps the children make personal connections to the story |

Ms. Tory:	*(Continues to read.) "She put on a straw basket to see what sort of hat it would make. Then she drew pictures. 'HAT-CHOO!,' she sneezed. 'Bless you, dear,' called her mother, 'and what are you doing?' 'I'm drawing a hat-erpillar—I mean a caterpillar,' answered Jennie."*

Have you ever heard anyone sneeze like that? (Children shake their heads, no.) What do you think a hat-erpillar is? | Asks *who, what, when, where, why,* and *how* questions |
Children:	*(Sit quietly for a moment.)*	
Dallas:	*(Points to the picture on the page.) Not a hat-erpillar, a caterpillar! See, there is the picture of the caterpillar!*	
Ms. Tory:	*Why do you think Jennie called it a* hat-erpillar? *(Children offer a variety of responses. Ms. Tory continues to read and ask questions.)*	Draws children's attention to initial consonant sounds by repeating a nonsense word
Carlos:	*The birds are following Jennie.*	
Ms. Tory:	*Hmm, I wonder why. (Pauses.)*	Uses open-ended comments to encourage thinking
Ms. Tory:	*(Reads text about the birds that swooped down, flapping and fluttering around Jennie's new hat. She makes swooping movements with her arms and flaps her hands as she does so. Invites the children to join her in making flapping, fluttering, and swooping motions.) Why were the birds following Jennie?*	Uses movement to clarify the meanings of new words and to spark interest in the story

Involves the children in physical activity

Asks *wh-* questions

Encourages children to talk about the story |

Children:	*To put things on her hat!*
Crystal:	*Jennie is happy now! But she wasn't at first, when she just had that plain hat.*
Dallas:	*The birds were Jennie's friends.*
Setsuko:	*Jennie's hat is beautiful now!*
Ms. Tory:	(Finishes reading the story.) *That's the end of the story!*
Sonya:	*Why did her mom wrap up her hat?*
Ms. Tory:	*What did the story say?* (She points to the last sentence and reads it again.) *"It would be saved and looked at and remembered for a long, long time." Do you have something that helps you remember a special day or a special experience?*
Sonya:	*I have a toy dolphin from my trip to the beach.*
Ms. Tory:	*Yes, your dolphin reminds you of your trip with your grandmother, doesn't it? Jennie's hat reminds her of the day the birds helped her. Well, I'll put* Jennie's Hat *in the Library area, along with this hat.* (Takes the hat off her head.) *You may read it on your own or with a friend.*

Ms. Tory line ("That's the end of the story!"): Uses book language, e.g., *The end*

Ms. Tory final line: Responds to a child's question and promotes comprehension skills by asking children to recall details of the story and by helping them connect the story to their own experiences

Showcases the book after reading

Two additional interactive approaches to reading books aloud with children are described on the following pages: repeated read-alouds and conversational reading. Each approach emphasizes the components of literacy in different ways.

Repeated Read-Alouds

The repeated read-aloud is a research-based approach to helping young children develop comprehension skills and expand their listening and speaking vocabularies.

According to McGee and Schickedanz (2007), teachers can enhance children's oral vocabulary development and listening comprehension by

- modeling higher-level thinking about why characters think, feel, and act they way they do and predicting what might happen next
- asking thoughtful questions about characters and story events
- prompting children to recall and retell a story
- reading a book more than once
- defining words and phrases during the reading of a story

Early childhood experts who watched hundreds of teachers read aloud to young children found that a high-quality storybook needs to be read at least three times in order for children to understand the complex ideas and story problems that the author presents. By reading the same book repeatedly, teachers help children gain confidence in their knowledge of the story and of print in general. Familiar books also support children's learning of new concepts within the context of recognizable story lines and vocabulary (Barclay, 2014) The types of books that are best suited for repeated read-alouds are sophisticated illustrated storybooks. Such picture books include stories where the listener or reader must infer characters' motives (why they act as they do or say certain things), feelings, and thoughts. High-quality books use rich vocabularies, especially words that are not often heard in children's typical conversations. A number of high-quality books that are appropriate for repeated interactive read-alouds are included in the *Teaching Strategies® Children's Book Collection*.

The repeated read-aloud approach has four components:

1. Book introduction: Read the title and show the front cover of the book. Then introduce the main characters and talk about their problem.
2. Vocabulary: Select 8–10 words that you want to highlight and define for children. Choose words that are essential to understanding the story. As you read, define the words in one or more of the following ways:
   - Point to an illustration or part of an illustration that shows the meaning of a word, e.g., point to the cradle as you read the word *cradle*.
   - Demonstrate the meaning of words by using facial expressions, movements, and other body language, e.g., tap your hand rhythmically on a hard surface as you read the phrase "tapped a rhythm on the side of the truck."
   - Give a very brief definition of a word as you read it in the text (e.g., *Shrink. That means get smaller and smaller.*)

3. Comments and questions: Make comments that show children how to think about the characters and events. Ask questions to help children understand the story in more depth. Do not comment or ask questions about every page, just at important points during the story when you want children to infer or deduce a character's motives, thoughts, and feelings or to predict what will happen next.

4. After-reading questions: Ask two or three open-ended questions that help children think about the characters' problem and interpret the characters' behavior.

Here is an explanation of what to do during each of the read-alouds.

First read-aloud

In the first reading, you introduce children to new ideas and ways of thinking. After telling the children the title and the names of the author and illustrator, tell them the names of the characters and hint at the problem the characters will face. During the reading, use the techniques listed earlier to define the words you chose. Comment about what the main character is doing, thinking, and feeling. Your comments encourage children to interpret the story, that is, to extend their thinking beyond the literal details of the story. Do not phrase these comments as questions. After you have finished reading the story, pose after-reading questions and be prepared to help children answer them.

Second read-aloud

The second reading should occur 1 or 2 days after the first read-aloud and includes the same components. While the book introduction, questions, vocabulary, and after-reading questions are similar to those of the first read-aloud, they should guide children to slightly more advanced thinking and language use. Before reading, help children recall some of the ideas that were introduced in the first read-aloud. Also help children name the characters and state the problem before you begin rereading the text. During the reading, ask questions about the characters and make comments as necessary to help children understand the characters' behavior, thoughts, and feelings. Continue to define the words you want to emphasize, this time adding more verbal explanations for words that you defined during the first read-aloud by pointing to illustrations or by dramatizing. Pose after-reading questions and guide children to answer more fully.

Third read-aloud

The third reading should occur within a week of the second read-aloud. At this point, children are better prepared to retell the story with your support. Invite two or three children to identify the main characters and to talk about the problem the characters face. To assist children in retelling the story, show illustrations and ask, "What is happening here?" or "What happens next?" Prompt children to provide more information by pointing to the illustration of a character and asking questions such as "What is he thinking?" or "What is she feeling?" Encourage children to use the vocabulary of the book as they explain what is happening in each illustration. Further emphasize some words by using them in a context that is familiar to the children but not related directly to the story. (Of course, when words have multiple meanings you will usually want to emphasize the meaning the author intended.) You may read some pages of the book between children's retellings to keep the pace lively and interesting, but maintain the focus on the children's retellings. Pose the after-reading questions and help children listen to each other's responses.

For more specific examples of the repeated read-aloud approach, refer to *Book Discussion Cards*™, which were developed for selected storybooks in the *Teaching Strategies® Children's Book Collection*. These cards are quick guides for you to use as you read a book aloud with a group of children. They include suggestions for introducing the book, short definitions of words to emphasize, examples of comments and questions for each read-aloud, after-reading questions, and additional questions related to the social–emotional objectives of *The Creative Curriculum® for Preschool*.

Conversational Reading

Conversational reading is modeled on the reciprocal way families and children read together. This technique is an early version of interactive book reading, of which dialogic reading (Whitehurst & Lonigan, 2001) is an extensively studied version. Conversational reading has several features in common with interactive book reading, including active engagement and questioning. Other features also make it appropriate for both teachers and families to use with preschool children. The approach

- includes conversational exchanges
- is appropriate for nonverbal as well as verbal children
- is used with one or two children at a time
- employs an easy "3S" strategy

The flexible "see, show, say" (3S) strategy helps you recognize and then respond to a child's actions while reading a book together. On the basis of the child's developmental level, you choose among three interactive strategies:

See—Point to, talk about, and name the pictures in the book, and run a finger under the words while reading them. Watch for the child's looking and listening responses. Observe the child to be sure that he or she is looking at the picture your finger is on. Then stop pointing to some of the more familiar pictures and watch the child's eyes to see if he or she still looks at the pictures (or details of an illustration) that you are naming but not pointing to. Make sure the child is positioned so that you can watch his or her eyes.

Show—Instead of pointing to and naming pictured characters and objects as you read, give directions such as "Touch the little boy's hat" or "Show me who's jumping." Wait for the child to respond by using some form of motion, such as patting, touching, or pointing to the character or object on the page.

Say—As you read, ask the child questions such as "What's this?" or "What will the girl do next?" Accept any verbal response from the child, from one- or two-word phrases to a detailed paragraph.

The "see" and "show" strategies give young children—especially nonverbal children and children whose first language is not English—a way to use their receptive language skills and respond successfully before they are able to use the necessary expressive language. With verbal children for whom the "say" strategy is appropriate, you can use many of the conversational reading and other interactive story reading strategies discussed earlier. See chapter 4 of this volume for more discussion of strategies related to interactive story readings.

Tips to Share With Families

- Surround your child with books. Borrowing books from the public library is free, so help your child get a library card. Take your child to the library for story time. Books from bookstores can be expensive, but you can get inexpensive books at garage and yard sales, thrift shops, and library book sales.

- Choose books that both you and your child enjoy. Tell your child how much you enjoy looking at books together. Reread favorite books.

- Let your child choose which books to read. Letting your child read what interests him or her is one way for reading to be meaningful and enjoyable.

- Choose books in your first language if that is what you speak and read best.

- If you are not comfortable reading aloud, or if you do not know English and would like your child to hear stories in English, you may borrow books with accompanying audio recordings from the library. There are also computer programs and apps and games for the tablet that highlight words on the screen as a voice speaks. Children can choose to hear the story and play related games in English or other languages.

- If you are not comfortable reading aloud, choose wordless books in which the story is told through pictures.

- Find a comfortable place and make your book-sharing time special.

- Use gestures and facial and vocal expression as you read.

- Talk about what is happening in the story and, when possible, how the story relates to your child's life.

- Ask your child questions and give him or her time to respond. Discuss what happens in the story and point out details of the illustrations. Ask questions such as "What do you think will happen next?" or "Why is she doing that?".

- Let your child ask questions. Stop and answer, even if that interrupts the story.

- Occasionally run your fingers under the words as you read. Point out how words are read from left to right and from top to bottom (or in whatever direction is appropriate to the language you are reading). Explain that words are separated by spaces.

- Take books with you in the car or on the bus or subway.

- Let your child tell you the story or take a turn "reading" the book to you.

Storytelling

Storytelling, one of the oldest art forms, is a common form of entertainment and a way people pass their beliefs, values, and traditions from one generation to the next. It helps children learn social skills, such as how to relate to and get along with others. Oral storytelling supports children's literacy learning, knowledge and understanding of the world, and social–emotional well-being.

Storytelling encourages children's emotional involvement with literature. When a story is well-told, interactive, and fun, children view **literacy as a source of enjoyment**. They are filled with the wonder and excitement of stories and are motivated to become storytellers as well as listeners and readers.

Storytelling helps children build **vocabulary and oral language** skills by teaching them how to communicate complex messages verbally. Through storytelling, children gain experience with a broad range of language: new vocabulary, unfamiliar expressions, rhymes, dialogue, and the structure of extended narrative. Storytelling also teaches children that they can communicate their thoughts, ideas, and feelings with words and body language, including gestures and facial expressions. Adult storytelling encourages children to act out and retell stories, thereby promoting the children's language and cognitive development.

Many stories use rhymes, tongue twisters, and other forms of word play. When children hear patterns repeated again and again by the storyteller, and when they actively participate in the storytelling or retell these stories on their own, they gain **phonological awareness**.

As children hear many stories, they develop understandings about story structure that contribute to their **understanding of books**. They learn that the setting, characters, and the theme of a story are introduced in the beginning. They also learn that storytellers recount important events (in the middle), and they end the story by stating a moral or with another conclusion (ending). Storytelling introduces children to various types of narrative, such as folktales, fairy tales, and fables, and it enhances children's later reading skills by inspiring them to read stories they have heard. It also supports children's ability to communicate their own experiences. Telling a simple story is a skill essential to children's later independent writing; children who are able to compose a story to tell orally are more able to write a story or dictate a story for someone else to write down.

Certain storytelling strategies contribute to children's **knowledge of print**. For example, a story clothesline helps children understand the left-to-right progression that is used in text. Depictions of the major events of the story are clipped to the clothesline from the children's left to the children's right.

Listening to stories enhances children's **comprehension**. In order to find meaning, they must focus on the story's setting, characters and their problems, and the sequence of story events. The interactions that occur between the storyteller and the listener before, during, and after the telling of a story are very important to greater comprehension.

How to Begin

Storytelling is possible for everyone. It requires no equipment, only the story and the imaginations of the storyteller and listeners. It is sometimes more challenging than reading because you do not have the language and illustrations of a book to support your narration, but storytelling can be learned. These ideas will help you get started:

- Think of yourself as a storyteller.
- Select appropriate stories.
- Prepare for storytelling experiences.

Thinking of Yourself as a Storyteller

Think about a time when you used a phrase such as "Once I…" or "Remember when…?" as you began to recount an experience that was important to you. You were introducing a story. As social beings, we want to express ourselves, share our life stories with others, and hear their stories. Even very young children eagerly tell their families, teachers, and other children about the latest events and experiences in their lives.

Selecting Appropriate Stories

Like reading aloud, storytelling requires planning. By knowing the needs, interests, and abilities of the children in your class, you will be able to select appropriate stories, modify their length and the pace at which they are told, and determine ways for children actively to participate.

Finding stories that are well-suited to the age and interests of the children in your class is important. There are many kinds of stories to choose from, such as folktales, fairy tales, tall tales, and trickster stories. For young children, you may wish to begin with a folktale that has simple story elements.

Recall the stories that captured your attention as a young child and identify the characteristics that made them appealing to you. They probably had one or more of the following qualities:

- a simple plot (an easily followed sequence of events), e.g., *The Enormous Turnip* (Kathy Parkinson)
- repeated words or phrases, e.g., *The Gingerbread Boy* (Bonnie Dobkin)
- predictable or cumulative storylines, e.g., *I Know an Old Lady Who Swallowed a Fly* (Simms Taback)
- strong or interesting characters, e.g., *The Three Billy Goats Gruff* (Bonnie Dobkin)
- interesting, entertaining, or humorous situations, e.g., *Anansi and the Moss-Covered Rock* (Eric A. Kimmel)
- action or suspense, e.g., *Where the Wild Things Are* (Maurice Sendak)
- an exciting or satisfying conclusion, e.g., *Henny Penny* (Paul Galdone)

Your enthusiasm for a story can be contagious. The stories that are meaningful to you will probably become the children's favorites, and they will attempt to retell them on their own.

Preparing for Oral Storytelling

Oral storytelling requires interaction between the teller and listeners. When children listen to stories without the use of a book, they must use their imaginations differently from when illustrations are provided. As a storyteller, you must think about ways to capture and hold the children's attention. Your childhood memories of listening to stories can be helpful. Think of your feelings during the telling of a story, the storyteller's portrayal of the characters, and the ways in which the storyteller involved you in the telling. Keep in mind that the storytelling experience will be more valuable for children if the story and the storyteller are engaging.

Once you have chosen a story, spend time with it. It may take a number of tellings to find an effective way to engage children fully. The following tips will help you prepare for storytelling.

Think about the details of the story characters. Develop a clear image of each character and describe each with many varied words. Think about how the characters look, smell, feel, speak or otherwise sound, move, and behave. Practice portraying the characters.

Develop a strong beginning. Begin the story with an opening phrase such as "Once upon a time…" or "Long, long ago, in a land far away…" to signal to the children that they are leaving reality and entering the world of make-believe. As you begin, establish the mood of the story and introduce the characters, setting, and theme. Call upon the children's imaginations by describing sights, sounds, tastes, touch sensations, and smells in detail.

Learn the story. Most traditional stories are plot-driven, that is, they are based upon a particular sequence of events. If you understand the plot, you can tell the story simply by recounting what happens in your own words. It is not necessary to memorize the words as someone else has told the story. After you have learned the plot, let your imagination work. Imagine each event and think about the language—the descriptive words and phrases—the children will understand. Then tell the story out loud to yourself in your own words. Decide when to lower your voice, when to pause for effect, and when to speak faster. Create different versions of the story and practice telling it to different listeners. Telling slightly different versions of a story is part of a long oral tradition. Of course, if the telling is enlivened by refrains, you will want to use them.

Develop an ending. Tales traditionally end with a sentence that lets the children know the story is over and that brings them back to reality. Some familiar endings include "That's a true story!" and "They all lived happily ever after."

Telling Stories With Children

Before storytelling, make sure that classroom distractions are minimized, that the area is comfortable enough for children to relax, and that they can be near you. Place any storytelling props where you can reach them easily.

The following chart provides an example of how two teachers, Ms. Tory and Mr. Alvarez, capture children's imaginations with an oral story. The children recently went to a petting farm where they handled and fed animals. They seemed to be especially interested in the goats, so Ms. Tory thought it was a perfect time to tell the Norwegian folktale "The Three Billy Goats Gruff." The notes on the right explain the teachers' strategies and prompts.

	Ms. Tory places a globe, a toy troll, and a tone block in the Library area. Then she invites the children to join her for a story.	Collects the props and materials in advance

---

Ms. Tory:	*Today Mr. Alvarez and I are going to tell you a story. We won't be reading the story from a book and showing you the pictures, so you will have to listen carefully to imagine what is happening in the story. Is everyone comfortable and ready to listen and think?* (Children nod their heads, "Yes.")	Prepares the children for listening and makes sure that they are comfortable
	The story is an old Norwegian folktale called "The Three Billy Goats Gruff." A folktale is a story that people have told over and over and over again. This story has been told so many times, we really aren't sure who the author was.	Introduces the story and gives a little background information about the type of story, its author, and its source
	When I was a little girl, my dad used to tell me stories that his dad told him. Now I tell the same stories to my son. Do any of your parents or grandparents tell you stories from long ago that someone else told them?	Fosters children's understanding by drawing on their personal experiences Asks for personal contributions
Carlos:	*My great-grandmother tells me stories about when she was a little girl in Mexico, before she came to the U.S.*	

Ms. Tory:	*Well, this story was first told in the country Norway. Norway is far, far away—even farther away than Mexico. See? Here is where we live, and here is Norway.* (She uses a globe to show the children where Norway is in relation to their homes. Children comment on how far away Norway seems to be. Ms. Tory settles the children and then continues.)	Gives background information about the story's origin Makes a connection between the setting of the story and where the children live
	Does anyone know what a billy goat is?	Asks a question that will help children learn about the main characters
Susie:	*A goat. Like the ones we saw at the farm.*	
Ms. Tory:	*It is a goat. But what do you think a* billy *goat is?*	
Juwan:	*I have a friend named Billy.*	
Ms. Tory:	*Is your friend a boy?* (Juwan nods his head, "Yes.") *That might give you a hint.* (Ms. Tory pauses and waits for a child to respond. She continues.) *Even though some girls are also named Billie, a billy goat is a male, or boy, goat. So this is a story about three boy goats. Let's begin.*	Explains or defines unfamiliar words to help children's build their vocabularies and understanding Allows time for children to answer and proceeds when they do not

Ms. Tory:	*Once upon a time, in a land far away, there lived three billy goats. The last name of all three billy goats was Gruff.*	Opens the story with a statement that encourages children to enter an imaginary world
Ms. Tory:	*The youngest billy goat Gruff was very, very small. He had two little horns just starting to show on the top of his head, and he spoke in a soft voice.* (Each time Ms. Tory introduces a new character, she changes the pitch of her voice and uses her hands to show the size of the goat and its horns.)	Uses her voice and gestures to help children imagine the characters
	The second billy goat Gruff was a medium-sized goat. He had horns, too, and he had a few whiskers on his chin.	
	The last and oldest was great big billy goat Gruff. He was huge*! He had long, pointed horns—almost like spears; big hooves; and a beard. He made his two brothers feel safe because he was so big and strong.*	
Ben:	*My brother Broderick is strong!*	

Ms. Tory:	*Does anyone remember what billy goats like to eat?*	Asks a question to help children connect their farm visit with the story
Zach:	*Grass and seeds.*	
Carlos:	*And sometimes old shoes and stuff like that!*	
Ms. Tory:	*Well, these billy goats loved to eat sweet, juicy green grass more than anything else. One day when they were grazing on grass near their home, one of them noticed a lush hillside not too far away. The grass looked green and tasty, and when the breeze blew the goats could smell its sweet smell. They just had to have it, so they decided to go up to the hillside to get some of the grass.*	
	But there was a problem. (Ms. Tory pauses and looks at the children's eyes.). *You see, to get to the other hillside, the billy goats had to cross a bridge. Now the bridge wasn't the problem, but what lived under the bridge was a* big *problem!*	Makes eye contact with the children and maintains it throughout the telling (This helps hold the children's attention and provides information about whether and how storytelling strategies should be modified.)
	What do you think lived under the bridge?	
Children:	*A monster!*	

Ms. Tory:	(Ms. Tory lowers her voice, moves a little closer to the children, and speaks slowly and deliberately.) *Under the bridge lived a* troll. (Ms. Tory takes out a toy troll and shows it to the children.) *This is a toy troll. But the troll that lived under the bridge was* big *and* ugly *and very, very mean!*	Uses her voice to emphasize story details
	His eyes were as big as saucers, so he could spot a goat a mile away. His nose was as long as a fireplace poker, so he could smell a goat a mile away. (Mr. Alvarez stands nearby and makes gestures to indicate the size and nature of the troll.)	Uses simple, natural gestures
Kate:	*He would scare me! He's so big and mean and ugly!*	
Ben:	*Yeah! I bet he gets the billy goats when they cross the bridge. Huh, Ms. Tory?*	Encourages children to comment while the story is being told

Ms. Tory:	*Well, the first billy goat to cross the bridge was the small billy goat Gruff. He went trip-trap, trip-trap, trip-trap over the bridge.* (Ms. Tory uses the tone block to make faint, fast, trotting sounds.) *About that time the troll roared in the meanest, loudest voice you've ever heard.*	Uses props, as appropriate, to enhance storytelling
Mr. Alvarez:	*Who's that tripping over my bridge?* (Clenches his fist and uses a deep, roaring voice.)	Uses movement and a dramatic voice
Ms. Tory:	(Responds in a quivering, high-pitched voice.) *It is I, the tiniest billy goat Gruff. I'm going to the hillside to make myself fat.*	
Mr. Alvarez:	*I'm coming to gobble you up!*	
Ms. Tory:	(Again in a tiny, pleading voice.) *Oh, no! Please don't take me. I'm much too little. Wait for my brother, the medium-sized billy goat Gruff. He's much bigger and meatier than I am.*	
Mr. Alvarez:	*Very well. Be off with you!*	
Susie:	*That billy goat tricked you!* (She points to Mr. Alvarez.)	
Mr. Alvarez:	*You're right. I may need some help! Let me hear you say, in your meanest troll voices, "Now I'm coming to gobble you up!"* (Children respond.)	Involves children in the telling
	Ms. Tory continues to play the part of each billy goat. To represent the difference in the size and strength of each goat, she plays the tone block more and more slowly, loudly, and deliberately, and she alters the pitch, tone, and volume of her voice. Mr. Alvarez plays the troll.	
Ms. Tory:	*Pretty soon all three billy goats were on the hillside eating that sweet, juicy green grass. They ate so much that they got really, really fat and could hardly make it home. In fact, they are probably still fat. And so—snip, snap, snout—this tale's told out.* *What did you think about that story?*	Concludes the story with a sentence that signals the end of the story and the return to reality Asks an open-ended question

Various children:	*It was good! That big billy goat wasn't afraid of the troll.*	
	At first I was scared! But I'm not now.	
Ms. Tory:	*Stories can be a little scary. Do you think that story really happened, or do you think it was make-believe?*	Acknowledges children's opinions and feelings and asks a question to help them distinguish between reality and fantasy
Carlos:	*Make-believe, because goats don't really talk.*	
Ben:	*And there's no such thing as a troll.*	

Ms. Tory affirms their responses and continues the discussion. She asks the children if they would like to hear the story again. She and Mr. Alvarez make plans to create puppets and a backdrop to use next time. After that, they will invite the children to use the props to retell the story, and they will add the props to the Library area for the children to use at choice time.

Ms. Tory is a skilled storyteller, so she used few props to tell the story. However, it is appropriate to use props, or visual aids, with young children as long as they do not distract children from listening to the story. A few simple props can be useful in holding young children's attention during storytelling, and placing them in the Library area encourages children to tell and retell stories on their own. A discussion of various storytelling props and techniques can be found in the section "Story Retelling."

Your Teaching Practice

Think about where you are most comfortable telling stories. Do you prefer a quiet room with everyone watching you? Do you think the outdoors could work as an appropriate setting? Take a few moments to reflect on your ideal circumstances for telling stories. Think about how you can feel the most comfortable so that storytelling can be enjoyable for the children and you.

Tips to Share With Families

- Make up stories about a character who has the same name as your child.

- Tell stories about when you and other family members were children.

- Tell stories about your child when he or she was younger.

- Tell stories about a main character who does what your child did that day. The main character does not have to be a child.

- Invite family members to share stories about their life experiences.

- Use familiar storytelling phrases, such as "Once upon a time...," "They lived happily ever after," "In a far-away land...," and "The end."

- Change your voice to portray different characters.

- Involve your child by having him add sound effects or motions.

- Involve your child by encouraging her to repeat a refrain or supply a missing word.

- Take turns telling parts of the story.

- Use props, such as an old hat, puppets, household items (e.g., a pot for a helmet and a piece of fabric for a cape).

- Laugh and have fun.

Story Retelling

Reading aloud and telling stories are effective strategies for promoting children's literacy learning. However, what happens before, during, and after these experiences is also important to children's literacy development. Research confirms that story retelling, when children recount in their own words a story they have heard or read, is one of the most effective strategies for supporting children's comprehension and their understanding of story structure. Retelling activities support the development of many other components of literacy as well. Young children's ability to retell a story in a basic order of events and with some detail is linked directly to future social and academic success (Barclay, 2014).

Retelling activities enable children to experience **literacy as a source of enjoyment**. Positive experiences make it more likely that children will choose to engage with books and other literacy activities during choice time.

Oral retellings provide opportunities for children to increase their **vocabularies and oral language** skills as they experiment to confirm their understanding of new words and expressions. As children assume the roles of the characters in the story, they use dialogue from the story and inflect their voices. Oral retelling can help improve English-language learners' facility with English. Retelling is particularly effective for children who have had few literacy experiences, because these children are more likely to engage in active literacy experiences than in those that require them to listen more passively.

Many stories for young children are told with refrains or rhymes. Many focus children's attention on the separate sounds of language and encourage them to experiment with the sounds. When children have opportunities to retell stories with these features and to repeat particular words or phrases, they gain **phonological awareness**.

Retelling helps children **understand books** by giving them experience with story structure. Children learn to introduce the story with its setting, characters, theme, and initial events (beginning); to give an organized, sequential account of the story's plot (middle); and to offer a resolution (ending).

Retelling is not simply recalling events or facts from a story. Retelling requires that children think about the whole story and organize the details of the characters, setting, and plot. By doing so, they develop understandings about story structure. Retelling also requires them to infer and interpret how characters think, feel, speak, and act (develop **comprehension**).

See *Intentional Teaching Card* LL06, "Dramatic Story Retelling," to learn more about retelling stories with children.

How to Begin

Retelling skills must be taught. Children need guidance, support, and lots of practice. These suggestions will help you begin:

- Select appropriate stories and model ways to retell them.

- Use props for oral retellings.

Selecting Appropriate Stories and Modeling Ways to Retell Them

Choose stories that you have already read to the children and that have simple plots (e.g., *The Mitten* by Alvin Tresselt), familiar characters (e.g., *The Three Little Pigs* by Paul Galdone), repetitive phrases (*Do You Want to Be My Friend?* by Eric Carle) or familiar sequences (*The Very Hungry Caterpillar* by Eric Carle). The predictability of simple texts helps children succeed in their early attempts at retelling.

Children benefit from listening as you retell stories. Always be sure to include a clear beginning, middle, and end, and relate events in the same sequence as the version you read earlier. Explain to the children that storytellers must tell the story in a way that even listeners who never heard it before will understand. They must include all of the information that the audience needs to know, and they must organize the information so that it makes sense. As you model story retelling, explain how you decide what to tell. Demonstrate the use of various props. Discuss and model what the characters say and how their voices sound.

Using Props for Oral Retellings

Props are visual prompts for young children. They provide concrete references for story details, help children organize their thoughts, and suggest to children what to do or say. Some props (e.g., puppets and costumes) help children play the parts of the characters. Here are some ideas:

Provide objects as props. Collect toys or other objects to represent particular characters or events in a story. For example, for the story *Jump, Frog, Jump!* by Robert Kalan, you might use a toy fly, frog, fish, snake, turtle, net, and basket. A piece of blue felt, paper, or fabric could represent the pond in which the story is set. As you tell the story, place the appropriate object on whatever represents the pond.

Make clothesline story props. Create pictures to represent important story events and characters. Hang a clothesline in a section of the Library area that is out of the line of traffic. Place a basket of clothespins nearby. As you retell the story, clip the appropriate picture to the clothesline, in sequence from the children's left to the children's right.

Offer picture props. Create pictures that represent the important events of a story on felt, fabric, or sturdy card stock (colored and laminated for durability). Fasten self-stick hook-and-loop fastener material or a magnetic strip to the back of each picture. Retell the story by putting the pictures on a felt or magnetic board in the order they are mentioned in the story. You can create individual story boxes by lining the inside of a pizza box with felt. Accompanying story pieces can be made and stored inside each box. When children are ready to retell a story, they simply open the box, remove the pieces, and retell the story, using the lid as a felt board. Likewise, cookie sheets can serve as magnetic storyboards.

Use costumes and dramatic play props. Dramatic story enactments are particularly effective for young children because they love to dress up and pretend. As they work together to enact a story, children explore the roles of various characters. Set the stage by providing simple costumes (e.g., old clothing, large pieces of fabric, uniforms, hats or headbands, and masks) and props to help children get into character. Create the setting by drawing a simple scene on a sheet or large cardboard box. Explain to the children that you will read a story and then they will act it out by pretending to be the characters. Ask them to pay special attention to what the characters say and do and how they express their feelings. After reading, lead a discussion about the story and invite children to volunteer for each part. Provide support by serving as the narrator and prompting children when necessary. Once children know the process, they will be able to act out the story on their own or with minimal support.

Collect puppets. Puppets are especially useful for retelling stories that have repetitive dialogue, such as *Chicken Little, The Little Red Hen,* and *The Three Billy Goats Gruff.* Timid children often feel more secure when they may use puppets during retellings. After selecting a story, decide which type of puppet (e.g., hand, stick, finger, or body) to use and assemble a collection to represent the story characters. Although commercial puppets are available for purchase, puppets can be made out of almost anything (e.g., oven mitts, wooden spoons, cardboard tubes, paper plates, or hair curlers) and children enjoy the variety. Next, prepare children for the retelling by following the same procedure described in the paragraph just above (reading, discussing the characters, and prompting when necessary).

Supporting Children's Story Retelling

Retelling activities can involve the whole class, a small group, or an individual child. After modeling the retelling of a familiar story, give children a variety of opportunities to retell the story. Each way involves a different level of support. For example, you may work individually with a child, encouraging him to retell a portion of the story (the beginning or ending) while you retell the rest. You can engage the whole class in retelling a story by using clothesline props or another technique, or you can work with a small group of children to enact a story while you narrate it.

Young children usually need a lot of support during early retelling experiences. You can assist them by offering open-ended prompts. For example, to help children get started, you might say, "Tell us what characters the story is about," or ask, "Where did the story take place?" To help children who have difficulty recalling the story events, you might ask, "What happened next?" To prompt children to extend their description of a character you might say, "Tell me more about this character." Prompts such as these help children understand that all parts of a story are important when it is being retold.

Teachers help children develop and refine their retelling skills by creating a special place in the classroom where children can retell stories they have heard during story time. In *The Creative Curriculum®* classroom, teachers usually designate a portion of the Library area specifically for retelling stories. Books and related props are stored there and used by children during choice time.

In the example that follows, Ms. Tory models and guides a group of children in retelling *Jennie's Hat* by Ezra Jack Keats, one of the children's favorite books. The notes on the right explain what she is saying and doing.

Ms. Tory places the following props on a shelf in the Library area: a hatbox with a plain straw hat inside, a basket, a lamp shade, a flower pot, a TV antenna, a shiny pot, and a hat covered with flowers. She places other props in a basket, including artificial flowers, plastic eggs, greeting cards, a paper fan, colored leaves, and an artificial bird's nest. She gathers a small group of children together at story time.

Plans in advance to have ready the props she needs

Provides objects to use as visual prompts

Ms. Tory:	*Children, today I would like you to help me tell one of your favorite stories. It is from the book* Jennie's Hat. *Do you remember the story?*	Involves the children in discussing the story before the retelling
Derek:	*Yeah. It's about a girl who gets a hat, and she doesn't like it.*	
Crystal:	*In the end she likes it.*	
Sonya:	*Yes, because the birds put all kinds of things on it.*	
Leo:	*Like flowers and leaves and eggs and sticks.*	
Ms. Tory:	*You remember a lot about the story. Let's start at the beginning of the story and think about everything that happened.*	Acknowledges the children's responses

Ms. Tory:	*Once there was a girl named Jennie. She was waiting for a present from her favorite aunt. She was sure her aunt was sending her a big, beautiful hat covered with lots of flowers.*	Introduces the story setting and characters
	The present finally came, and Jennie was very excited. But when she opened the box... (Ms. Tory pauses and opens the hatbox to take out the plain straw hat.) *there was only a plain hat like this one. Jennie was very disappointed. Do you remember what Jennie's mom said?*	Introduces the story theme Uses props to help children remember the story Prompts children to recall story details
Crystal:	*She said she thought it was a nice hat. But Jennie still didn't think so.*	
Ms. Tory:	*That's right. Do you remember what Jennie did next?* (She pauses and points toward the props on the shelf.)	Recalls and prompts children to recall the plot episodes
Derek:	*She tried to use a bunch of other things for hats.*	

| Ms. Tory: | *Yes, first she tried on a basket. Then she tried on a lampshade, a flower pot, a TV antenna, and a shiny pot. (Ms. Tory puts each on her head.) None of them would do. (Ms. Tory glances at her watch.) Just about that time, Jennie noticed that it was time to feed the birds. She got some bread crumbs, went to the park, and began scattering the crumbs. (Ms. Tory pretends to throw crumbs on the ground.) What happened then?* | Uses a prop for each important story detail

Acts out story details to focus children's attention

Asks a question to give children an opportunity to be part of the retelling |
| Children: | *The birds came fluttering all around. They hopped on Jennie's head, and they ate up all the food.* | |

Ms. Tory:	*Jennie had so much fun at the park that she forgot about her hat until she started to walk home. She wanted her hat to be just a little fancier.*	
	The next day Jennie got up and peeped out of the window. Do you remember what she saw?	Asks a question that will help move the story line along
Leo:	*A lot of ladies wearing hats with flowers.*	
Crystal:	*A lot of ladies at her church had flower hats, but Jennie just had her plain hat.*	
Ms. Tory:	*You're right. Jennie had to wear her plain hat to church. However, when Jennie and her parents were leaving the church…(Ms. Tory pauses.)*	Prompts children to recall the resolution
Sonya:	*The birds came.*	
Leo:	*They brought lots of stuff to put on Jennie's hat.*	
Ms. Tory:	*Like what?*	Prompts children to recall details
Crystal:	*Lots of flowers and eggs.*	
	Ms. Tory puts the flowers and eggs on the hat. Then she shows the children the box of props and adds each prop to the hat as it is named.	Uses props as visual prompts
Derek:	*Leaves.*	
Sonya:	*Cards and valentines.*	
Leo:	*A fan and a bird's nest.*	
Ms. Tory:	*At last Jennie had a beautiful hat! She waved to the birds and said, "Thank you!"* (Children wave.) *Do you remember how the story ended?*	Prompts children to recall the ending of the story

Derek:	*Yes. Jennie thought her hat was so beautiful that she and her mom wrapped the hat.*	
Ms. Tory:	*She wrapped it up so it could be saved and looked at for a long, long time.*	Accepts the detail the child contributed and adds additional information
Ms. Tory:	*Thank you for helping me to retell the story. You remembered all the things that happened.*	
Ms. Tory:	*I'm going to put these things* (motions to the hat and decorations) *in the Library area for you to use to retell the story on your own.*	Encourages independent retelling

Tips to Share With Families

- Use stuffed animals, toys, and other household items as props to retell stories.

- Act out stories that you have read with or told to your child, with both of you assuming roles.

- Encourage your child to tell the story while looking at the pictures in a book.

- Let your child tell the story in his or her own words.

- Retell stories with your child, taking turns to tell different parts.

- Give prompts freely when your child needs assistance in telling a story (e.g, if you are retelling *The Mitten*, ask, "What happened after he lost the mitten?").

Writing

When given opportunities, children experiment with writing and explore different ways to convey messages in print. Research confirms that reading and writing develop together as interactive and interrelated processes. Writing is an essential part of preschool literacy programs and supports children's development with regard to several components of literacy. Although teachers demonstrate letter formation, the main focus in preschool is on writing as a communication tool rather than on handwriting instruction.

Young children enjoy the process of writing, the social relationships they develop during the process, and the sense of accomplishment they feel as they use writing to express themselves. They experience **literacy as a source of enjoyment**.

Children increase their **vocabulary and oral language** skills as they read and as they talk about their early writing and drawing. As they realize that what they think and say can be written down, their oral language becomes the basis of what they write.

Writing with children helps them to understand the sound structure of words (**phonological awareness**). For example, a child may become more aware of syllables if a teacher, while writing Leo's name, exaggerates their segmentation and says "Leeee" (while writing *Le*) and "ooooo" (while writing *o*). When writing a word, the teacher calls attention to each phoneme by saying the sound aloud as she writes the letter(s). Once children become aware that words are a sequence of sounds represented by letters, they begin to try to sequence letters in a conventional way.

Interactive writing helps children develop their **knowledge of print.** As teachers model writing and talk about their purposes, thinking, and actions while writing, children learn that print conveys meaning and that what they say can be written and then read. As adults model writing, children develop understandings about left-to-right directionality, the correspondence between spoken and written words, spacing, punctuation, and capitalization. By offering children opportunities to create a variety of texts (e.g., stories, lists, letters, cards, and recipes) through interactive writing, they learn that print is organized differently for different purposes.

As teachers talk with children about print while they model writing, children learn about **letters and words**. They learn specific letter names, become aware of letter features, and see how letters are formed (the line segments used to form each letter and the direction and sequence in which the segments are written). Children also learn that letters represent one or more sounds, that letters are grouped together in a particular order to represent words, and that written words have meaning.

The writing process helps promote children's understanding of **books**. As children attempt to compose their own stories by dictating or writing them on their own, they develop and refine their sense of story. When children explore a variety of genres by writing their own books, they learn about the features and structure of each type. For example, when children create their own alphabet books, they learn that alphabet books typically introduce one letter per page, with pictures of objects whose names begin with the sound (phoneme) represented by the letter.

How to Begin

Both teacher-initiated and child-initiated writing experiences should be a part of daily life in the classroom. Teachers must

- consider the strengths, needs, and interests of their children

- plan a variety of writing experiences

- provide materials and opportunities for children to write on their own

Considering Children's Strengths, Needs, and Interests

In any class, children are at different levels of development in their awareness of print and the purposes of writing. Children demonstrate their knowledge and understanding of written language through their own writing, dictation, and comments. Teachers can use the curricular objectives to guide their observations and to reflect on what children are doing. Then they plan experiences and interact with children in ways that help children develop understandings about written language.

Support can take many forms: responding to children's writing (regardless of the format) and acknowledging their writing as attempts to communicate; modeling the mechanics of writing (e.g., demonstrating letter formation, directionality, and spacing); answering children's questions; offering information; and, when appropriate, asking questions that help children think about written language.

Planning Writing Experiences

Teachers who use *The Creative Curriculum*® engage children in learning about and producing many kinds of written language. Meaningful writing experiences are included in various events of the day so that children learn how written language is used for various purposes. Some of these experiences are teacher-directed; others are child-initiated and offer children opportunities to explore writing on their own. Here are strategies that encourage children to write:

Write names. When teachers plan activities that require children to recognize and write their names, they help children learn that written language can be used to express identity and show ownership. Teachers give children reasons to write their names, such as signing their names on

- attendance sheets upon arrival each day

- drawings, stories, greeting cards, letters, and other products

- sign-up sheets for a popular activity

- "question of the day" charts

To help children learn to write their names, provide name cards written conventionally with upper- and lowercase letters. Children's ability to write their names develops over time, depending upon their level of motor control, knowledge of letters as discrete units, and awareness of the distinguishing features of letters. Many children's first attempts at name writing are scribbled shapes or lines and contain no letters at all. As children practice writing and become more aware of print, they begin including letter-like forms and letters in their signatures.

Make lists. When teachers involve children in making lists, children learn that written language can be used to satisfy needs and desires (e.g., to recall information or to have a turn with a particular toy). List-making is an effective strategy because it is a brief activity and each child may contribute more than once. Class lists are useful for documenting

- things to do to prepare for a special event
- what children saw on a neighborhood walk or a study trip
- supplies needed for making snacks
- children who want a turn with a particular toy or piece of equipment
- favorite things (foods, places to go, colors)
- story characters

Write cards, letters, and notes. These writing experiences show children that written language enables them to communicate with others. Children can

- make greeting cards for family members and friends
- write thank-you notes or letters to classroom volunteers, guest speakers, and the sponsor of a class field trip
- participate in a pen pal program with another preschool class and write letters to one another
- use a message board or post office in the classroom and write notes to each other

Write instructions. When teachers write instructions, children learn that written language can be used to tell others what or how to do something. Teachers can

- involve the children in making signs, labels, or notices for the classroom
  (e.g., *Do not touch, Please flush, Exit, and Please be quiet.*)
- involve the children in making class rules, writing them down, posting them, and reviewing them regularly
- create simple picture and word recipes

Record information. When teachers create various written documents, children learn that written language is used to communicate information. Teachers can

- make a telephone and address book with the children (after getting families' permission to share contact information) and refer children to it during play; place note pads and pencils nearby to encourage children to write messages
- invite children to help make written announcements or invitations for special events, such as a family breakfast or class art show
- create a picture dictionary or word wall of common words for children to refer to when they are writing independently
- create a log for children to record their observations, such as changes in a tadpole or the growth of bean sprouts
- chart children's experiences during a class trip or special school event

Take dictation and create journals. When teachers take dictation and offer opportunities for independent journal writing, children learn that written language is a way to express their thoughts, ideas, feelings, and opinions. Teachers can

- encourage children to dictate captions (words or sentences) or stories about a drawing, painting, or photo
- record on a chart, on the class calendar, or in a class journal children's thoughts about daily classroom events, experiences related to a study topic, exciting outdoor discoveries, and new information
- give each child a personal journal in which to draw, dictate, or write about self-selected topics

Write in response to literature. Offering children opportunities to respond in writing to literature helps them understand that written language is a tool for self-expression. Teachers can

- encourage children to create and dictate the narrative for a story originally published as a wordless book; record children's language on sticky notes
- invite children to draw and write (using pen and paper or typing on the computer or tablet-writing) about a character who appears in a series of books (e.g., the monkey Curious George)
- have children create experience stories; record the stories on a chart
- have children create and dictate stories for a chart or book, using predictable books as a model
- use other types of books (e.g., nonfiction and alphabet books), poems, rhymes, songs, and chants to encourage children's expressive language development

Providing Materials and Opportunities for Children to Write

Children first notice print in real-life settings where writing is used for a variety of purposes. For many children, print is not part of everyday experiences, so they do not develop the insight that it carries messages. Preschool teachers must offer meaningful opportunities for children to write and read, especially through teacher-directed activities such as those described in the previous section.

Teachers also need to encourage child-initiated writing. Children need time, opportunities, and materials to explore writing on their own. They need to try the ideas about writing they form through their observations of and interactions with others.

In *The Creative Curriculum®* classroom, the Library area is the primary place for children to explore writing by creating cards, drawing, dictating, writing stories, and making books. In *The Creative Curriculum® for Preschool, Volume 2: Interest Areas*, you will find an extensive list of writing materials to include in the Library area.

Reading and writing materials are also important in the Dramatic Play area. Through dramatic play, children explore real-world situations in which reading and writing are useful. As children explore adult roles in their play, they imitate writing behavior in order to understand its purpose and conventions. For example, in a pretend doctor's office, the child assuming the role of the doctor is likely to write on patient charts or scribble prescriptions, while the receptionist might sign patients in or keep an appointment book.

Writing is not limited to just the Library and Dramatic Play areas. Teachers encourage children to explore reading and writing in all interest areas by placing paper, writing tools, and other print props alongside toys, games, blocks, and so on. By providing literacy materials in all interest areas, children have opportunities to explore print in their own way, deciding when, what, and how to write. For more ideas and information about incorporating literacy in interest areas, see chapter 4 of this volume and *The Creative Curriculum® for Preschool, Volume 2: Interest Areas.*

Writing should also be integrated with content activities for math, science, social studies, the arts, and technology. With each topic of study, materials can be added and experiences offered to encourage writing and reading (e.g., books and bookmaking, experience charts, graphs, and journal writing).

Supporting Children's Writing

Materials alone are not enough. Teachers must thoughtfully and intentionally model reading and writing, and they must interact with children to promote their literacy learning. One of the most powerful strategies teachers use to help children learn about written language is to talk about it when they write, themselves. When teachers describe their thoughts and actions as they write, children learn about the functions and conventions of print (e.g., letter names, letter features, how letters are formed, letter–sound associations, spacing, punctuation, directionality, etc.). Children come to understand that letters can be grouped together to form words, that words have meaning, and that words are ordered to record sentences.

The vignette that follows shows how one teacher, Mr. Alvarez, used writing during a large-group meeting to introduce many literacy skills and concepts. The notes on the right indicate the teachers' reflections about what they are doing.

The children sit on the rug, facing Ms. Tory for their morning meeting.

Ms. Tory:	*Our morning meeting is almost over. Who can tell what we will do next?* (The children recite in unison as Ms. Tory points to the words *Choice time.*)	Shows the importance of functional print
	Before you go to interest areas, Mr. Alvarez is going to show you some new things. (Mr. Alvarez takes Ms. Tory's place in front of the children.)	
Mr. Alvarez:	*I have three new things to share with you today. Let me make a short list of them on this chart paper so I won't forget what they are.*	Demonstrates and talks about a purpose of print

The first thing we need to discuss is a new toy for the Sand and Water area. It's a pump, so I'll write the word pump. *Let's see. I'll start here.*	Demonstrates left-to-right directionality
(He points to the top-left side of the paper and names each letter as he writes.) P-u-m-p, pump.	Calls attention to letters and demonstrates how they are formed
The second thing we need to talk about is today's snack. I'm writing a list, so I'll write snack *underneath* pump: s-n-a-c-k. Snack.	Talks about the format of a list

Shawn: *That's my name!*

Setsuko
and Sonya: *And mine!*

Mr. Alvarez:	Your names do begin with an S, *but there is one difference. Let's see if anyone can tell the difference.* (He says each child's name aloud and then writes it on the chart.)	Acknowledges the children's responses and challenges them to think further about the information

Jonetta: *It's bigger!*

Mr. Alvarez:	*You are watching closely, Jonetta. Their names begin with a capital, or uppercase* S, *and the word* snack *begins with a lowercase* s. *The letters are formed the same way, but they are different sizes. See?* (Mr. Alvarez writes Ss so the children can see the difference.)	Calls attention to the features and forms of letters

Setsuko: *I have both.*

Mr. Alvarez:	*You certainly do, Setsuko. You have an uppercase* S *at the beginning of your name and a lowercase* s *in the middle of your name.* (Mr. Alvarez draws a line under each *s* as he speaks.)	Confirms Setsuko's observation
	The third thing I would like to share is the set of pictures from our trip to the apple orchard. Let's see. What should I write?	Involves the children in generating language

Malik: *How about* pictures?

Mr. Alvarez:	*What do the rest of you think?* (The children nod their heads, "Yes.") Pictures. (Mr. Alvarez repeats the word as he writes it on the chart.) *Look,* pictures *and* pump *start with the same letter,* p.	Draws children's attention to a particular letter

---

	(Mr. Alvarez returns to the top of the list and reads *pump.*) *Have you ever seen a pump before? Can you guess what it does?* (He takes the pump from a nearby box and explains that a pump is a tool that people use to help move water from one place to another. He has prepared a tub of water so he can demonstrate how it works. The children ask several questions and take turns working the handle. Mr. Alvarez records their questions on chart paper and repeats their words as he writes.)	Plans a way to introduce a new toy
		Links a new word to prior knowledge
		Calls children's attention to the correspondence between a spoken word and a written word
		Shows that he values the children's questions by writing them on the chart
Mr. Alvarez:	You've asked some very interesting questions! I bet you'll discover some of the answers when you use the pump in the Sand and Water area. I've written your questions on the chart so we can come back and talk more about them at our next meeting.	Talks about a purpose of print
Mr. Alvarez:	We need to make a pegboard label for the pump so you will know where to put it when you are finished using it. (Mr. Alvarez has cut a picture of the pump from a catalog and glued it on card stock. Together he and the children make a label. He talks as he writes *p-u-m-p*.)	Prepares the materials he needs in advance
	(He reads the word slowly, sweeping his hand under the word.) *Does anyone notice anything special about the word* pump?	Calls attention to features of words
Alexa:	*It has two of the same letter.*	
Mr. Alvarez:	*That's right, Alexa. It has two* ps, *one at the beginning of the word and one at the end. Listen and you'll hear the sound that the letter* p *makes.* (He reads the word slowly again to call attention to the /p/ sounds in the word.) *I'll put this label on the pegboard in the Sand and Water area, along with the pump. Be sure to try it when you work there today.*	Calls attention to the sounds represented by letters
	I'll cross out the word pump *now, because we talked about it.*	

Mr. Alvarez and children:	(Mr. Alvarez looks at the list again and then takes the snack menu out of the box. He holds it so all the children can see.) *Today's snack is trail mix. You will have an opportunity to make your own trail mix in the Cooking area.*

Let's look at the recipe and read the list of ingredients. (He holds up a picture/word recipe made with labels from familiar food products. He sweeps his hand under the words.) *Cheerios®, pretzels, raisins, almonds.* (The children call the almonds *nuts.* He explains that almonds are one type of nut and points out the word *Almonds* on the package. He continues to read the directions with the children and tells them that the recipe will be posted for them to follow.)

Introduces new words

Mr. Alvarez:	*Who remembers what to do if you want to prepare snack but the Cooking area is too crowded?*

Talks about a purpose of print

Zack:	*Write your name on the snack sign-up sheet.*

Mr. Alvarez:	*Zack, will you please show everyone the sign-up sheet?* (Zack shows the children the new sign-up sheet for the day, and Mr. Alvarez reminds them that the sign-up sheet helps to make sure that everyone has a turn to make snack. He reminds them to cross their names off of the list when they have finished preparing snack and to let the next person on the list know it is his or her turn.)

Provides children with a meaningful reason to write

I will cross snack off our list. (He draws a line through the word.)

Do you remember the third thing we need to talk about? (He points to the word *pictures* on the list.)

Helps children see the connections among speaking, writing, and reading

All children:	*Pictures!* (Mr. Alvarez takes a photo album out of the box and shows a few pictures to the children.)

Mr. Alvarez: *I'm going to put these in the Library area for you to look at. I'll be visiting the area today so you can dictate a few sentences about the pictures. That way, your families will be able to read about all the things that happened on our trip to the apple orchard.*

(Puts a line through the word pictures.) That's the last thing on our list. I think it's time for you to choose the area in which you want to play.

Talks about a purpose of print

Tips to Share With Families

- Help your child develop small-muscle strength and coordination by offering materials such as molding dough, clothespins, beads and string.

- Tell your child what you are doing when you write (e.g., *I'm making a shopping list so I can remember what to get at the store*).

- Have a box or another place in which your child can keep writing and drawing supplies.

- When your child tells you stories, write them down and read them back.

- Encourage your child to write cards and letters to family members and friends in English or any language you speak at home.

- Encourage your child to make signs related to what he or she is playing.

- Write simple notes to your child.

- Help your child recognize his name and show him how to write it.

- Together, make words with magnetic or other toy letters.

- Bring writing supplies when you travel, such as paper and pencils, a magnetic drawing board, or a magic slate.

- Outdoors, write letters in dirt or sand by using sticks or fingers, or use chalk on the sidewalk.

Meaningful Play

Children explore the world and construct understandings through their play. Teachers support children's literacy learning by incorporating reading and writing materials into children's play so they can experiment with them. Literacy skills are promoted through play and the social interactions that occur in the context of play.

When play is child-initiated, child-directed, open-ended, creative, and relatively risk-free, children enjoy learning. When reading and writing are incorporated in their play, children begin to understand **literacy as a source of enjoyment**.

As children play in interest areas and interact with adults and peers, they have opportunities for **vocabulary and language** development. They learn the names of props, ask and answer questions, exchange ideas, and explain what they are doing. In sociodramatic play, they must communicate with others and negotiate roles and events. They also enact real-life experiences and use increasingly sophisticated language as they negotiate and act out various roles.

By using literacy materials in their play, children explore their **knowledge of print**. They attempt to imitate what they have seen adults and older children doing when they read and write. Children use written language to communicate for different purposes during their play (e.g., making signs and labels for constructions, making greeting cards for friends and family members, and signing their names on waiting lists to use equipment).

Children learn about **letters and words** as they manipulate alphabet materials, play matching letter games, and write. When print materials, such as labeled picture cards, are coupled with alphabet manipulatives, children can explore how letters are put together to form words.

Play is essential to building children's **comprehension** skills. Through play, children gain background knowledge and discover the meaning of language they later encounter in print. Firsthand experiences enable children to link new information with what they already know, thereby constructing understandings about what they hear and read.

During play, children have opportunities to see, handle, and create various kinds of **books and other texts**. Labels and signs are used to organize materials in every interest area; menus and recipes are found in the Cooking and Dramatic Play areas; and charts, graphs, and photos with descriptions that document children's learning are displayed. Written directions for routine procedures are also posted so children can manage independently (e.g., cleanup, handwashing, and toothbrushing procedures). As children read and listen to books, retell stories, and talk about their experiences, their sense of story structure is enhanced.

How to Begin

In *The Creative Curriculum®* classroom, teachers arrange the environment carefully. They

- plan the physical environment to support literacy learning
- include literacy materials for meaningful reading and writing experiences

Planning the Environment

The physical environment is arranged in clearly defined interest areas that are equipped with props and materials that facilitate children's play. These small, intimate spaces encourage children's social interaction and use of language. The interest areas are organized by using labels, signs, lists, and charts so that children know what to do and so that they learn important literacy skills. Teachers stock these areas with interesting props and an abundant supply of reading, writing, and oral language materials. They make sure that there is adequate space for children to work, that the areas are clean and well-lit, and that the materials are stored where children can reach them easily.

Research confirms that children learn language as they observe and interact with others in social situations. When teachers provide opportunities for children to play with peers in literacy-rich settings, children learn collaboratively about reading and writing. They help each other figure out the meaning of print (e.g., *That says love.*), coach one another in literacy-related tasks (e.g., *This is how you make a T.*), and help each other understand literacy-related roles (e.g., *The doctor writes prescriptions, not the patient.*).

Selecting Materials Thoughtfully

The Library area is the hub of literacy learning in *The Creative Curriculum®* classroom and usually the place where most of the literacy materials are stored. However, literacy materials are included in all interest areas. Teachers carefully select materials that reflect the interests, backgrounds, and real-life experiences of the children so that literacy learning is meaningful for them. For example, including writing materials, informational books, posters, and charts about the growth cycle of frogs in the Discovery area, along with an aquarium with tadpoles, encourages interested children to use literacy as a learning tool. Meaningful experiences enable children to understand purposes for literacy, and they are able to explore reading and writing at their own paces and in their own ways. For more ideas about how to support literacy learning in interest areas, see chapter 4 of this volume.

Supporting Children's Play

Interactions between teachers and children during play are critical to children's language and literacy development. Teachers need to observe children's play carefully to determine the most appropriate amount and type of support to offer. When adults become too involved or controlling, children lose interest and stop playing.

When teachers understand the components of literacy, they can interact with children deliberately to encourage them to explore literacy in ways that the children might not try on their own. Consider this example:

> *A teacher noticed that the children in the Dramatic Play area have many pretend phone conversations. To promote children's awareness that print has meaning and can be used to communicate with others, the teacher added paper and pencils to the area. She then pretended to have a phone conversation and to take an important message for one of the children. Then she read the message to the child.*

Teachers' enthusiasm about children's early attempts to read and write also influences children's view of themselves as readers and writers. By respecting children's efforts—however conventional or unconventional they might be—teachers can help children to feel confident and competent, and to know that the classroom is a place where they can experiment safely with oral and written language.

Teachers assume various roles during play in order to support children's literacy learning. These roles include being an observer, facilitator, player, and leader.

Observer

Sometimes children are deeply involved in play, and the teacher only needs to observe, offer encouragement through a smile or nod of the head, or acknowledge a child's effort. Here is an example:

Malik:	(Has a doll in her lap, holds the phone receiver to her ear, and is writing on a notepad.) *Give her one spoonful of medicine before she goes to bed and one when she wakes up. Okay, I'll bring her to see you tomorrow. Thank you, Doctor.*
Ms. Tory:	(Looks at the pad on which Malik wrote.) *I see you wrote down what the doctor said. Good thing you were able to talk with him on the phone. Doctors are sometimes very busy.*

Facilitator

As a facilitator, the teacher does not participate in the children's play but supports them by providing props and materials or by helping children arrange an area for a particular kind of play. The following conversations took place between Crystal; Ben; Dallas; and their teacher, Mr. Alvarez, as they set up a restaurant in the Dramatic Play area.

Ben:	(Looks at Mr. Alvarez.) *We need a sign or paper that tells people what they can buy at the restaurant.*

Mr. Alvarez:	*A sign?*
Ben:	*Yeah, so people will know what kind of food we have and how much it costs.*
Mr. Alvarez:	*Oh, yes. Some restaurants post that information on signs, and some have smaller menus. Here are some menus.* (Mr. Alvarez hands Ben menus from a familiar local restaurant.)
Mr. Alvarez:	*This is a nice place you have here. What is the name of your restaurant? I want to tell all of my friends about it.*
Crystal:	*We don't have a name yet.*
Mr. Alvarez:	*Well, when you decide the name, let me know. I will be happy to help you make a name sign and hang it up so everyone will know about your restaurant.*
Dallas:	*I'm going to be the waiter!*
Mr. Alvarez:	*Here are some pads so the waiter or waitress can write the customers' orders.*

Player

As a player, the teacher participates in children's play at their invitation. Assuming a role or character, the teacher extends children's play through dialogue or literacy activities related to the play theme. This encourages children to assume roles and to talk about what they are doing. In the scenario below, the children have positioned chairs in rows of two to make a pretend bus. Kate is seated in the driver's seat while Setsuko, Sonya, and Carlos are pretending to be passengers.

Kate:	*Ms. Tory, do you want to go on a bus trip?*
Ms. Tory:	*I would love to.*
Kate:	(Holds out her hand.) *Where's your ticket?*
Ms. Tory:	*I didn't know I need a ticket. Where do I get one?*
Carlos:	*You have to buy one. I'll get you a ticket.* (Carlos pretends to get off the bus and goes to a nearby table. Ms. Tory follows him.)
Ms. Tory:	(Acts in character.) *Excuse me. Is this where I get a bus ticket?*
Carlos:	*Yes. How many do you want?*
Ms. Tory:	*Just one.*
Carlos:	*Here you go.* (Carlos scribbles on a piece of paper and hands it to Ms. Tory.)
Ms. Tory:	*How much money do I owe you?*
Carlos:	*Fifty dollars.*

Ms. Tory:	*Fifty dollars! That's a lot of money! Let me see if I have enough.* (She pretends to search her pockets.)
Ms. Tory:	*Hmm. I'm all out of cash. Will you take a check?*
Carlos:	*I guess so.*
Ms. Tory:	(Ms. Tory reaches for a blank piece of paper and thinks aloud as she writes.) *Kate's Bus Company. Fifty dollars. Ms. Tory.*
Ms. Tory:	(Hands the paper to Carlos.) *Here you go.*
Carlos:	*Okay. Let's go.* (Carlos returns to his seat on the bus.)
Ms. Tory:	(Gives the ticket to Kate, sits in a chair, and continues the role of bus passenger.)

Leader

As a leader, the teacher directs aspects of children's play, not by controlling the play but by intentionally introducing new ideas. In the following example, a spring holiday is approaching and the children in an oceanside community have been talking about going to the beach. Mr. Alvarez is in the Dramatic Play area with Crystal and Juwan. They are pretending that they are going to the beach, and they have asked him to pretend that he is their dad. Sonya is also in the Dramatic Play area, but she is not initially involved in Crystal's and Juwan's play. Notice how Mr. Alvarez skillfully introduces literacy into the children's play.

Juwan:	*We need to go to the store to buy food and stuff for our trip.*
Mr. Alvarez:	*You're right. Before we go, we need to make a list. You know how often I forget things.*
Crystal:	*Okay. Hand me that paper, and I'll start the list. Let's see. We're gonna need snacks and suntan lotion, beach towels, and hats to keep the sun out of our eyes.*
Sonya:	*Hi. What are you doing?*
Crystal:	*Making a list so we can remember what to get at the store. We're going on a trip to the beach!*
Sonya:	*Who's going?*
Crystal:	*Me and Dad* (motions to Mr. Alvarez) *and Juwan.*
Sonya:	*Who's gonna keep your baby brother?* (She points to the doll in the high chair.)
Crystal:	*Hmmm.* (She puts her finger to chin as though she is thinking.) *You mean while we go to the store or to the beach?*
Sonya:	*To the store. Want me to keep him?*

Crystal:	*Yeah! We might be gone for a few hours, and he might get fussy.* (She picks up keys and looks at Mr. Alvarez.) *Let's go, Dad. Juwan come on. Sonya is gonna keep the baby.*
Mr. Alvarez:	*We can't go until we give her instructions for taking care of the baby, especially because he has been a little fussy. Here.* (He hands Crystal a memo pad.)
Crystal:	(Talks as she writes.) *Give him a bottle in 20 minutes. Rock him and then put him in his crib. He likes for you to sing "You Are My Sunshine." That is his favorite song.*

While four roles have been described, it does not mean that the teacher assumes only one role exclusively when interacting with children. Often the teacher assumes multiple roles during a play episode, according to the strengths and needs of the children.

Incorporating literacy in children's play enables them to construct understandings about literacy experiences they have in other contexts. It is also a way to provide developmentally appropriate instruction.

Tips to Share With Families

- Do things together that you both enjoy (e.g., taking a walk, baking muffins, or swimming) and talk about what you notice and what you are doing, thinking, and feeling.

- Encourage your child's dramatic (pretend) play by asking questions and sometimes assuming a role. (*Are you making a sandwich for me? I like cheese sandwiches with mustard. I'd like to take a trip on your airplane. Where are you going?*)

- Collect empty food containers, grocery bags, paper and pencils to make shopping lists, and some play money to encourage your child to pretend that he is going to the grocery store.

- Offer old clothes, hats, suitcases, plastic dishes, empty food containers, and writing materials so your child can play house. If possible, make office supplies available as well.

- Provide writing materials for your child to use as she plays.

- Offer your child different kinds of art materials and talk about how they can be used.

- Encourage your child to talk about what he is doing and thinking as he plays.

Studies: Using Literacy to Learn

The Creative Curriculum® for Preschool encourages the use of studies as a way of helping children build content knowledge and helping children develop process skills (see *Volume 1: The Foundation*). A study is an in-depth investigation of a topic worth learning more about. As children work on studies, they find the answers to their questions. They practice and apply literacy skills in order to learn about the topic.

Beginning the Study

To understand how children use literacy to learn, consider the study that evolved in Ms. Tory's and Mr. Alvarez's class.

> *It was spring, and the children began to notice changes outside. Outdoors they began picking wildflowers and wild onions. They brought them back to the classroom and used them in a variety of ways. They arranged them in vases to display in the Dramatic Play area and glued them on the fronts of folded card stock to create greeting cards. Some children blew the dandelions and watched to see where the seeds landed. At group time, the teachers talked with the children about the flowers and asked them to describe the different ways they used them. They also recalled seeing flowers in other places. As their interest continued to grow, Ms. Tory and Mr. Alvarez realized that a study of flowers would offer many opportunities for the children to learn content.*

The teachers then created a web of big ideas to identify the content children could learn. They started by brainstorming words that relate to flowers. In addition to helping them identify the content, this also enabled them to record important vocabulary that could be taught. After generating a long list of words on sticky notes, they grouped the words into categories on a piece of chart paper. They drew a circle around each group and labeled it. The labels identified the big ideas of the topic.

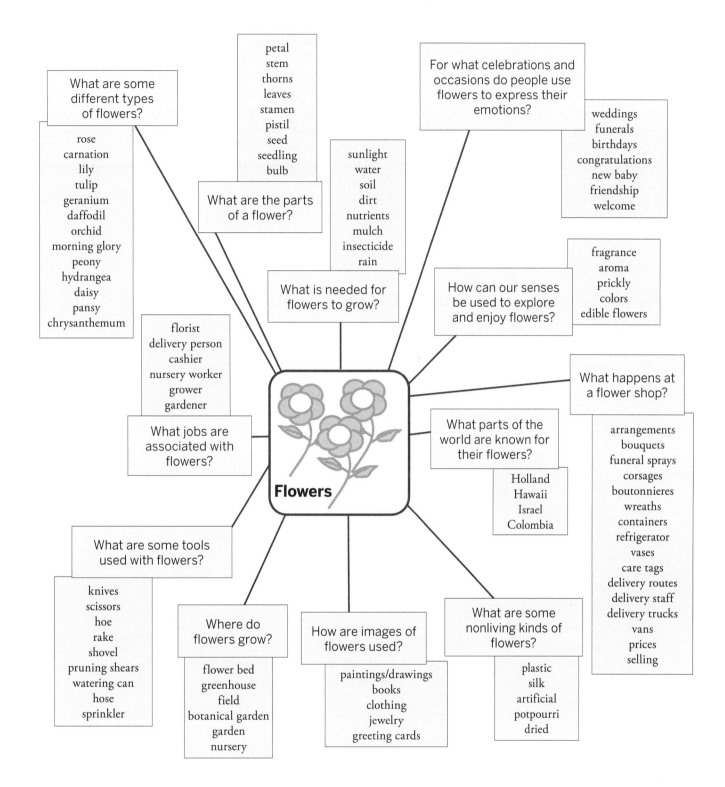

What are some
different types
of flowers?

rose
carnation
lily
tulip
geranium
daffodil
orchid
morning glory
peony
hydrangea
daisy
pansy
chrysanthemum

petal
stem
thorns
leaves
stamen
pistil
seed
seedling
bulb

What are the parts
of a flower?

sunlight
water
soil
dirt
nutrients
mulch
insecticide
rain

What is needed for
flowers to grow?

For what celebrations and
occasions do people use
flowers to express their
emotions?

weddings
funerals
birthdays
congratulations
new baby
friendship
welcome

fragrance
aroma
prickly
colors
edible flowers

How can our senses
be used to explore
and enjoy flowers?

florist
delivery person
cashier
nursery worker
grower
gardener

What jobs are
associated with
flowers?

Flowers

What happens at
a flower shop?

arrangements
bouquets
funeral sprays
corsages
boutonnieres
wreaths
containers
refrigerator
vases
care tags
delivery routes
delivery staff
delivery trucks
vans
prices
selling

What parts of the
world are known for
their flowers?

Holland
Hawaii
Israel
Colombia

What are some tools
used with flowers?

knives
scissors
hoe
rake
shovel
pruning shears
watering can
hose
sprinkler

Where do
flowers grow?

flower bed
greenhouse
field
botanical garden
garden
nursery

How are images of
flowers used?

paintings/drawings
books
clothing
jewelry
greeting cards

What are some
nonliving kinds of
flowers?

plastic
silk
artificial
potpourri
dried

Mr. Alvarez and Ms. Tory thought of the many ways that they could address literacy, math, science, social studies, the arts, and technology through the study of flowers. They reviewed the information found in chapter 3 of *The Creative Curriculum® for Preschool, Volume 1: The Foundation* to see how their web addressed important science and social studies concepts and skills. Both teachers considered how children could use literacy and math skills to learn content. They also discussed how this topic relates to their program's learning standards.

A good study begins with what children know and then leads them beyond their everyday experiences. Ms. Tory led a discussion about the children's flowers to find out what they already knew. She commented, "I wonder how the wildflowers grew all of a sudden, like magic." The children offered ideas, which Ms. Tory recorded on a chart.

During their discussions at group time, Ms. Tory kept a list of the children's questions:

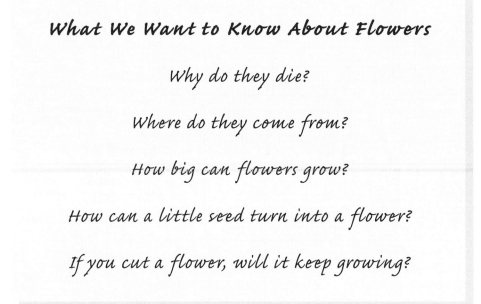

What We Want to Know About Flowers

Why do they die?

Where do they come from?

How big can flowers grow?

How can a little seed turn into a flower?

If you cut a flower, will it keep growing?

She continued to add to the list each day as the children wondered aloud. This list of questions became the heart of their study. The experiences that Ms. Tory and Mr. Alvarez offered and encouraged were designed to help the children find answers to their questions. Ms. Tory wrote a letter to families to let them know about the flower study and ways they might participate.

Investigating the Topic

Ms. Tory and Mr. Alvarez first thought of possible experiences that would help the children find answers to their questions and gain deeper understandings about flowers. The following were some of their ideas for incorporating literacy skills.

Flower Experiences	Ways to Use Literacy Skills
Site visit to a flower shop (or nursery or garden)	Help children formulate questions for the florist and practice asking them before the visit.
	Provide clipboards for children to write or draw observation notes.
	Read informational books about flower shops and flowers before the visit.
	Take photos of print at the flower shop or nursery and display them.
	Collect samples from the florist of printed materials, e.g., care tags, flyers, advertisements.
	Compose a thank-you note with the children and address the envelope together.
	Write an experience story after the site visit.
Plant flowers	Explore with children the letters and words on seed packets; create matching games.
	Read and follow directions for planting seeds with the children; make a book with seed packets.
	Create a job chart for plant care.
	Keep journals to document observations of growing plants.
	Look at books and catalogs with pictures of flowers from around the world.
	Read books about flowers, such as *The Tiny Seed* (Eric Carle); *The Dandelion Seed* (Joseph P. Anthony); *Gardening Tools* (Inez Snyder); *Bumble Bee, Bumble Bee, Do You Know Me?: A Garden Guessing Game* (Anne Rockwell); and *Planting a Rainbow* (Lois Ehlert).

Flower Experiences	Ways to Use Literacy Skills
Arrange flowers	Help children write letters to their families, asking for flowers from their yards.
	Look at magazines, flyers, books, and florist Web sites to see flower arrangements.
	Learn new vocabulary words, such as *container, vase, arrangement, bouquet,* and *corsage.*
	Learn the names of the flowers in the children's arrangements, such as roses, daisies, and zinnias.
	Learn descriptive words, such as *fragrant, thorny,* and *fragile,* and record them on a chart.
	Write enclosure cards for flower arrangements.
	Discuss the occasions and celebrations for which people use flowers.
	Make up rhymes or poems to deliver with flowers (e.g., *Roses are red, violets are blue, sugar is sweet, and so are you*); call children's attention to the rhyming words.
	Make a book with magazine pictures of bouquets, corsages, boutonnieres, and sprays.
Create a flower shop in the Dramatic Play area	Refer to the photos taken on the site visit to the florist; create signs with the children.
	Write on chart paper a list of what to include in the flower shop.
	Create advertisements, brochures, enclosure cards, care tags, and identification labels.
	Make a poster that identifies the types of flowers for sale.
	Provide order forms for flower arrangements.
	Add a local map and delivery instructions.
Conduct experiments with flowers	Place white carnations in containers of colored water. Make a chart of the children's predictions about what will happen; discuss results.
	Experiment with flowering plants (light–no light; water–no water; plant food–no plant food). Write predictions and record findings.

There were far too many experiences to be completed in a week. Learning takes time. Mr. Alvarez and Ms. Tory used the "Weekly Planning Form" (see *The Creative Curriculum® for Preschool, Volume 1: The Foundation*) to record the materials they needed and to identify what they hoped to accomplish each week. They adjusted their plans on the basis of their observations of the children engaged in the study.

Over the next few weeks, the teachers guided children through various investigations and activities to help them find the answers to their questions. They used open-ended questions to help children plan, predict, and solve problems. Here are examples of the questions and prompts they used to help the children build understandings and to encourage language development:

I wonder why the tall flower topples over when you put it in the short vase. What can you do so it won't fall over?

What do you think will happen if we don't water the geranium?

How do you think the florist gets the flowers that are in the cooler?

How do you think this tiny sunflower seed becomes a plant that grows to be so tall?

Ms. Tory and Mr. Alvarez displayed the children's documentation of their study.

Concluding the Study

To close their study of flowers, the children planned a flower show for their families and other visitors. The children created invitations, welcome banners, and programs. They worked in groups to create floral arrangements. They followed recipes to prepare a snack. When the guests arrived, each group told about their arrangement, the types of flowers they used, and the process of creating it. The guests were given a tour of the flower garden the children had planted. After the celebration was over, the children delivered their arrangements to residents in a nearby nursing home.

As you can see, this study of flowers uses literacy in ways that are meaningful and relevant to children. The study helps children understand purposes for reading, writing, listening, and speaking, and it helps them practice literacy skills.

Literacy Learning in Interest Areas and Outdoors

The Library Area: The Hub of Literacy Learning   126
Creating an Effective Library Area
Observing and Responding to Children
Interacting With Children in the Library Area
Special Challenges in the Library Area

Literacy in the Block Area   135
Using Blocks to Teach Literacy Skills
Observing Children's Understanding

Literacy in the Dramatic Play Area   139
Using Dramatic Play to Teach Literacy Skills
Observing Children's Understanding

Literacy in the Toys and Games Area   145
Using Toys and Games to Teach Literacy Skills
Observing Children's Understanding

Literacy in the Art Area   148
Using Art Materials to Teach Literacy Skills
Observing Children's Understanding

Literacy in the Discovery Area   153
Using Discovery Materials to Teach Literacy Skills
Observing Children's Understanding

Literacy in the Sand and Water Area   158
Using Sand and Water to Teach Literacy Skills
Observing Children's Understanding

Literacy in the Music and Movement Area   161
Using Music and Movement to Teach Literacy Skills
Observing Children's Understanding

Literacy in the Cooking Area   166
Using Cooking to Teach Literacy Skills
Observing Children's Understanding

Literacy in the Technology Area   172
Using Technology to Teach Literacy Skills
Observing Children's Understanding

Literacy Outdoors   177
Using the Outdoors to Teach Literacy Skills
Observing Children's Understanding

Literacy Learning in Interest Areas and Outdoors

In programs that use *The Creative Curriculum*®, children spend a significant part of each day in child-initiated play in interest areas and outdoor spaces designed thoughtfully by teachers. When each interest area and the outdoors are organized with literacy in mind, children's play is meaningful and literacy learning is maximized. This chapter describes how to make each interest area and the outdoors valuable places for literacy learning. It also shows how teachers interact with children in ways that support each component of literacy. Although the Library area has the most significant number of books and other literacy materials, each area of the classroom and part of the outdoors must be places where children's literacy-skill development is promoted in purposeful, integrated ways.

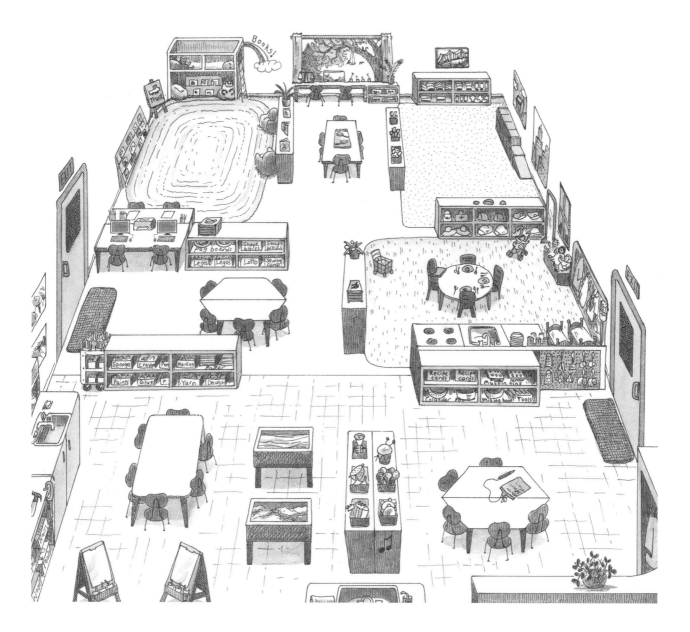

The Library Area: The Hub of Literacy Learning

The Library area is a resource area and the place where concentrated literacy learning often occurs. An effective Library area helps children develop the motivation and skills necessary to read and write. As they hear stories read aloud every day, look through books on their own, listen to recorded stories, retell familiar stories, and make up their own stories, children have many opportunities to progress in all areas of development and learning.

Creating an Effective Library Area

The Library area should include places for looking at books, listening to recordings, writing, retelling familiar stories, and perhaps using a computer. When arranged attractively and stocked with materials thoughtfully, the Library area can be one of the most popular places in the classroom. Consider the books, tapes, writing materials, and storytelling props that are most appropriate and appealing for the children in your classroom. Organize and display the materials so that children are drawn to them and able to use them easily.

Selecting Books

As with all materials, keep the ages and interests of the children in mind when you select books. In general, younger preschool children like books with a simple, predictable plot about familiar experiences; colorful, bold illustrations that are clear and detailed; and rich language (rhymes, nonsense words, and repetition). Older preschool children have a longer attention span and can follow more complicated plots. They appreciate humor and fantasy and begin to enjoy stories about faraway places.

Instead of displaying all of your books at one time, put out a manageable number of books and rotate them regularly. That way, the children will notice new books and will be excited by old favorites they have not seen for a while. As new interests emerge, add relevant books. Select books that

- relate to the interests and life experiences of children and that will help them develop understandings about the world
- are predictable and encourage children to participate by supplying words and phrases
- enrich children's language development
- help children gain knowledge of the alphabet and phonological awareness
- are of a variety of genres
- portray diversity and promote inclusion

For children whose first language is not English, provide books written in their primary languages. This practice sends the message to children and their families that each first language is honored and respected.

Materials for Story Retelling

After children have heard a story several times and have observed the story retold with props, they will want to retell it independently. In the Library area, include materials that encourage children to tell and retell stories, such as flannel boards and puppets. For more guidance about books and props for story retelling, see chapter 3, "Teaching Strategies."

Materials for Listening

Include recordings of familiar stories so children can practice following a story in a book as they listen, turning the pages at the appropriate time and matching the narration with the pictures. If possible, the Library area should include a few small CD players and a variety of CDs for children to select. Headphones enable children to listen without disturbing others.

The same general guidelines for selecting books apply to selecting story CDs. The best stories are short, lively, unbiased in content, and narrated by both men and women. In selecting recordings, begin with stories that are familiar to the children or that accompany books you have in the classroom. You can make audio recordings, yourself, reading books that the children particularly love. As you record the story, include sound effects or other cues to let children know when to turn the page. To encourage children to supply a word or phrase, pause occasionally while recording the story. Invite family members and community volunteers to make recordings for the children as well.

Materials for Writing

A place for writing offers children opportunities to write for different purposes, such as creating greeting cards or writing messages to each other. The Library area should include a table and chairs as well as a shelf for storing an assortment of writing materials. At a minimum, include

- alphabet strips
- name cards
- various kinds of paper, including envelopes and stationery
- a variety of writing tools (pencils, markers, and crayons)
- stencils and letter stamps
- bookbinding supplies

For a complete list of materials, see *The Creative Curriculum® for Preschool, Volume 2: Interest Areas*.

Observing and Responding to Children

Some children have had many experiences with books at home and come to school with early reading and writing skills. Others have had little experience with language and literacy. Teachers can guide children's learning when they know what particular reading and writing skills children are acquiring.

Skills for Engaging With Books

Learning to read is a complex process that involves developing many skills. Look for and promote these skills as children progress to reading and writing:

Listening for understanding. Listening and reading are closely related. As children listen to stories, they learn the meaning of new words. They try to make sense of words by connecting them with their own experiences. Later, when children begin reading, they figure out words more easily when they already know their meanings. Listening to stories improves children's understanding of grammar and the structure of language. That understanding helps pave the way for making sense of the text.

Exploring books. Imitating adults and older children, young children like to pretend to read. Even though children may not actually be reading, they explore many reading-like behaviors. They hold the book correctly and turn the pages appropriately. Children also want to have books read to them, frequently asking for the same picture book again and again at one sitting. Adults often tire of rereading a story long before the children tire. Repeated readings support the development of children's understanding of story structure and their efforts to learn the conventions of print.

Understanding how stories work. Children gradually recognize that stories have a beginning, middle, and end. They use picture cues to remember the details of their favorite stories and to confirm their growing understanding of print concepts. You might hear children use story language such as "Once upon a time…" or "That's the end of the story." After hearing a story repeatedly, children call on their memory, comprehension, and verbal skills to retell the story.

Understanding the function and value of print. Readers understand why and how print is used. From meaningful print throughout the classroom, such as a menu, a daily schedule, and names on cubbies, children learn that print provides information. Children use books as a source of information, such as when they want to identify a leaf they found on the playground or a shell in the Discovery area.

Recognizing that written words are meaningful. When children are first introduced to books, they follow the story through the pictures. With multiple experiences and adult guidance, they gradually learn that printed words function differently from pictures but that both express ideas and feelings.

Connecting written symbols with sounds. As children explore the sounds and rhythms of language, they begin to understand that spoken words are ordered sounds that are represented by the letters of the alphabet. For example, when a child listens to the story of the duck named Ping, she may say, "That starts the same way as my name!"

Matching words with the printed text. You may see children run their fingers along the text or point to individual words as a book is being read. They may begin matching spoken with printed words by pointing. These behaviors indicate that they are beginning to understand the concept of a word, although they may not read words correctly.

Recognizing written words. Children who are learning this skill take an active interest in the text and are curious about finding words they know on the page. They may ask questions, such as "What does this say?" or "Where does it say that?" Children develop a sight vocabulary. They notice words from favorite books or commercial products and excitedly point them out in less familiar books and in the environment.

Developmental Levels of Writing

Long before children come to school, they see writing created and displayed, and they see people use it. When children have opportunities to write in the context of everyday activities, they learn many important literacy skills. They construct understandings about print conventions and the functions of print, and they develop phonological awareness.

The Creative Curriculum® for Preschool, Volume 6: Objectives for Development & Learning shows the developmental levels of children who are learning to write. The typical progression of skill development is presented to help teachers understand Objective 19, "Demonstrates writing skills. That objective has two dimensions: "Writes name," and "Writes to convey ideas and information." The progression, which is also included in the appendix of this volume, shows a rating scale, indicators, examples, and age-range expectations for each dimension. The information can be used as a guide to analyzing children's writing. Note that many of the characteristics of each stage of writing one's name and writing to convey meaning are very similar.

Responding to Each Child

Because the Library area offers many opportunities for learning, visit the area, observe, and talk with children when they are working there. An appropriate starting point for your observations is to look for the reading and writing behaviors described earlier. While observing a child's use of the Library area, notice whether the child

- shows a preference for certain topics or books and often connects them to personal experiences
- talks about the story, pretends to read it, and identifies words in the text
- handles a book appropriately and follows print from left to right, top to bottom, and front to back (or in whatever direction is appropriate to the language in which the book is written)
- retells stories in his or her own words and by using props
- writes or scribbles messages to communicate meaning

Your observations can be used to plan specific activities to extend each child's development and learning. For further guidance, review the "Observe, Reflect, Respond" charts in *The Creative Curriculum® for Preschool, Volume 2: Interest Areas.*

Interacting With Children in the Library Area

Teachers are role models for young children. If you show children how much you enjoy books and if they see you writing often and for a purpose, children will want to imitate you. The Library area is a place where you can share books, retell stories, listen to recordings, and write with individuals and small groups of children.

Reading Books With Small Groups and Individual Children

The Library area is ideal for sharing books with small groups of children. The intimate setting enables you to interact with children positively and enhance their language and literacy learning. The following chart shows the kinds of questions you might ask and comments you might make.

Interactive Story Reading

Kind of Question or Comment	Example
Completion—Omit a word at the end of a sentence and pause to let the children fill it in.	*Run, run, as fast as you can. You can't catch me. I'm the Gingerbread _____!*
Open-ended—Ask the children a question that will encourage them to think of several answers.	*What do you think the Gingerbread Man is doing in this picture?* *I wonder why the Gingerbread Man wanted to run away. What do you think?* *How would you feel if you were a gingerbread man?*
Who, what, when, where, why, and how—Ask the children these kinds of questions about the narrative and the illustrations.	*What did the baker use to make the Gingerbread Man?* *What did the little old man say when the Gingerbread Man ran away?* *Where did the fox want the Gingerbread Man to go?* *Why do you think the fox wanted the Gingerbread Man to ride on his head across the river?* *How did the fox trick the Gingerbread Man?*
Connections—Help the children see how the story relates to their own experiences.	*Have you ever eaten gingerbread?* *Did anyone ever try to trick you?*

You may also choose to use the repeated read-aloud approach if you are reading sophisticated storybooks and nonfiction books. See chapter 3 of this volume, "Teaching Strategies," for a more complete description of this approach.

When you read a book with just one child, you can focus on particular skills. Here are some strategies:

Before reading:

Have the child sit comfortably beside you or in your lap.

Note the child's preferences: *This must be your favorite book. You've picked it out every morning this week. Tell me what you like best about it.*

Look at and discuss the book's cover: *The title of this book is… I wonder what the story is about.*

Take a "picture walk" with the child by talking about the illustrations and asking the child to predict what will happen: *I wonder why the insects are hiding in the grass. What do you think will happen to them?*

During reading:

Reinforce the child's correct handling of books: *The careful way you are turning the pages tells me that you really know how to take care of books.*

Encourage the child to think critically: *What would you do if you were Andrew? Why do you think Peter's mother said, "No"?*

Help the child think of and express new ideas and solutions: *The glue on her shoes really slowed her down, didn't it? What would you do?*

Encourage the child to anticipate the story line as you read: *What do you think will happen next?*

Explore feelings: *Have you ever felt like Francis?" "Have you ever stayed overnight at a friend's house? I bet you know just how Ira felt about sleeping away from home.*

Relate what is happening in the story to the child's own life: *The little boy in this story has a new baby brother, just as you do, Tasheen.*

Encourage the child to point to words: *Can you find where it says dog? It starts like your name, Derek.*

After reading:

Discuss the completed story with the child: *What did you like about this story? Who was your favorite character?*

Encourage the child to retell or act out the story: *Would you like to use flannel board pieces to tell the story?*

You may also choose to use the conversational reading strategies discussed in chapter 3 of this volume.

Retelling Stories With Children

Children also try to retell familiar stories and to make up new stories. You may assume one of many roles during these retellings:

- Narrator—You narrate the story as children act it out.
- Player—You assume a role in the retelling at the children's request.
- Resource person—You assist in finding props.
- Observer—You observe the action as children retell the story with props they choose independently.

Carefully follow the children's lead during their retelling and determine when children need additional support. For more information about retelling stories, see chapter 3 of this volume.

Listening to Audio Recordings With Children

Take the time to join one or two children in listening to a recorded story. You may need to turn the pages of the book to help some children keep pace with the recorded voice. Other children might be able to do this on their own.

Some children may be reluctant to select a story on their own, or they may be unsure about how to operate the audio equipment. Sometimes the assistance of another child is all that is needed. Once children learn to operate the equipment, they can listen to recorded stories independently.

Promoting Children's Writing

Keep writing tools and paper readily available. Show an interest in writing and in what children do. Try these approaches:

Model writing and explain your purpose: *I need to write a note to the director to remind her that we have a study trip next week.*

Comment on each child's work: *I see you've been busy writing. Will you read to me what you wrote?*

Describe what you see: *You made a whole row of As and then a row of Ms.*

Help children use equipment and materials: *Let me help you find a way to put the caps on the markers.*

Ask questions or make statements that help a child solve a problem: *Do you want to know how to write Alexa's name? I wonder if we can find her name on something in the classroom.*

A teacher's genuine interest and involvement in the Library area helps to encourage children's growing interest in writing and reading.

Special Challenges in the Library Area

Children who have fine-motor difficulties and children who have trouble attending to and processing language may not seem to be particularly interested in Library area activities. The following suggestions can help children with special challenges participate actively in the Library area with their peers.

If a child...	Try these strategies...
shows variable attention during listening and reading activities	Encourage the child's involvement by offering hands-on experiences. For example, adapt pop-up or flap books by cutting off the flaps, laminating them for durability, and then re-attaching them to the book with hook-and-loop fasteners. The child can interact with the book by pulling each item off or putting it on as you read the story.
	Use related props with every story so that the child has something to hold and manipulate (e.g., a spider ring for the book Itsy-Bitsy Spider).
	Use books that repeat phrases frequently, to support the child's learning and engagement.
	Encourage the child to be the lead storyteller, to encourage his or her attention and participation.
has difficulty hearing, understanding, or seeing as books are read aloud	Have the child sit close to you.
	Speak slowly to allow time for the child to process the language and information. Repeat text as necessary.
	Use exaggerated facial expressions, intonation, and gestures.
	Encourage the use of a magnifying glass, binoculars, or "third eye" magnifying lens.
	Use a peer reading buddy to provide individualized support to the child while looking at books.
is an English-language learner or has a language delay	Use simple gestures and point to specific characters or details in illustrations.
	Use American Sign Language for basic words in a story, rhyme, or song.
	Adapt vocabulary, sentences, and text length to fit the child's level of understanding.
	Use teacher-made or commercial books that present songs that are sung in the classroom and books that have photographs of particular interest to the child.

If a child...	Try these strategies...
has trouble holding and manipulating reading materials	Use adaptive equipment such as book trays or holders.
	Ask a peer reading buddy to turn the pages.
	Attach hook-and-loop fastener tabs on page edges to make page turning easier.
avoids writing	Include large writing tools in many interest areas.
	Encourage the child who is interested in playing with magnetic letters and numbers to trace around them and to make words with them.
has difficulty holding and manipulating writing tools and materials	Use adaptive equipment to encourage writing, such as pencil grips, very large crayons, and hook-and-loop fastener hand or wrist straps to hold writing tools.
	Consult with an assistive technology professional about the latest tools available to support children with fine-motor and visual–motor problems.

Literacy in the Block Area

Blocks are a powerful tool for representing stories and enacting real events, for sparking conversations, for communicating and negotiating ideas, and for inspiring writing. Take advantage of children's love of block play to help them develop important literacy skills.

Examples of What a Child Might Do	Examples of Related Objectives	Examples of How This Relates to Literacy
Build a fire truck with blocks	14. Uses symbols and images to represent something not present a. Thinks symbolically	Understanding that the block structure represents a real object, which is an important step in understanding that letters represent sounds and that words express ideas and feelings
Use a plank to create a drawbridge and talk about how it goes up and down	9. Uses language to express thoughts and needs a. Uses an expanding expressive vocabulary	Using specialized vocabulary to communicate ideas
Build a skyscraper with another child and figure out how to keep it from falling	10. Uses appropriate conversational and other communication skills a. Engages in conversations 11. Demonstrates positive approaches to learning c. Solves problems e. Shows flexibility and inventiveness in thinking	Solving a problem and using language to talk with a peer about the problem and solutions
Write a sign that says, "Do not knock down."	19. Demonstrates writing skills b. Writes to convey ideas and information	Understanding the purpose of writing; using writing to express an idea
Match blocks with shape labels when returning them to the shelf	13. Uses classification skills	Matching shapes, which relates to matching and discriminating letters and words
Place blocks on top of one another carefully	7. Demonstrates fine-motor strength and coordination a. Uses fingers and hands	Developing important pre-writing skills, such as eye–hand coordination, visual perception, and small-muscle control

Adding literacy-related props to the Block area not only supports the development of language and literacy skills, but it also inspires children to build more creatively. Placed in the Block area, books can spark children's creativity and be a source of building ideas.

Materials

books and pictures about construction, buildings, workers, tools, construction and emergency vehicles, architecture, repairs, roads, bridges

advertisements for construction materials and tools

blueprints

floor plans

graph paper

logos of local businesses and familiar products

memo pads

newspapers

repair manuals

traffic signs

Suggested Books

(Titles preceded by an asterisk are included in the *Teaching Strategies® Children's Book Collection*.)

Alphabet City (Stephen Johnson)

Alphabet Under Construction (Denise Fleming)

As the Crow Flies: A First Book of Maps (Gail Hartman)

Bear About Town (Stella Blackstone)

Block City (Robert Louis Stevenson)

Bridges Are to Cross (Philemon Sturges)

Bruno the Carpenter (Lars Klinting)

*Build It From A to Z (Trish Holland)

*Building a House (Byron Barton)

*Buildings, Buildings, Buildings (Judith Bauer Stamper)

Cars and Trucks and Things That Go (Richard Scarry)

*Changes, Changes (Pat Hutchins)

City Signs (Zoran Milich)

Dig Dig Digging (Margaret Mayo)

Freight Train (Donald Crews)

Get to Work, Trucks (Don Carter)

Henry Builds a Cabin (D. B. Johnson)

The House in the Meadow (Shutta Crum)

*House, Sweet House (Judith Bauer Stamper)

How a House Is Built (Gail Gibbons)

How I Learned Geography (Uri Shulevitz)

I Read Signs (Tana Hoban)

Inside Freight Train (Donald Crews)

*Los tres pequeños jabalíes/The Three Little Javelinas (Susan Lowell)

Me on the Map (Joan Sweeny)

Mike Mulligan and His Steam Shovel (Virginia Lee Burton)

New Road! (Gail Gibbons)

On the Road (Susan Steggall)

*The Three Pigs (David Weisner)

*The True Story of the 3 Little Pigs (Jon Scieszka)

Using Blocks to Teach Literacy Skills

Understanding the developmental stages of block play will help you think about how to promote literacy in the Block area. (Also see *The Creative Curriculum® for Preschool, Volume 2: Interest Areas*). You may have a child in your class who is at Stage I, "Carrying blocks." This child is exploring the physical properties of blocks and what she can and cannot do with them. Your interactions with this child might involve talking about how heavy or how long a block is. Your conversations with a child who is at Stage IV, "Building elaborate constructions," might be entirely different. This child might use blocks to build a castle, a fire truck, or a city and then use the construction in sociodramatic play. You might offer additional literacy materials, such as books about the topic or paper for signs. The key is to observe the block play and match your interactions to the child's stage of development.

Here are examples of what you might say and ask as children use the materials:

Unit blocks

This is a really interesting construction. Will you tell me about it?

Would you like to make a "Do not knock down" sign to keep your building safe?

I noticed that your tower keeps falling when you build it on the carpet. I wonder why that happens.

You know, the skyscraper you built today is even taller than the one you built yesterday. How did you make it so tall?

This road you made curves just like a letter S.

You made a house out of wood and a house out of bricks for the three little pigs. What could you use for the third house? Let me know when you're ready to act out the story. I'd love to watch you.

Let's match these blocks to the shapes on the shelf while we clean up.

I see that you're making a bridge. How is your bridge like the one in this book?

Hollow blocks

You made the top of your castle just like the one in the book. You put one block standing up; then you left a space; then you stood another block up. I wonder why castles were built like that.

You made a drive-through window for the bank just like the one where your mother works. Would you like to make a sign for your bank to let everyone know that it is open for business?

Block accessories (vehicles, animals, people)

Have you ever seen a front-loader? What do you think it is used for?

Would you like to make a license plate for this car? Here's a piece of paper. You can write the letters and numbers on it.

I have a driver's license that shows I know how to operate a car and follow the rules of the road. Would you like to make your own driver's license with words about you and with your picture on it?

I see you made a zoo. Have you ever been to a zoo? Zoo is an easy word to spell: z-o-o. It almost sounds like boo!

Would you like to make a sign for your entrance?

You placed all the dolls in the bed you made out of blocks. Do you think they would enjoy hearing you read a bedtime story?

Do you remember what the Little Engine said? "I think I can! I think I can!"

Loose parts (PVC pipes, cardboard tubes and boxes, rain gutters, newspaper rolls)

You're using the box just as they did in the story. First the children used the box as a cave. Let me think… How else did they use the box?… How will you use the box?

That piece of pipe curves like the letter J. Some children in our class have names that begin with J. Do you know one?

The house you're building is enormous. Tell me all about it.

Signs

I see you're making a stop sign so the cars won't crash. Stop begins the same way as your name: **St***ephen;* **st***op.*

It looks as though you're making a neighborhood like ours. Do you want to cut this grocery store name from the newspaper and make a sign for your store?

Observing Children's Understanding

While children are engaged in block play, look for these indications of literacy understanding:

- using language to communicate their ideas
- talking with peers and adults about their constructions
- describing what they are doing with the blocks
- controlling the muscles of their hands and wrists as they stack blocks carefully
- describing size, shape, and position
- using words learned in a different context
- matching shapes when they return blocks to the shelves
- writing signs for their constructions

Literacy in the Dramatic Play Area

Children's oral language and literacy skills progress when their dramatic play experiences encourage the use of rich, expressive language and when they explore reading and writing as they play. Children explore literacy in meaningful ways as they enact real-life situations. They write phone messages, read to dolls, and have conversations about being adults. As they play, children gain experience as readers and writers.

Examples of What a Child Might Do	Examples of Related Objectives	Examples of How This Relates to Literacy
Pretend that a pot is a drum	14. Uses symbols and images to represent something not present a. Thinks symbolically	Using symbols in dramatic play helps the child use other symbols, e.g., letters to represent sounds, and words to express ideas and feelings
Talk about print on empty food containers	17. Demonstrates knowledge of print and its uses b. Uses print concepts	Making connections between written language and spoken language
Button, buckle, snap, and zip dress-up and doll clothes	7. Demonstrates fine-motor strength and coordination a. Uses fingers and hands	Developing hand strength and coordination, which are needed for using writing tools
Talk on a play telephone, pausing to listen	10. Uses appropriate conversational and other communication skills b. Uses social rules of language	Learning that conversations involve alternating speakers
Write a shopping list	19. Demonstrates writing skills b. Writes to convey ideas and information	Exploring a purpose of print and how to use it to assist recall
Place a stack of baseball caps on his head and say, "Caps for sale! Caps for sale! Fifty cents a cap!"	18. Comprehends and responds to books and other texts c. Retells stories and recounts details from informational texts	Recalling the events and details of a story that was read aloud

Think about the materials you can add to the Dramatic Play area to support language and literacy development. When selecting books for the Dramatic Play area, choose those that enhance children's thematic play, such as playing house, office, and restaurant scenarios. Also consider the individual needs of the children in your class. Books can help children deal with significant events such as a new baby, death, or moving to a new neighborhood. The following lists offer helpful suggestions for this interest area.

Materials

blank address books

books and magazines

calendars, date books, and appointment books

clipboards

empty food containers

maps

menus, recipe cards, and cookbooks

message boards

newspapers

notepads

old checkbooks

pencils, pens, and markers

photo albums

price lists

receipt books

signs

stationery, greeting cards, and envelopes

telephone book

typewriter or computer keyboard

Suggested Books

(Titles preceded by an asterisk are included in the *Teaching Strategies® Children's Book Collection*.)

Amazing Grace (Mary Hoffman)

Albert the Fix-It Man (Janet Lord)

*Caps for Sale (Esphyr Slobodkina)

Ella Sarah Gets Dressed (Margaret Chodos-Irvine)

Elizabeti's Doll (Stephanie Stuve-Bodeen)

Friends at School (Rochelle Bunnett, Matt Brown)

*The Girl Who Wore Too Much (Margaret McDonald)

Go Away, Big Green Monster (Ed Emberly)

Going to the Dentist (Fred Rogers, Jim Judkis)

Going to the Doctor (Anne Civardi)

Goodnight Moon (Margaret Wise Brown)

Guess How Much I Love You (Sam McBratney)

Hats, Hats, Hats (Ann Morris)

How Do Dinosaurs Get Well Soon? (Jane Yolen)

How Do Dinosaurs Say Goodnight? (Jane Yolen)

I Pretend (Heidi Goennel)

Jesse Bear, What Will You Wear? (Nancy White Carlstrom)

Jonathan and His Mommy (Irene Smalls)

Suggested Books, continued

Kevin and His Dad (Irene Smalls)

Let's Talk About It: Adoption
(Fred Rogers, Jim Judkis)

Let's Talk About It: Extraordinary
Friends (Fred Rogers, Jim Judkis)

Lilly's Purple Plastic Purse
(Keven Henkes)

Making Friends
(Fred Rogers, Jim Judkis)

*Mama and Papa Have a Store
(Amelia Lau Carling)

Mama, Do You Love Me?
(Barbara M. Joosse)

Manners (Aliki)

Miss Spider's Tea Party (David Kirk)

*The Mitten (Jan Brett)

"More, More, More," Said the Baby
(Vera Williams)

My First Day at Preschool
(Edwina Riddell)

The Napping House (Audrey Wood)

New Baby (Fred Rogers, Jim Judkis)

Not a Box (Antoinette Portis)

Papa, Do You Love Me?
(Barbara M. Joosse)

*The Paper Bag Princess
(Robert Munsch)

*Peter's Chair (Ezra Jack Keats)

*The Quinceañera
(Judith Bauer Stamper)

*Something from Nothing
(Phoebe Gilman)

Talk, Baby! (Harriet Ziefert)

Tell Me Again About the Night
I Was Born (Jamie Lee Curtis)

The Trip (Ezra Jack Keats)

*Uncle Nacho's Hat
(adapted by Harriet Rohmer)

What Is Your Language?
(Debra Leventhal)

When a Pet Dies
(Fred Rogers, Jim Judkis)

Where's Spot? (Eric Hill)

*Who Wears What?
(Judith Bauer Stamper)

William's Doll (Charlotte Zolotow)

*Wemberly Worried (Kevin Henkes)

Literacy Props for Dramatic Play Settings

Bank—checkbooks; sample or defunct credit cards; deposit slips; and signs (e.g., *Open/ Closed, Do not enter, Next window, Thank you, Today is _____*)

Camping—blank books for nature journals; field guides; brochures; first-aid manual or poster; maps, camping magazines; and signs (e.g., *Camping site, Do not feed the bears, First aid, No swimming, Picnic area, Please put out the campfire*)

Garage—car manuals; repair guides; books about cars and trucks; auto store or car dealership ads; and signs (e.g., *Gas, Keys, Parking, Pay here, Tire sale, Waiting area, Do not enter*)

Dentist's or doctor's office—appointment books and cards; books about dentists, teeth, and oral hygiene; eye charts; file folders; magazines; and signs (e.g., *Please be seated, Smile!, The dentist/doctor is in/out*)

Restaurant—coupons; tray liners; order pads; food containers; Braille menus; nutrition charts; newspaper ads; books about food; logos on uniforms; and signs (e.g., *Drive through, Open/Closed, Order here, Pay here, Trash, Thank you, Come again*)

Florist—books and magazines about flowers and plants; price list; seed and flower arrangement catalogs; enclosure cards; care tags; order forms; newspaper ads; and signs (e.g., flower names, *Today's special, Cash and carry*)

Grocery store—coupons; newspaper inserts; receipts; grocery lists; food containers; and signs (e.g., areas of the store, *Recycle your bags, Today's specials, Pay here, Checkout*)

Police station—books about police officers and safety; clipboards; file folders; driver's licenses (expired or teacher-made); parking tickets; badges; street maps; and signs (e.g., traffic signs, *Dial 911, Driver's Licenses, Lost and Found, Parking Tickets*)

Post office—envelopes; stationery; stamps, rubber stamps and ink pads; greeting cards; address labels; postcards; books about mail, letters, mail carriers, and the post office; signs (e.g., *Local mail, Special delivery, Express mail, Zip codes, Next window, Stamps, U.S. mail*)

Shoe store—catalogs; shoe boxes; shoe ads; order forms; receipts; and signs (e.g., *Sizes 1–4, Checkout, Women, Men, Children, Open/Closed, Big sale today*)

Veterinarian—books and brochures about pets and animal care; identification tags; breed and pet care posters; appointment book and cards; and signs (e.g., *Pet Supplies, Quiet please—sick pets, Wait here*)

Using Dramatic Play to Teach Literacy Skills

In the Dramatic Play area, teachers observe children's play and consider ways to help them discover purposes for reading and writing. By talking with children, by suggesting additional roles and play scenarios that involve the use of reading and writing, and by providing literacy materials that children can use in their play, you promote skill development. Here are examples of what you might say and ask:

Dress-up clothes

Where are you going with your briefcase? Do you need another pencil to write with at your office?

You look like you're getting ready to do some work in those overalls. What will you work on? What tools do you need?

Are you on your way to put out a fire? Here's a map to help you find the office building.

The design on your shirt is very interesting. I see a reddish stripe here…That color is called burgundy. It's right next to a beige stripe. Where else do you see these colors in our classroom?

Food containers (environmental print)

What kinds of cereal do you have in your store today? How can you tell what is inside the box?

I see some words on these containers that begin the same way as your name begins. Can you find them?

Would you like to look in our box of coupons to see what we should buy at the store? Coupons help us save money.

Did you say that you want to bake some bread? Here's some paper and a pencil to write your shopping list. What ingredients do you need to buy?

Telephone, telephone book, address book, and message board

Hello! My name is Mr. Alvarez. What's your name? How are you today? I've been thinking about taking a trip to the city. What do you think I will see when I get there?

Would you like to call Tasheen? Let's look for her name in our class telephone book. Let's see. What letter does her name begin with? We need to turn to the T pages.

Are you talking to the doctor about your sick baby? Why don't you write what he tells you to do on the pad so you can remember?

Dolls and stuffed animals

Your baby is fussy today. Maybe he will calm down if you rock him and read him a story.

I see that you are pretending to be Goldilocks. Would you like me to help you gather some things to help you act out the story?

Doctor's office play

Doctor, my baby is sick. Will you write a prescription for some medicine so she can get better?

Let's check your eyes so we know whether you see correctly. Can you read the letters on our chart?

I need to make an appointment for next week. Will you please write my name in the doctor's appointment book?

Observing Children's Understanding

When you observe children engaged in dramatic play, look for these indications of literacy understanding:

- pretending to read
- telling or retelling a story to a doll, a stuffed animal, or another child
- recognizing letters, especially those in their own names and on food containers
- returning materials to their proper locations, using picture and word labels or matching silhouettes
- attempting to write a list or message
- recognizing a name in a class phone or address book
- conversing with children and adults in a series of exchanges and talking about topics that do not involve only the here-and-now
- using fine-motor skills to button, buckle, zip, snap, and tie
- using new vocabulary to converse
- using symbols in play
- using invented, or developmental, spelling that indicates a beginning understanding of sound–symbol relationships

Literacy in the Toys and Games Area

In the Toys and Games area, children are surrounded by letters and words. They describe how they are putting together a puzzle or sorting a collection of objects. They talk about objects as they play, comparing size, shape, and color. While using beads, pegboards, puzzles, dominoes, and collectibles, they develop reading skills such as progressing from left to right, visual discrimination, and matching similar objects. As they use magnetic letters and alphabet blocks, children explore letters, and then arrange and rearrange them to form words. As they play with letter and word materials, they construct important understandings about language.

Examples of What a Child Might Do	Examples of Related Objectives	Examples of How This Relates to Literacy
String beads	7. Demonstrates fine-motor strength and coordination a. Uses fingers and hands	Building fine-motor skills that are important for holding and controlling writing tools and handling print materials
Play with magnetic letters	16. Demonstrates knowledge of the alphabet b. Identifies letter–sound correspondences	Beginning to understand how letters are ordered to form words
Participate in a game of alphabet bingo	16. Demonstrates knowledge of the alphabet a. Identifies and names letters	Matching and recognizing letters
Sew a lacing card	7. Demonstrates fine-motor strength and coordination a. Uses fingers and hands	Developing eye–hand coordination that is important for writing
Describe a rocket built with plastic building bricks	9. Uses language to express thoughts and needs a. Uses an expanding expressive vocabulary	Engaging in conversation and using descriptive language

Some specific literacy-related materials and books for the Toys and Games area are listed here. Just as books in your home are not confined to one room, books and other print materials in *The Creative Curriculum®* classroom are placed in each interest area.

Materials

alphabet bingo	magnetic letters
alphabet blocks	matching games
alphabet puzzles	name games
basic vocabulary pictures and games	rhyming picture games
environmental print puzzles	sequence cards
labeled picture cards	sorting and classification materials
letter sorting and matching games	

Suggested Books

(Titles preceded by an asterisk are included in the *Teaching Strategies® Children's Book Collection.*)

Alexander and the Wind-Up Mouse
(Leo Lionni)

*Button, Button, Who's Got the Button?
(Trish Holland)

*Can You See What I See?: Picture
Puzzles to Search and Solve*
(Walter Wick)

*Chicka Chicka Boom Boom
(Bill Martin and John Archambault)

I Spy (Walter Wick)

Look Alikes Jr. (Joan Steiner)

Max's Toys (Rosemary Wells)

Olivia and the Missing Toy
(Ian Falconer)

Pattern Fish (Trudy Harris)

Too Many Toys (David Shannon)

Using Toys and Games to Teach Literacy Skills

As you interact with children in the Toys and Games area, your conversations can help them learn important literacy skills. When you talk with children, first encourage them to describe what they are doing. Observe how they are playing with the materials and talk with them about what you see. Here are examples of what you might say and ask:

Magnetic letters

What letters do you need for your name?

How is this letter like this one?

Can you find a letter like this one somewhere else in the classroom?

Environmental print puzzles, lotto games, concentration games

Have you ever seen this word before? Tell me about it.

Someone in our class has a name that begins the same way as the word soup. Who is that?

Some of these words from food containers start the same way. Listen: Juicy Juice®, Blue Bonnet®, Fiddle Faddle®, Peter Pan®. I wonder what would happen if we changed some of the first letters. (Play with one example: Peter Pan, Meter Man, Deter Dan. Then encourage the child to try other letter substitutions.)

Sequence cards

Would you like to make up a story about these pictures? What do you think happened first? What happened next? How will you end your story?

Have you ever seen (done) this before? Tell me about it.

Name games (name puzzles, memory games, matching names with photos)

May I read your name? Juwan. (Read slowly, moving your finger under the name.)

I see two letters in your name that are the same. Can you find them?

Sonya, your name begins the same way as sun, seed, sit, and six. What are some other words that begin the same way?

The names of some children in our class are very short, like Ben. Other names are longer, like Setsuko. Do you think your name is a short name or a long name?

Construction toys

Tell me about what you are building. Would you like to make a sign for it?

Did you ever see a _____ like this before? Tell me about it.

What do you think would happen if you…?

I wonder how you could make this move.

Toys featuring storybook or nursery rhyme characters

Do you remember the story about _____ (e.g., Curious George)? Tell me about it.

Hey, diddle diddle, the cat and the fiddle. Diddle and fiddle rhyme! Do you see any puzzle pieces that show things that rhyme? Yes, moon and spoon rhyme.

Observing Children's Understanding

As you observe children playing with toys and games, look for these indications of literacy understanding:

- recognizing their names in name games
- recognizing and talking about letters and creating words as they use alphabet manipulatives
- matching letters or numerals while playing bingo
- using fine-motor skills to grasp and manipulate small toys, beads, and other small objects
- talking about pictures on games and puzzles
- conversing with each other, solving problems, and negotiating and interpreting the rules of games
- recognizing environmental print
- talking about print on the toys and games, e.g., a puzzle with street signs or words

Literacy in the Art Area

Art experiences provide ideal opportunities to promote language and literacy skills. Children want to talk about their creations and to hear the ideas of others, thus motivating them to develop expressive and receptive language. They can learn many new words, such as *bright, dull, shiny, gooey, messy, sticky, pound*, and *roll*. Through art, children express the stories that they are thinking about as well as other ideas and feelings.

Examples of What a Child Might Do	Examples of Related Objectives	Examples of How This Relates to Literacy
Paint lines and shapes	7. Demonstrates fine-motor strength and coordination 　a. Uses fingers and hands	Making basic lines and curves that make up the letters of the alphabet
Draw and color with pencils, crayons, and markers	7. Demonstrates fine-motor strength and coordination 　b. Uses writing and drawing tools	Refining fine-motor skills necessary for writing
Pound and shape clay	7. Demonstrates fine-motor strength and coordination 　a. Uses fingers and hands	Strengthening hand muscles and building stamina for writing
Sponge paint a patterned border	23. Demonstrates knowledge of patterns	Developing the ability to detect patterns in letters and words
Draw a picture of a storybook character	18. Comprehends and responds to books and other texts 　c. Retells stories and recounts details from informational texts	Developing the ability to comprehend and recall story details
Follow directions for handling glue properly	8. Listens to and understands increasingly complex language 　b. Follows directions	Developing listening comprehension skills

Stock the Art area with literacy-related materials so children have the opportunity to handle and use print materials in a variety of ways. This encourages children's curiosity about the letters and words on materials, and it enables children to use print in their artwork, sign their work, copy print, or just observe other children as they use print. When they explore books related to art, children begin to think in more complex ways about their own representations. The following lists offer suggestions.

Materials

alphabet cookie cutters	colored pens and pencils
alphabet rubber stamps	greeting cards
alphabet sponges	magazines and newspapers
blank books to illustrate	titled posters of famous artwork
brochures and pamphlets	Wikki Stix®
chalkboards and colored chalk	

Suggested Books

(Titles preceded by an asterisk are included in the *Teaching Strategies® Children's Book Collection*.)

A Piece of Chalk
(Jennifer A. Ericsson)

The Art Lesson (Tomie dePaola)

Babar's Museum of Art
(Laurent De Brunhoff)

The Black Book of Colors
(Menena Cottin)

*Colors! ¡Colores!
(Jorge Luján & Piet Grobler)

*Don't Lose It – Reuse It!
(Nancy Noel Williams)

The Dot (Peter H. Reynolds)

Elephants Can Paint Too!
(Katya Arnold)

Hands: growing up to be an artist
(Lois Ehlert)

Harold and the Purple Crayon
(Crockett Johnson)

I Spy: An Alphabet in Art
(Lucy Micklethwait)

Legend of the Indian Paintbrush
(Tomie dePaola)

Little Blue and Little Yellow
(Leo Lionni)

Look! Look! Look! (Nancy Elizabeth
Wallace with Linda K. Friedlaender)

Matthew's Dream (Leo Leonni)

Mouse Paint (Ellen Stoll Walsh)

Museum ABCs
(Metropolitan Museum of Art)

My Crayons Talk (Patricia Hubbard)

The Pencil (Allan Ahlberg)

*The Pot That Juan Built
(Nancy Andrews-Goebel)

When Pigasso Met Mootisse
(Nina Laden)

Books with illustrations that inspire the use of particular art techniques

Pictures give children a chance to see the world in many different ways. Illustrations in children's picture books can inspire children to experiment with different media and techniques. After sharing one of the books listed below, place it in the Art area, along with the appropriate materials, so children can recreate a page or scene from the book. They might also want to use the illustrator's technique to create an original page or book.

collage	*The Very Hungry Caterpillar* (Eric Carle)
watercolor	*Sand Castle* (Shannon Brenda Yee)
charcoal	*Marshmallow* (Clare Turlay Newberry)
pastels and chalk	*Gilberto and the Wind* (Marie Hall Ets)
block printing	*Millions of Cats* (Wanda Gag)
color mixing	*Mouse Paint* (Ellen Stoll Walsh)
crayons	*Harold and the Purple Crayon* (Crockett Johnson)
black ink on white paper	*Where the Sidewalk Ends* (Shel Silverstein)
painting on cloth	*Tar Beach* (Faith Ringgold)

Using Art Materials to Teach Literacy Skills

Introduce literacy in the Art area carefully and informally so as not to interrupt the children's creative processes. Look for the right moment to engage children in conversation. As you interact, observe what children are doing with the art materials and think about incorporating literacy in a way that will enhance their art experiences. Here are examples of what you might say and ask:

Paint

You mixed yellow and blue to make green, just like in our book Little Blue and Little Yellow. What would you mix together to make purple?

You painted many circles on your page, Olivia. They are like the letter O, which begins your name.

How does that finger paint feel? Can you write your name in it?

How should we paint the backdrop for our "Little Red Hen" show? Let's look in the book for some ideas.

Clay and art doughs

You rolled your clay like a snake. Can you make the letter S with your clay?

Would you like to sing our song about clay while we work?

Pounding, pushing, poking, pulling;
Playing with clay is fun!
Squeezing, squishing, smashing, shaping;
Now we're almost done.

You worked very hard to make your clay dog. Here's a card for you to write the word dog so we can put it on our display shelf. Don't forget to add your name, because you are the sculptor.

Printmaking

You carved the letter B into the foam meat tray and made a print with it. What do you notice about the printed B?... You're right: It came out backwards! What do you think will happen if you make a rubbing of it?

Your grandmother will enjoy the card you made. Would you like to write a note to her on the inside?

Woodworking

Why is this tool called a C-clamp?... a T-square?

Let's look at our safety rules on this sign before you begin sawing.

Collage

You worked hard to organize our beautiful junk for collages. Let's label the containers so we'll know what's inside. I'll write shiny things *on this label. What other labels do we need to write?*

Leo Lionni illustrated Swimmy *by cutting and gluing tissue paper shapes, just as you're doing.*

Three-dimensional constructions

Would you like to make craft stick puppets so we can act out today's story? What characters do we need to make?

How can this cardboard tube be used in the machine you're building?

Markers, crayons, and colored pencils

Tell me about your picture. Would you like me to write your story on paper so we can share it with others?

Your rubbings help me guess how your objects feel. This one looks like it might be bumpy, and this one looks like it might be smooth.

Observing Children's Understanding

As children explore in the Art area, look for these indications of literacy understanding:

- controlling the small muscles of their hands while coloring, cutting, and drawing
- drawing or painting basic shapes and line segments
- noticing the letters and words on magazines, newspapers, art materials, and labels
- talking about letter shapes in their creations, such as an *S* made with a clay coil and a *Z* made with paint
- representing story characters or scenes in their artwork
- writing their names on their artwork
- listening and following directions for using art materials
- using words and expanded sentences to describe what they are doing
- conversing with children or adults about their artwork

Literacy in the Discovery Area

In the Discovery area, children use literacy skills to help learn about the world around them. While engaged in scientific discoveries, they learn new words, ask and answer questions, make predictions, and explain why and how. To represent what they have learned, they may begin to write in journals, on charts, and on other materials. In the Discovery area, children learn to use informational books as resources to find answers to their questions.

Examples of What a Child Might Do	Examples of Related Objectives	Examples of How This Relates to Literacy
Take care of the class pet	11. Demonstrates positive approaches to learning d. Shows curiosity and motivation	Learning new vocabulary and acquiring background knowledge (life science)
Sort a collection of leaves	13. Uses classification skills	Using visual discrimination skills that are important for noticing similarities and differences among letters and among words
Use a screwdriver to take an old toaster apart	7. Demonstrates fine-motor strength and coordination a. Uses fingers and hands	Building hand muscles that are important for writing; acquiring background knowledge
Plant seeds in a cup and label it with the seed packet	17. Demonstrates knowledge of print and its uses b. Uses print concepts	Using print to label objects in a functional way
Follow directions for mixing "oobleck"	8. Listens to and understands increasingly complex language b. Follows directions	Developing listening comprehension skills and an understanding of sequence
Look in a book to find the name of an insect	18. Comprehends and responds to books and other texts a. Interacts during reading experiences, book conversations, and text reflections	Understanding that books are resources for finding information

Here are suggested materials and books to the Discovery area in order to enhance scientific thinking and literacy learning.

Materials

clipboards	pencils, pens, markers, crayons
graph paper	pet care books and posters
index cards, note pads	plant care instructions
journals	plant and animal identification cards
nature magazines	seed catalogs and packets

Suggested Books

(Titles preceded by an asterisk are included in the *Teaching Strategies® Children's Book Collection.*)

Picture books

The Adventures of Gary and Harry (Lisa Matsumoto)

The Carrot Seed (Ruth Kraus)

First the Egg (Laura Vaccaro Seeger)

The Grouchy Ladybug (Eric Carle)

A House for Hermit Crab (Eric Carle)

Mickey's Magnet (Ruth Kraus)

On My Beach There Are Many Pebbles (Leo Lionni)

Our Tree Named Steve (Alan Zweibel)

Pablo's Tree (Pat Mora)

Parts (Tedd Arnold)

Rainbow Fish (Marcus Pfister)

Round Trip (Ann Jonas)

The Salamander Room (Ann Mazer)

The Snail's Spell (Joanne Ryder)

The Snowy Day (Ezra Jack Keats)

Some Smug Slug (Pamela Duncan Edwards)

Two Bad Ants (Chris Van Allsburg)

The Very Busy Spider (Eric Carle)

The Very Hungry Caterpillar (Eric Carle)

The Very Quiet Cricket (Eric Carle)

Informational books (nonfiction)

Bugs! Bugs! Bugs! (Bob Barner)

A Color of His Own (Leo Lionni)

Diary of a Wombat (Jackie French)

Diary of a Worm (Doreen Cronin)

The Emperor's Egg (Martin Jenkins)

Growing Trees (Judith Bauer Stamper)

Leaf Man (Lois Ehlert)

The Magic School Bus Inside a Beehive (Joanna Cole)

Me and My Amazing Body (Joan Sweeney)

Me and My Senses (Joan Sweeney)

Move! Steve Jenkins

My First Body Book (Christopher Rice)

My Visit to the Aquarium (Aliki)

A Tree Is For... (Judith Bauer Stamper)

Trees, Trees, Trees (Nancy Noel Williams)

Waiting for Wings (Lois Ehlert)

Watch Them Grow (Linda Martin)

The Way Things Work (David Macaulay)

Suggested Books, continued

What Do You Do With a Tail Like This? (Steve Jenkins & Robin Page)

What Do Wheels Do All Day? (April Jones Prince)

Alphabet Books

African Animals ABC (Sarah Schuette)

The Alphabet Tree (Leo Lionni)

Animalia (Graeme Base)

The Butterfly Alphabet (Kjell Sandved)

Eating the Alphabet (Lois Ehlert)

*When the Monkeys Came Back (Kristine Franklin)

*Who Lives In Trees? (Trish Holland)

Why? (Lila Prap)

An Edible Alphabet (Bonnie Christenson)

The Flower Alphabet Book (Jerry Pallotta)

The Icky Bug Alphabet Book (Jerry Pallotta)

Old Black Fly (Jim Aylesworth)

The Yucky Reptile Alphabet Book (Jerry Pallotta)

Using Discovery Materials to Teach Literacy Skills

Your interactions with children in the Discovery area can promote language and literacy skills and encourage more complex scientific thinking. Here are examples of what you might say and ask:

Animals

How can we warn other children to be careful about keeping their fingers out of the rabbit cage?

Do you have any ideas about how a spider spins a web? This book shows us many different kinds of spiderwebs.

How do you think our new baby chicks will change? We can take a picture of the chicks every day and write about how they change.

Please write your name on the chart after you have fed the fish.

Plants, seeds, and flowers

I notice that our plant seems to be dying. Let's list all of the things that might be wrong so we can solve the problem.

Let's make a leaf book! You can glue your leaves on paper, and we'll write the name of the tree underneath them. If we don't know the name of the tree, we'll look it up in a book.

I see that you are making a beautiful arrangement of flowers for your mother. You used many wildflowers. Here's a card so you can write a note to her.

The directions on this seed packet say that we should only plant the seeds about an inch deep.

Natural materials and collections

How has this leaf changed from when it was on a tree?

Which kinds of rocks do you prefer to handle: rough or smooth?...flat or round?

I wonder what kind of animal lived in this shell. How can we find out?

Can you form your name with the twigs?

Your pebble looks like the one in Sylvester and the Magic Pebble. *What do you think would happen if you made a wish when you hold it?*

Physical science materials (magnets, discovery bottles, gears, pulleys, balls, mirrors)

Do you have an idea about how I can use these materials to move this marble in different ways?

Write your name or a letter on this card and hold it up to a mirror. What do you notice?

Your horseshoe magnet is just like the one in Mickey's Magnet. *What do you think it will pick up? Let's write your prediction.*

Sensory table or sensory tubs

Tell me how the gak feels. I'll write down the words you use to describe it: cold, slimy, gooey, creepy, squishy. Later we can make up a poem with those words.

I wonder why some of the rocks stayed in the colander after you sifted the soil.

Thanks for helping shuck the corn. Have you ever heard someone say, "Aw, shucks"? It's the same word, but it means something different.

I see that you have written an S in the shaving cream, Sarah. It's the first letter of your name. It sounds like this: /s/. Do you know any other words that begin with the /s/ sound?

Take-aparts

Tell me how you think this clock worked.

Have you found the on–off switch? What other words are important on this old radio?

Before you take this apart, would you like to draw what's inside? I'll help you label the parts so you can have a diagram to look at later.

Observing Children's Understanding

As children explore in the Discovery area, look for these indications of literacy understanding:

- looking in books for information
- recording their predictions and findings
- describing what they are doing and why
- asking and answering questions
- using new vocabulary
- conversing with children and adults about their discoveries
- connecting what they are learning to previous experiences
- using fine-motor skills to handle tweezers, tongs, or other tools

Literacy in the Sand and Water Area

Sand and water play gives children many opportunities to develop language and literacy skills. New vocabulary, such as *gritty, grainy, coarse, fine, sieve, colander, texture, empty, full, pour, trickle, sprinkle, sink, float, drip, mold,* and *measure,* can be incorporated easily into conversations about sand and water. Children develop expressive and receptive language by conversing with children and adults during their play. Children often become quite talkative at the sand and water table as they exchange ideas, ask and answer questions, create scenarios, and retell stories with the materials.

Examples of What a Child Might Do	Examples of Related Objectives	Examples of How This Relates to Literacy
Pour water carefully from one container to the other	7. Demonstrates fine-motor strength and coordination a. Uses fingers and hands	Strengthening and controlling the hand muscles necessary for writing
Use a finger to write a name in the sand	19. Demonstrates writing skills a. Writes name	Using touch and movement, which are important for kinesthetic learners
Work with a friend to figure out how to put water in a sandcastle moat	10. Uses appropriate conversational and other communication skills a. Engages in conversations 11. Demonstrates positive approaches to learning e. Shows flexibility and inventiveness in thinking	Using language to communicate ideas and solve problems
Make pretend birthday cakes out of wet sand	14. Uses symbols and images to represent something not present b. Engages in sociodramatic play	Engaging in symbolic play, which supports the child's understanding of letters as symbols for sounds
Pour sand into a sieve and hold it up as the sand trickles through	9. Uses language to express thoughts and needs a. Uses an expanding expressive vocabulary 11. Demonstrates positive approaches to learning d. Shows curiosity and motivation	Learning the meaning of new words, such as *sift, sieve,* and *trickle,* with teacher guidance

Literacy-related props enhance the Sand and Water area. While hands-on, active involvement is the primary experience in this area, many books inspire children's play. Here are some suggestions of materials and books.

Materials

alphabet cookie cutters or sand molds

chart with recipe for sand pies

ice cubes with small plastic letters frozen inside

laminated name cards, words, or letters

list of rules generated by the children about sand and water play

local business logos attached to popsicle sticks or drinking straws

posters of sand castles and boats

prediction charts ("What Will Happen?")

signs printed with permanent markers on polystyrene meat trays

sink-or-float sorting charts

sponge or foam letters

storybook characters (laminated or plastic) and related props (twigs for trees, plastic building bricks, plastic houses, vehicles)

street or traffic signs

vinyl bathtub books

Suggested Books

(Titles preceded by an asterisk are included in the *Teaching Strategies® Children's Book Collection*.)

At the Beach (Ann Rockwell)

Beach (Elisha Cooper)

Beach Day (Karen Roosa)

Better Not Get Wet, Jesse Bear (Nancy White Carlstrom)

Bubble, Bubble (Mercer Mayer)

Curious George Goes to the Beach (H. A. Rey)

A Drop of Water (Gordon Morrison)

In the Middle of the Puddle (Mike Thaler)

In the Sand (Kate Burns)

Let's Try It Out in the Water (Seymour Simon)

The Quicksand Book (Tomie dePaola)

Sally Goes to the Beach (Stephen Huneck)

Sand (Ellen Prager)

The Sand Castle (Brenda Shannon Yee and Thea Kliros)

Sandcastle (Mick Inkpen)

Sea, Sand, Me! (Patricia Hubbell)

Splish, Splash (Stephen M. Scott)

A Swim Through the Sea (Kristin Joy Pratt)

Wash and Dry (Trish Holland)

Wave (Suzy Lee)

Who Sank the Boat? (Pamela Allen)

Will It Float or Sink? (Melissa Stewart)

Using Sand and Water to Teach Literacy Skills

After creating a literacy-rich Sand and Water area, ask meaningful open-ended questions to help children express their thoughts verbally and to develop literacy skills. Here are some examples:

Sand and sand props

Which letters can you write in the sand?

How does the sand feel?

Tell me about what you are building.

You're making a street like the streets in our neighborhood. What signs would you like to add?

All of your dump trucks are going in the same direction. Which sign could you add to let others know that there is only one way to travel?

You molded the sand into a letter M. Do you know any children whose names begin with the letter M?

Here are some props for retelling Goldilocks and the Three Bears *as you play in the sand. Do you remember how the story goes? What happened first?*

You made a funny word with your letters. You wrote BATNIP: B-A-T-N-I-P. Do you think there is such a thing as batnip? I see a little word I know in batnip: bat. Can you find it?

The sand you packed in the bucket feels cool and damp. Now that you have it in the bucket, what will you do next?

This sand is hard and sticks to the bucket. I wonder why.

Water and water props

You're adding plastic people to the boat, one at a time. That is just like today's book, Who Sank the Boat? *I wonder how many people made from plastic building blocks can fit on the boat before it sinks?*

Can you arrange these sponge letters to spell your name?

I wonder why some things sink and some things float. Would you like to predict which of these toys sink and which float? Here are cards with the words sink and float. You can use them to label the groups of toys you sort.

When you finish at the water table, I'll help you look in a book to find a picture of a boat like this one. Then we'll know what to call it.

Have you ever been to a beach (river, lake, or swimming pool)? Tell me about it. I'll write what you say to share with others at group time.

"You made your tugboat push this other boat. It's called a barge. What is your barge carrying? Where is it going?"

Observing Children's Understanding

As children explore in the Sand and Water area, look for these indications of literacy understanding:

- using language to solve problems and communicate their ideas
- understanding and using new words
- representing ideas through symbolic play
- using fine-motor skills to sift, pour, build, and squeeze
- talking about and recognizing print found on props
- connecting sand and water play to prior knowledge
- engaging in conversations about what they are doing
- using print in sand and water play

Literacy in the Music and Movement Area

Music and movement activities can play an important role in language and literacy development. Songs promote an awareness of sounds and ways to experiment with language. Children can be encouraged to attend to the features of sounds, such as pitch (high–low), volume (loud–soft), and rate (fast–slow). They can make up new lyrics to songs, learn new vocabulary, and hear and create rhythms. The repetition in songs parallels repetition in books. As children read picture books that use familiar songs as the texts, they sing and begin to recognize written words.

Movement activities encourage children to follow directions and practice other language skills. With their bodies, they demonstrate comprehension of directions, songs, and stories, and they express the ways that music and language make them feel. They also develop the coordination necessary for writing.

Examples of What a Child Might Do	Examples of Related Objectives	Examples of How This Relates to Literacy
Make up a birthday song	9. Uses language to express thoughts and needs a. Uses an expanding expressive vocabulary	Expressing thoughts and feelings verbally
Make up nonsense words to a familiar song	15. Demonstrates phonological awareness, phonics skills, and word recognition a. Notices and discriminates rhyme	Developing phonological awareness, isolating words, and manipulating sounds
Hop, skip, and jump to music	4. Demonstrates traveling skills 34. Explores musical concepts and expression	Learning the meaning of *hop*, *skip*, and *jump* through firsthand experience
Tap rhythm sticks to songs	15. Demonstrates phonological awareness, phonics skills, and word recognition c. Notices and discriminates discrete units of sound	Isolating words and syllables in a song
Sing about a boa constrictor or a kookaburra	9. Uses language to express thoughts and needs a. Uses an expanding expressive vocabulary	Learning new words in a fun, meaningful way
Sing *Down by the Bay* while turning the book pages	17. Demonstrates knowledge of print and its uses a. Uses and appreciates books and other texts	Following print from left to right, top to bottom, and front to back; using picture cues to assist comprehension of the story; beginning to recognize words in print

Children's books and music often go together easily. You can support children's literacy development in the Music and Movement area by adding print or other materials that focus on reading, writing, listening, and speaking skills. Songs are an important tool for encouraging phonological awareness. Some songs help children focus on one aspect of language, such as rhyming. Others help children focus on other aspects, such as alliteration and phoneme manipulation.

Materials

alphabet songs on tape or CDs

color-coded music cards to use with xylophones, tone bells, or melody bells

posters of musical instruments

rebus (picture) movement cards

song charts and cards

songs for following oral directions (e.g., "Hokey Pokey" or "Looby Loo")

taped listening activities

Suggested Books

(Titles preceded by an asterisk are included in the *Teaching Strategies® Children's Book Collection*.)

Books About Music and Movement

Abiyoyo (Pete Seeger)

Angelina Ballerina (Helen Craig)

Ballerina Dreams – A True Story (Lauren Thompson)

The Bat Boy and His Violin (Gavin Curtis)

Ben's Trumpet (Rachel Isadora)

Best-Loved Children's Songs from Japan (Yoko Imoto)

Cada Nino: Every Child: A Bilingual Songbook for Kids (Tish Hinojosa and Lucia Angela Perez)

Charlie Parker played bebop (Chris Raschka)

The Deaf Musicians (Pete Seeger and Paul Dubois Jacobs)

Getting to Know You!: Rodgers and Hammerstein Favorites (Richard Rodgers)

How Sweet the Sound: African-American Songs for Children (Wade and Cheryl Hudson)

Hush!: A Thai Lullaby (Minfong Ho)

I See a Song (Eric Carle)

Jamari's Drum (Eboni Bynum and Roland Jackson)

Max Found Two Sticks (Brian Pickney)

M Is for Music (Kathleen Krull)

Music, Music for Everyone (Vera B. Williams)

My Mother Had a Dancing Heart (Libba Moore Gray)

Philadelphia Chicken: A Too Illogical, Zoological Musical Review (Sandra Boynton and Michael Ford)

Rap a Tap Tap: Here's Bojangles – Think of That! (Leo Dillon and Diane Dillon)

The Remarkable Farkle McBride (John Lithgow)

Song and Dance Man (Karen Ackerman)

Take Me Out of the Bathtub and Other Silly Dilly Songs (Allen Katz)

Tessa's Tip-Tapping Toes (Carolyn Crimi)

A Tisket, A Tasket (Ella Fitzgerald)

Willie (Virginia Kroll)

Suggested Books, continued

Song Storybooks

A-Hunting We Will Go!
(Stephen Kellogg)

Baby Beluga (Raffi)

Do Your Ears Hang Low?: A Love Story
(Caroline Jayne Church)

Down by the Bay (Raffi)

Inch by Inch: The Garden Song
(David Mallet)

Just the Two of Us (Will Smith)

Mary Had a Little Lamb
(Mary Ann Hoberman)

*Mary Wore Her Red Dress and Henry
Wore His Green Sneakers*
(Merle Peek)

Miss Mary Mack
(Mary Ann Hoberman)

*Neighborhood Song (Trish Holland)

Simple Gifts (Chris Raschka)

*There Once Was a Man Named
Michael Finnegan*
(Mary Ann Hoberman)

*There Was an Old Lady Who
Swallowed a Fly* (Simm Taback)

Today is Monday (Eric Carle)

What a Wonderful World (George
David Weiss and Bob Thiele)

Songs That Promote Phonological Awareness

"Apples and Bananas"

"Baby Bumblebee"

"Down by the Bay"

"Eensy-Weensy Spider"

"Hokey Pokey"

"I've Been Working on the Railroad"

"John Jacob Jingleheimer Schmidt"

"My Bonny Lies Over the Ocean"

"The Name Game"

"Polly Wolly Doodle"

"A Sailor Went to Sea, Sea, Sea"

"Willoughby, Wallaby, Woo"

Using Music and Movement to Teach Literacy Skills

As children engage spontaneously with music and movement, try not to interrupt them. Time your interactions so that they encourage children to experiment in new ways and to develop important language and literacy skills. Here are examples of what you might say and ask:

Singing and songs in print (song charts, cards, and books)

Each time you hear a word that rhymes with late, clap your hands.

What do you think a _____ (e.g., water spout, tuffet, or dell) is?

*You're listening to the song called_____ (e.g., "On Top of Spaghetti").
What happens in the song?*

Where do you begin when you are reading the song on this chart?

The first letter in your name is M. Here is an M on the song chart. How many more Ms can you find on this chart?

Can you make up some silly words for this song?

Can you sing the ABC song to a different tune? How about to the tune of "Mary Had a Little Lamb"?

Movement Props and Experiences

This music is slow, so you're taking slow steps like a turtle. Now the music is fast! How will you move to it?

Can you move your scarf around in a circle like the letter O? How about like the letter S?

Move your streamer up high in the air when I show the card that says, "Up." Hold it low to the ground when I raise the card that says, "Down." The arrows on the cards will give you a hint.

Can you make a gigantic motion when you hear the loud sounds in this song?

Wave your wand each time you hear the /b/ sound in the song.

Musical Instruments

Which song would you like to sing very, very slowly? Which song would you like to sing quickly?

When you hit the drum hard, it made a loud sound. What will happen when you hit it softly?

Can you tap the sticks to your name?

How should I play this tambourine to show that we are happy? …sad? …mad? …scared?

Can you copy the pattern I make with the rhythm sticks? Will you tap a pattern for me to copy?

Each time you see a colored note on this card, ring the bell that is the same color. Would you like to try to read and play this song?

Which song would you play if you were Abiyoyo from today's story?

How can we use the instruments to make sounds effects as we retell our story?

Observing Children's Understanding

As children explore in the Music and Movement area, look for these indications of literacy understanding:

- making up new lyrics to songs
- detecting patterns in songs and rhythmic movements
- following the words on a song chart, from top to bottom and left to right
- demonstrating listening comprehension by using appropriate motions to songs and in movement activities
- following directions during movement activities
- using language to describe their movements
- including songs and movement as they retell stories
- talking about the story line of a song

Literacy in the Cooking Area

Cooking activities provide many opportunities to enhance literacy learning. Children can find a favorite recipe in a cookbook, make a shopping list, locate newspaper coupons, read product labels, and follow instructions for preparing food. They learn the names of foods as well as words to describe how they taste. They also learn the names of various cooking tools and processes. Cooking is a way for children to use all of their senses as they learn to read and write.

Examples of What a Child Might Do	Examples of Related Objectives	Examples of How This Relates to Literacy
Follow the steps on a picture and word recipe	17. Demonstrates knowledge of print and its uses b. Uses print concepts	Understanding that print has a purpose; tracking print from left to right and top to bottom; understanding sequencing concepts
Identify an ingredient by recognizing print on the packaging	17. Demonstrates knowledge of print and its uses b. Uses print concepts	Learning the meaning of particular written symbols
Grate, chop, stir, knead, pound, cut, pour, measure, and peel	7. Demonstrates fine-motor strength and coordination a. Uses fingers and hands	Strengthening and controlling the small muscles necessary for writing

Examples of What a Child Might Do	Examples of Related Objectives	Examples of How This Relates to Literacy
Find newspaper coupons for a shopping trip	17. Demonstrates knowledge of print and its uses b. Uses print concepts 18. Comprehends and responds to books and other texts	Learning about forms of print other than books
Use descriptive words (e.g., *yummy, sweet, bitter, sour, salty, crunchy*)	9. Uses language to express thoughts and needs a. Uses an expanding expressive vocabulary	Learning the meaning of words through firsthand experiences
Follow safety directions	8. Listens to and understands increasingly complex language b. Follows directions	Building listening comprehension skills
Write a shopping list	19. Demonstrates writing skills b. Writes to convey ideas and information	Understanding that written language assists memory

The following list suggests literacy-related materials to add to your Cooking area. You will also find children's storybooks and cookbooks that are related to food and cooking.

Materials

alphabet cookie cutters

blank recipe cards

calendar for recording snack helpers

cookbooks

coupons

graphs and charts, for example,

   "Did you like the soup?" "Yes/No"

   "How many of each type of fruit did we use in our salad?"

   "Healthy Foods/Unhealthy Foods"

grocery store circulars

labels for utensils and ingredients

letter molds

menus

nutrition charts

paper

picture and word recipe cards

print on containers of ingredients

recipe charts

writing tools

Suggested Books

(Titles preceded by an asterisk are included in the *Teaching Strategies® Children's Book Collection.*)

Storybooks

At Grandpa's Sugar Bush (Margaret Carney)

Bear Wants More (Karma Wilson)

Bee-bim Bop! (Linda Sue Park)

Bread and Jam for Frances (Russell Hoban)

Bread, Bread, Bread (Ann Morris)

Chato's Kitchen (Gary Soto)

Cloudy with a Chance of Meatballs (Judi Barrett)

Corn Is Maize: A Gift from the Indians (Aliki)

Dim Sum for Everyone (Grace Lin)

**Doorbell Rang* (Pat Hutchins)

Eating the Alphabet (Lois Ehlert)

Everybody Cooks Rice (Nora Dooley)

Growing Colors (Bruce McMillan)

Growing Vegetable Soup (Lois Ehlert)

How Are You Peeling? (Saxon Freymann and Joost Elffers)

The Hungry Thing (Jan Spepian)

I Know an Old Lady Who Swallowed a Pie (Alison Jackson)

In My Momma's Kitchen (Jerdene Nolen)

In the Leaves (Huy Voun Lee)

**Jalapeño Bagels* (Natasha Wing)

**The Little Red Hen* (retold by Bonnie Dobkin)

Magda's Tortillas (Becky Chavarria-Chairez)

Market Day (Lois Ehlert)

Matzah Ball Soup (Joan Rothenberg)

More Spaghetti, I Say! (Rita Golden Gelman)

Pancakes for Breakfast (Tomie dePaola)

**Peeny Butter Fudge* (Toni Morrison and Slade Morrison)

Pickles to Pittsburg (Ron Barrett)

**Rice Is Nice* (Nancy Noel Williams)

Strega Nona (Tomie dePaola)

Today is Monday (Eric Carle)

Tony's Bread (Tomie dePaola)

The Tortilla Factory (Gary Paulsen)

**Too Many Tamales* (Gary Soto)

The Ugly Vegetables (Grace Lin)

The Very Hungry Caterpillar (Eric Carle)

Who Took the Cookie from the Cookie Jar? (Bonnie Philemon and Lass Sturges)

Wild Boars Cook (Meg Rosoff)

Children's cookbooks

Betty Crocker Kids Cook! (Betty Crocker Editors)

Blue Moon Soup (Gary Goss)

Children's Quick and Easy Cookbook (Angela Wilkes)

Cooking with Herbs: The Vegetarian Dragon (Julie Bass)

**Come Cook With Me* (Heather Baker, Kai-Leé Berke, and Sherrie Rudick)

Delicious Dishes: Creole Cooking for Children (Berthe Amos)

Kids Cooking: A Very Slightly Messy Manual (Klutz Press)

Suggested Books, continued

Kids First Cookbook
(American Cancer Society)

The Kids Multicultural Cookbook: Food and Fun Around the World (Deanna F. Cook)

Mother Goose Cookbook: Rhymes and Recipes for the Very Young
(Marianna Mayer)

Once Upon a Recipe: Favorite Tales, Food and FUNtivities (Judy Edelman)

Pretend Soup and Other Real Recipes for Preschoolers and Up
(Mollie Katzen)

The following chart suggests a few cooking activities related to children's stories.

Blueberries for Sal (Robert McCloskey)	Make blueberry jam.
Chicka Chicka Boom Boom (Bill Martin and John Archambault)	Prepare and taste a coconut.
Eating the Alphabet (Lois Ehlert)	Make and eat fruit kabobs.
Green Eggs and Ham (Dr. Seuss)	Add green food coloring or chopped spinach to scrambled eggs.
Harold and the Purple Crayon (Crockett Johnson)	Make and eat purple cows (ice cream and grape juice).
How Many Bugs in a Box? (David A. Carter)	Prepare and eat "ants on a log" (celery sticks, cream cheese, and raisins).
The Little Mouse, The Red Ripe Strawberry and THE BIG HUNGRY BEAR (Don Wood and Audrey Wood)	Clean, slice, and eat strawberries.
The Little Red Hen (Paul Galdone)	Bake bread.
Miss Spider's Tea Party (David Kirk)	Make and compare solar tea and brewed tea.
Strega Nona (Tomie dePaola)	Cook and eat pasta.

Using Cooking to Teach Literacy Skills

You can teach literacy skills in the Cooking area as you interact with children. Talk about different ingredients; food preparation steps; changes that occur as foods cook; and children's favorite part: tasting. Here are examples of what you might say and ask:

Foods

I wonder why some bananas are green and some are yellow.

How are these two cheeses alike? How are they different?

From where does milk come? How does it get to the store?

Have you ever heard the word beverage? What do you think it means?

Zucchini starts with the letter z. Do you know any other words that begin with z?

Little Miss Muffet ate some curds and whey. What do you think they are?

Let's make a list of things you like to eat with butter.

I hear two little words in pancake. Listen: pan…cake.

Examine the melons we have today. How do they feel when you touch them? What colors are they on the outside? Can you guess what color they will be on the inside? Let's cut them open to find out.

Recipe cards, cookbooks, recipe charts

Let's read the recipe before we begin cooking. We want to make sure we have all the ingredients before we start.

This recipe asks us to bring the soup to a boil and then simmer it. How will we do that?

Here are some picture and word cards that tell us how to make a cream cheese and jelly sandwich. Let's put them in the right order. What happens first? What happens next? Now we can follow the steps to make our sandwiches.

The directions for cooking rice are right here on the box. Let's read them to see what we should do.

Would you like to create your own recipe? Tell it to me, and I'll write it down. If you like, you can draw a picture of your dish, and we'll add it to our class cookbook.

When you see an uppercase T on a recipe, it means to use a tablespoon. Can you guess how much to use if we see a lowercase t?

Cooking utensils and equipment

Today we need to use a hot plate for cooking. What safety rules do we need to remember? Let's write them on a chart so we won't forget.

We need to turn the mixer on high speed. I wonder which of the words is High. I know that it begins the same way as Hannah's name does.

How many Cs can you find on this measuring cup?

Strega Nona had a magic pasta pot. What made her pot so magical? What would happen if our pasta pot were magical?

This special pan is called a wok. The word is on the handle: w-o-k. Have you ever heard of a wok before? What kinds of foods can you cook in a wok? Setsuko's family often uses a wok when they cook.

We're going to use a griddle today, just like in the book we read called Pancakes for Breakfast. *Have you ever used a griddle at home? What did you make?*

Tasting

The popcorn tastes very salty. Let's add the word salty to our list of taste words.

Which fruit tastes sweet? Which tastes sour?

How do cooked carrots taste different from raw carrots?

What is the strangest ice cream flavor you ever tasted?

You said the granola was crunchy. What are some other words that begin the same way as crunchy?

Food Preparation

How is folding eggs into batter different from folding a napkin?

Knead sounds just like another word I know. Can you guess what word I'm thinking about? How are these words different?

Why should we wash the beans?

Can you form the letter C with your pretzel dough?

Observing Children's Understanding

As children explore in the Cooking area, look for these indications of literacy understanding:

- using new words as they cook
- following recipe directions and sequences
- using eye–hand coordination to pour, measure, and cut
- building hand muscles while kneading, pounding, and squeezing
- making connections with previous cooking experiences at home
- talking about the letters and words on food containers
- following print from left to right and top to bottom on recipe charts and cards and in cookbooks

Literacy in the Technology Area

When used appropriately, the Technology area can promote language and literacy development. Technology tools and mobile digital devices, such as tablets and computers, can help children learn new words and gain background knowledge. As children work together sharing a tablet or working together at the computer, they talk, make predictions, share experiences, and solve problems. They use literacy-related apps, games, and computer programs and games to develop understanding about print concepts and to practice and refine their skills. Select technology tools even enable children to send and receive information. With the help of adults and classmates, they can use tablets and computers and other mobile digital devices to find the answers to their questions. With drawing programs, games, and apps, children can express their ideas and feelings.

Examples of What a Child Might Do	Examples of Related Objectives	Examples of How This Relates to Literacy
Type his or her name or key in his or her name on a touchscreen	16. Demonstrates knowledge of the alphabet a. Identifies and names letters	Recognizing letters on the keyboard and associating upper- with lowercase letters
Use icons to navigate an app	14. Uses symbols and images to represent something not present a. Thinks symbolically	Understanding that symbols are meaningful, which is a precursor to understanding that letters represent sounds
Use a computer mouse	7. Demonstrates fine-motor strength and coordination a. Uses fingers and hands	Developing the eye–hand coordination and other fine-motor skills necessary for writing

Write or dictate an explanation of a picture	17. Demonstrates knowledge of print and its uses
	     b. Uses print concepts
	 19. Demonstrates writing skills
	     b. Writes to convey meaning
		Communicating through writing and beginning to consider the audience who will be reading the message

Work with a friend to use an app or game on the tablet	10. Uses appropriate conversational and other communication skills a. Engages in conversations	Using language to state predictions, communicate ideas, and solve problems
Follow along with an interactive storybook on the computer	18. Comprehends and responds to books and other texts a. Interacts during reading experiences, book conversations, and text reflections	Developing an understanding of print conventions by following highlighted screen text from left to right and top to bottom; using equipment to hear stories read aloud

The decisions you make about apps, games, computer programs, and other materials in the Technology area affect literacy learning. Here are some suggestions about what to include.

Materials

chart with picture and word directions for using an app and navigating digital media

colored adhesive labels with words such as *off, on, enter, delete, up, down, forward, backward, print, stop, go, play, start*

hard copies of books related to interactive storybook computer programs

individual children's word banks (a collection of words that are important to them, written on cards and held together by a ring)

name cards for children to refer to when typing their names or those of their friends

picture dictionaries for reference when typing

printer, ink, and paper

sign-up sheets for computer use

sign with rules for Technology area safety and equipment care

supplies for binding books

Suggested Books

Children's books related to computers and digital media

Arthur's Computer Disaster (Marc Brown)

The Computer from A to Z (Bobbie Kalman)

Franklin and the Computer (Paulette Bourgeois and Brenda Clark)

A House With No Mouse (P. S. Tinsley)

Look Inside a Computer (Anna Curti)

The Magic Schoolbus Gets Programmed (Nancy White)

Patrick's Dinosaurs on the Internet (Carol Carrick)

When Charlie McButton Lost Power (Suzanne Collins)

ABCs of the Web: Alphabet Primer for Young Developers in Training (Andrey Ostrovsky & John C. Vanden-Heuvel Sr.)

Webster's Email (Hannah Whaley)

Dot. (Randi Zuckerberg)

Ada Byron Lovelace and the Thinking Machine (Laurie Wallmark)

Using Technology to Teach Literacy Skills

Adult interaction with children in the Technology area is just as important as in any other area of the classroom. It helps children learn new skills and concepts, collaborate with peers, share discoveries, and solve problems. Here are examples of what you might say and ask:

Technology tools

How do you think this computer works?

How do you think this tablet works?

Have you ever seen a computer before? Why did someone use it?

Have you ever seen a tablet before? Why did someone use it?

What happens when you move the mouse?

What happens when you touch the screen of the tablet?

Do you see any letters that you know on the keyboard? What happens if you push them?

That word is Backspace, and the key has an arrow. What do you think backspace means?

Do you think all of the letters of the alphabet are on this keyboard? How can you find out? I wonder why they are not in the same order as on our alphabet chart.

What do you think will happen if we press the escape key?

What do you think will happen if we tap this icon?

Peripheral technology devices (e.g., printers, digital cameras, scanners)

Let's print the photo you took today so you can write about it.

What can you find in the classroom that rhymes with sat? Would you like to use the camera to take pictures of those things? Then we'll make a rhyming book.

Would you like to scan the paper that you wrote your name on so we can e-mail it to your mother?

Word processing programs and apps

Would you like to write a story about our field trip? I will help you if you want. Let's think about what we did first.

You covered your screen with many Bs. Do you know any words that begin with the B sound: /b/?

Font means the way the letters and words look on the computer screen. You can make your fonts fancy or plain, large or small. Watch, and I'll show you. Would you like to change the font when you type your name?

Tell me about the story you just wrote. Would you like to print it for others to enjoy? You may share it at group time if you'd like.

Your name begins with an uppercase letter, and the rest are lowercase letters. I only see uppercase letters on the letter keys. What should we do to write your name just as it is on your name card?

Let's use the computer to write a thank-you letter to the dentist. How should we begin the letter?

Listen to what happens when you type your name by using this program. The computer reads it back to you! Would you like to type a word to see if the computer can read it?

Let's use this app to write a note to your cousin. We can invite him to visit our class next week.

Interactive storybook programs

What do you think this story is about?

Do you see any words (or letters) that you know on this page?

Watch! The words on the screen light up when they are read.

What do you think is going to happen next? To find out, click the arrow to turn to the next page.

I wonder why that happened.

Why did you like this story?

This program lets you play. What do you think will happen when you click on the different pictures?

Other apps and games

Tell me what you are doing.

How do you know what to do for this game?

What will happen if you tap this icon?

What words and pictures on the screen tell you what to do next?

I placed the photos we took on our study trip on the tablet. Will you tell me about the pictures?

Internet sites and e-mail

Would you like to send an e-mail to your mom to tell her what you did today? How would you like to begin your message?

I found an interesting Web site with lots of pictures of worms. Scroll up or down on the touchscreen device to look at them all. How is this worm like the one you found on the playground today? We can write a story about it later.

Observing Children's Understanding

As children explore in the Technology area, look for these indications of literacy understanding:

- navigating programs, games, and apps by using picture icons or words
- describing what they are doing and thinking
- using fine-motor skills to handle a computer mouse, the keyboard, and a touchscreen
- attending to the print on the screen
- talking about the letters on the keyboard
- combining letters to make words, using word-processing programs and apps
- following the story line while using interactive books
  - tracking print on the screen, from top to bottom and left to right
  - using new vocabulary related to computers, such as *icon, app, mouse, cursor, backspace, enter,* and *delete*
  - connecting letter sounds and symbols as they type

Literacy Outdoors

Children have many outdoor opportunities for using language and for developing the large- and small-muscle skills necessary for writing and handling print materials. As children play together outdoors, they use language to plan, negotiate, solve problems, and create. They learn new words for what they see (e.g., *cocoon*, *dandelion*, and *wasp*) and for the what they do (e.g., *gallop*, *stretch*, and *balance*). Writing in the sand, in dirt, or with sidewalk chalk gives children a chance to practice writing with different, yet fun, materials. Print in the outdoor environment, such as a traffic sign on the tricycle track, a bird identification sign hanging from a tree, and a seed packet label in the garden, helps children understand that print conveys meaning. In addition, every literacy activity that takes place indoors can be brought outdoors. Baskets of books, writing materials, and props for retelling stories promote literacy learning outdoors.

Examples of What a Child Might Do	Examples of Related Objectives	Examples of How This Relates to Literacy
Run, jump, hop, skip, gallop	4. Demonstrates traveling skills	Learning the meaning of *run*, *jump*, *hop*, *skip*, and *gallop* through firsthand experiences
Move through an obstacle course Follow directions and learning positional concepts and words, such as *over*, *under*, *left*, *right*, *behind*, *below*, and *on*	4. Demonstrates traveling skills 5. Demonstrates balancing skills 21. Explores and describes spatial relationships and shapes a. Understands spatial relationships	Following directions and learning positional concepts and words, such as *over*, *under*, *left*, *right*, *behind*, *below*, and *on*
Describe what is happening as a butterfly emerges from a cocoon Developing background knowledge and vocabulary that supports listening and reading comprehension, and decoding	9. Uses language to express thoughts and needs a. Uses an expanding expressive vocabulary 25. Demonstrates knowledge of the characteristics of living things	Developing background knowledge and vocabulary that supports listening and reading comprehension, and decoding

Plan with a group to be circus performers for an audience, using language to plan, negotiate, and communicate	3. Participates cooperatively and constructively in group situations
	   b. Solves social problems
	10. Uses appropriate conversational and other communication skills
	   a. Engages in conversations
		Using language to plan, negotiate, and communicate

Examples of What a Child Might Do	Examples of Related Objectives	Examples of How This Relates to Literacy
Play a hand-clapping game while singing	15. Demonstrates phonological awareness, phonics skills, and word recognition c. Notices and discriminates discrete units of sound	Developing increased phonological awareness while playfully saying rhymes

Here is a list of suggested materials to enhance your outdoor learning environment. Books also spark imaginative play and learning outdoors. In addition, children can take books outdoors to read—alone or in small groups-—as a quiet activity. When choosing books for outdoor use, consider informational books about nature as well as storybooks.

Materials

adhesive labels for resealable bags that hold natural collections

bird identification charts, laminated and displayed

blank books or journals

clipboards, paper, and writing tools

labeled muffin tins, egg cartons, or ice cube trays for collecting and sorting

labels for garden plants

laminated environmental print signs

nature guides, including plant and animal identification books

pretend driver's licenses

props for retelling stories

sidewalk chalk

traffic signs

Suggested Books

(Titles preceded by an asterisk are included in the *Teaching Strategies® Children's Book Collection*.)

Alpha Bugs (David A. Carter)

Around the Pond: Who's Been Here? (Lindsay Barrett George)

Bounce (Doreen Cronin)

Carl's Afternoon in the Park (Alexandra Day)

The Carrot Seed (Ruth Krauss)

Clifford and the Big Storm (Norman Bridwell)

Diary of a Worm (Doreen Cronin)

Dinosaur Woods (George McClements)

Franklin and the Thunderstorm (Paulette Bourgeois)

The Giving Tree (Shel Silverstein)

A Grand Old Tree (Mary Newell DePalma)

The Grouchy Ladybug (Eric Carle)

Growing Colors (Bruce McMillan)

Henry Hikes to Fitchburg (D. B. Johnson)

I Wish I Were a Butterfly (James Howe)

The Icky Bug Alphabet Book (Jerry Pallotta)

In the Small, Small Pond (Denise Fleming)

It Looked Like Spilt Milk (Charles G. Shaw)

Jack's Garden (Henry Cole)

Just Like Josh Gibson (Angela Johnson)

The Listening Walk (Paul Showers)

Miss Tizzy (Libba Moore Gray)

Planting a Rainbow (Lois Ehlert)

Play Ball! (Nancy Noel Williams)

The Rainy Day (Anna Milbourne)

Roxaboxen (Alice McLerran)

Say It! (Charlotte Zolotow)

The Snowy Day (Ezra Jack Keats)

Spring Changes (Ellen B. Senisi)

The Tiny Seed (Eric Carle)

The Very Hungry Caterpillar (Eric Carle)

We're Going on a Bear Hunt (Michael Rosen)

We're Going on a Leaf Hunt (Steve Metzger)

The Wind Blew (Pat Hutchins)

Using the Outdoors to Teach Literacy Skills

Take advantage of outdoor opportunities to enhance language and literacy learning. Help children develop skills by using open-ended questions and prompts. Here are examples of what you might ask and say:

Gross-motor equipment

What do you think will happen if you climb on the jungle gym while wearing your gloves?

Do you know what this sign says? You're right: STOP. S-T-O-P. Can you guess why we have that sign on our tricycle track?

Ben is bouncing a ball. I hear three words that begin the same way: Ben, bouncing, and ball.

When you hear a word that begins the same way as mouse, scurry under the parachute.

Would you like to walk across the balance beam and pretend to be a tightrope walker like the one in Olivia and the Circus?

Natural materials and experiences

You worked hard to plant the seeds. Will you help me find the right seed packet to mark the place where you planted? Look for the packet with a picture of a sunflower and a word that begins with the letter S.

Tell me about the bird you saw with the binoculars. Then we can look for its name in our bird book.

Can you tell what letters I am writing in the dirt with this stick? How big can you write your name?

Why did the worms crawl under the wet paper towel?

Will you write in our plant journal what you did today? That will help us remember.

Group games

Would you like to join me in a clapping game? Let's sing "Miss Mary Mack."

Pretend you are driving cars. When I hold up the word STOP, put on your brakes. When I hold up GO, start moving again.

Will you lead us in a bear hunt like the hunt in today's story? Where shall we begin?

Here's some sidewalk chalk. Would you like to write letters instead of numerals in the hopscotch squares?

Close your eyes. Let's listen to every sound.

Dramatic play

You're using rocks to make a house with rooms, just as in Roxaboxen. *What else happened in the story? What other materials can you use to create your own Roxaboxen?*

I see that you're acting out The Three Little Pigs. *What happened first in the story? What happened next?*

I see that you're pretending to be a police officer. Would you like some paper in case you need to write a traffic ticket?

Observing Children's Understanding

As children explore in the Outdoor area, look for these indications of literacy understanding:

- following directions
- coordinating movements
- using new vocabulary
- talking with friends to plan, negotiate play, and communicate
- identifying print in the outdoor environment
- retelling stories or imitating characters from books

References

Adams, M. J. (1990). *Beginning to read: Thinking and learning about print.* Cambridge, MA: MIT Press.

Adams, M. J., Treiman, R., & Pressley, M. (1998). Reading, writing, and literacy. In I. E. Sigel & K. A. Renninger (Eds.), *Handbook of child psychology: Vol. 4: Child psychology in practice* (5th ed.)(pp. 275–355). New York: Wiley.

Alexander, A., Anderson, H., Heilman, P., Voeller, K., & Torgesen, J. (1991). Phonological awareness training and the remediation of analytic decoding deficits in a group of severe dyslexics. *Annals of Dyslexia, 41*, 193–206.

Allen, L., Cipielewski, J., & Stanovich, K. E. (1992). Multiple indicators of children's reading habits and attitudes: Construct validity and cognitive correlates. *Journal of Educational Psychology, 84*, 489–503.

Anderson, R. C., & Freebody, P. (1981). Vocabulary knowledge. In J. Guthrie (Ed.), *Comprehension and teaching: Research reviews* (pp. 77–117). Newark, DE: International Reading Association.

Anderson, R. C., & Pearson, P. D. (1984). A schema–thematic view of basic processes in reading comprehension. In P. D. Pearson, R. Barr, M. L. Kamil, & P. Mosenthal (Eds.), *Handbook of reading research* (pp. 255–290). New York: Longman.

Anderson, R. C., Reynolds, R. E., & Montague, W. E. (1977). *School and the acquisition of knowledge.* Hillsdale, NJ: Erlbaum.

Anderson, R. C., Reynolds, R. E., Schallert, D. L., & Goetz, E. T. (1977). Frameworks for comprehending discourse. *American Educational Research Journal, 14*(4), 367–381.

Anderson, R. C., Spiro, R. J., & Montague, W. E. (1977). *Schooling and the acquisition of knowledge.* Somerset: John Wiley & Sons.

Apel, K. (1997). *Metalinguistic skills in school-age children: Building blocks for literacy.* Presentation at the Montana Speech, Language, and Hearing Association Summer Institute, Great Falls, MT.

Baker L., Afflerbach, P., & Reinking, E. (Eds.). (2012). *Developing engaged readers in school and home communities.* New Jersey: Routledge.

Baker, L., Fernandez-Fein, S., Scher, D., & Williams, H. (1998). Home experiences related to the development of word recognition. In J. L. Metsala & L. C. Ehri (Eds.), *Word recognition in beginning literacy* (pp. 263–287). Mahwah, NJ: Erlbaum.

Baker, L., Scher, D., & Mackler, K. (1997). Home and family influences on motivations for literacy. *Educational Psychologist, 32*, 69–82.

Ball, E. (1993). Assessing phoneme awareness. *Language, Speech, and Hearing Services in Schools, 24*(3), 130–139.

Ballantyne, K. G., Sanderman, A. R., & McLaughlin, N. (2008). Dual language learners in the early Years: Getting ready to succeed in school. Washington, DC: National Clearinghouse for English Language Acquisition. Retrieved January, 2009, from http://www.ncela.gwu.edu/files/uploads/3/DLL_in_the_Early_Years.pdf

Barclay, K. (2014). Conducting interactive reading experiences. *Young Children, 69*, 78-83.

Bardige, B. S., & Segal, M. M. (2005). *Building literacy with love: A guide for teachers and caregivers of children birth through age 5*. ZERO TO THREE. National Center for Infants, Toddlers and Families: Washington, DC.

Berk, L. E. (2012). *Child development*. (9th ed.). Boston: Pearson.

Bishop, D. V. M., & Adams, C. (1990). A prospective study of the relationship between specific language impairment, phonological disorders and reading retardation. *Journal of Child Psychology and Psychiatry and Allied Disciplines, 31*, 1027–1050.

Bloodgood, J. W. (1999). What's in a name? Children's name writing and literacy acquisition. *Reading Research Quarterly, 34*(3), 342–367.

Bond, G. L., & Dykstra, R. (1967). The cooperative research program in first-grade reading instruction. *Reading Research Quarterly, 2*, 5–142.

Bowey, J. A. (1994). Phonological sensitivity in novice readers and nonreaders. *Journal of Experimental Psychology, 58*, 134–159.

Bradley, L., & Bryant, P. E. (1978). Difficulties in auditory organization as a possible cause of reading backwardness. *Nature, 271*, 746–747.

Bradley, L., & Bryant, P. E. (1983). Categorizing sounds and learning to read: A causal connection. *Nature, 310*, 419–421.

Bransford, J. D., & Johnson, M. K. (1972). Contextual prerequisites for understanding: Some investigations of comprehension and recall. *Journal of Verbal Learning and Verbal Behavior, 11*, 717–726.

Braunger, J., Lewis, J., & Hagans, R. (1997). *Building a knowledge base in reading*. Portland, OR: Northwest Regional Educational Laboratory, National Council of Teachers of English.

Burgess, S. R., & Lonigan, C. J. (1998). Bidirectional relations of phonological sensitivity and prereading abilities: Evidence from a preschool sample. *Journal of Experimental Child Psychology, 70*, 177–141.

Burns, M. S., Griffin, P., & Snow, C. E. (Eds.). (1999). *Starting out right*. Washington, DC: National Academy Press.

Butler, S. R., Marsh, H. W., Sheppard, M. J., & Sheppard, J. L. (1985). Seven-year longitudinal study of the early prediction of reading achievement. *Journal of Educational Psychology, 77*, 349–361.

Campbell, C. (Ed.). (1998). *Facilitating preschool literacy*. Newark, DE: International Reading Association.

Chall, J. S. (1967). *Learning to read: The great debate.* New York: McGraw-Hill.

Chall, J. S., Jacobs, V. A., & Baldwin, L. E. (1990). *The reading crisis: Why poor children fall behind.* Cambridge, MA: Harvard University Press.

Chaney, C. (1992). Language development, metalinguistic skills, and print awareness in 3-year-old children. *Applied Psycholinguistics, 13,* 485–514.

Christie, F. (1984). Young children's writing development: The relationship of written genres to curriculum genres. In N. B. Bartlett & J. Carr (Eds.), *Language in education conference: A report of proceedings* (pp. 41–69). Brisbane, CAE, Australia: Mt. Gravatt Campus.

Christie, F. (1987). Factual writing in the first years of school. *Australian Journal of Reading, 10,* 207–216.

Christie, J. F. (1983). The effects of play tutoring on young children's cognitive performance. *Journal of Educational Research, 76,* 326–330.

Christie, J., Roskos, K., Vukelich, C., Enz, B., & Neuman, S. (1995). *Linking literacy with play.* Newark, DE: International Reading Association.

Clay, M. M. (1979a). *The early detection of reading difficulties* (2nd ed.). Auckland, New Zealand: Heinemann.

Clay, M. M. (1979b). *Reading recovery: A guidebook for teachers in training.* Auckland, New Zealand: Heinemann.

Clay, M. M. (1981). *Becoming literate.* Portsmouth, NH: Heinemann.

Clay, M. M. (1991). *Becoming literate: The construction of inner control.* Auckland, New Zealand: Heinemann.

Clay, M. (1993). *An observation survey of early literacy achievement.* Portsmouth, NH.: Heinemann.

Cochran-Smith, M. (1984). *The making of a reader.* Norwood, NJ: Ablex.

Collier, V. P. (1995). *Promoting academic success for ESL students: Understanding second language acquisition for school* (No. 1-883514-00-2). Jersey City, NJ: New Jersey Teachers of English to Speakers of Other Languages–Bilingual Educators.

Crain-Thoreson, C., & Dale, P. S. (1992). Do early talkers become early readers? Linguistic precocity, preschool language and emergent literacy. *Developmental Psychology, 50,* 429–444.

Cullinan, B. E. (1992). Leading with literature. In B. E. Culinan (ed.), *Invitation to read: More children's literature in the reading program* (pp. x–xxii). Newark, DE: International Reading Association.

Cunningham, A. E., & Stanovich, K. E. (1991). Tracking the unique effects of print exposure in children: Associations with vocabulary, general knowledge and spelling. *Journal of Educational Psychology, 83,* 264–274.

Cunningham, A. E., & Stanovich, K. E. (1998). Early reading acquisition and its relation to reading experience and ability 10 years later. *Developmental Psychology, 33*, 934–945.

Daniels, M. (1994). The effect of sign language on hearing children's language development. *Communication Education, 43*(4), 291–298.

Daniels, M. (1996). Bilingual, bimodal education for hearing kindergarten students. *Sign Language Studies, 90*, 25–37.

Davis, F. B. (1968). Research in comprehension in reading. *Reading Research Quarterly, 3*, 499–545.

Dickinson, D. K., & DeTemple, J. (1998). Putting parents in the picture: Maternal reports of preschoolers' literacy as a predictor of early reading. *Early Childhood Research Quarterly, 13*, 241–261.

Dickinson, D. K., & Smith, M. W. (1994). Long-term effects of preschool teachers' book readings on low-income children's vocabulary and story comprehension. *Reading Research Quarterly, 29*, 104–122.

Dickinson, D. K., & Tabors, P. O. (1991). Early literacy: Linkages between home, school and literacy achievement at age five. *Journal of Research in Childhood Education, 6*, 30–46.

Dickinson, D. K., & Tabors, P. O. (Eds.). (2001). *Building literacy with language: Young children learning at home and school*. Baltimore: Brookes.

Dole, J. S., Sloan, C. J., & Trathen, W. (1995). Teaching vocabulary within the context of literature. *Journal of Reading, 38*, 444–451.

Downing, J. (1986). Cognitive clarity: A unifying and cross-cultural theory for language awareness phenomena in reading. In D. B. Yaden, Jr. &. S. Templeton (Eds.), *Metalinguistic awareness and beginning literacy* (pp. 13–29). Portsmouth, NH: Heinemann.

Drevno, G. E., Dimball, J. W., Possi, M. K, Heward, W. L., Gardner, R., & Barbetta, P. M. (1994). Effects of active student response during error correction on the acquisition, maintenance and generalization of science vocabulary by elementary students: A systematic replication. *Journal of Applied Behavior Analysis, 27*(1), 179–180.

Duke, N. K., & Kays, J. (1998). "Can I say 'once upon a time'?": Kindergarten children developing knowledge of informational book language. *Early Childhood Research Quarterly, 13*(2), 295–318.

Durkin, D. (1966). *Children who read early*. New York: Teacher's College Press.

Echols, L. D., West, R. F., Stanovich, K. E., & Zehr, K. S. (1996). Using children's literacy activities to predict growth in verbal cognitive skills: A longitudinal investigation. *Journal of Educational Psychology, 88*, 296–304.

Ehri, L. C. (1984). How orthography alters spoken language competencies in children learning to read and spell. In J. Downing & R. Valtin (Eds.), *Language awareness and learning to read*. New York: Springer Verlag.

References

Ehri, L., & Wilce, L. (1985). Movement into reading: Is the first stage of printed word learning visual or phonetic? *Reading Research Quarterly, 20,* 163–179.

Espinosa, L. (2005). Curriculum and assessment considerations for young children from culturally, linguistically, and economically diverse backgrounds. *Psychology in the Schools, 42*(8), 837–853.

Espinosa, L. (2008). *Challenging common myths about young English language learners* (Foundation for Child Development Policy Brief No. 8). Retrieved January 7, 2009, from http://www.fcd-us.org/resources/resources_show.htm?doc_id=669789

Espinosa, L. (2009). *Getting it right for young children from diverse backgrounds: Applying research to improve practice.* Upper Saddle River, NJ: Pearson Publishing.

Fernandez-Fem, S., Scher, D., & Williams, H. (2013). Home experiences related to the development of word recognition. *Word Recognition in Beginning Literacy.* New York: Routledge.

Fowler, A. E. (1991). How early phonological development might set the stage for phoneme awareness. In S. A. Brady & D. A. Shankweiler (Eds.), *Phonological processes in literacy* (pp. 97–117). Hillsdale, NJ: Lawrence Erlbaum Associates.

Galda, L., & Cullinan, B. E. (1991). Literature for literacy: What research says about the benefits of using trade books in the classroom. In J. Flood, J. Jensen, D. Lapp, & J. R. Squire (Eds.), *Handbook of research on teaching the English language arts.* New York: Macmillan.

Gambrell, L. B. (2011). Seven rules of engagement: What's most important to know about motivation to read. *The Reading Teacher, 65,* 172–178.

Gambrell, L. B., Palmer, B. M., & Coding, R. M. (1993). *Motivation to read.* Washington, DC: Office of Educational Research and Improvement.

Garcia, E. E. (2003). *Student cultural diversity: Understanding and meeting the challenge.* Boston: Houghton Mifflin.

Genesee, E., Paradis, J., & Crago, M. B. (2004). *Dual language development and disorders: a handbook on bilingualism and second language learning.* Baltimore, MD: Paul H. Brookes.

Gibson, E., & Levin, E. (1975). *The psychology of reading.* Cambridge, MA: MIT Press.

Goatly, V. J., Brock, C. H., & Raphael, T. E. (1995). Diverse learners participating in regular education book clubs. *Reading Research Quarterly, 30,* 352–380.

Goatly, V. J., & Raphael, T. E. (1992). Non-traditional learners' written and dialogic response to literature. *Learner factors/teacher factors: Issues in literacy research and instruction: 40th yearbook of the National Reading Conference* (pp. 313–322). Chicago: National Reading Conference.

Goswami, U., & Bryant, P. E. (1990). *Phonological skills and learning to read.* Hillsdale, NJ: Erlbaum.

Griffith, P. O., & Olson, W. (1992). Phoemic awareness helps beginning readers break the code. *The Reading Teacher, 45*(7), 516–523.

Gundlach, R., McLane, J., Scott, F., & McNamee, G. (1985). The social foundations of early writing development. In M. Farr (Ed.), *Advances in writing research: Vol. 1: Children's early writing development.* Norwood, NJ: Ablex.

Gunn, B., Simmons, D., & Kameenui, E. (1995). *Emergent literacy: Synthesis of the research* (Tech. Rep. No. 19). Retrieved June 2004, from http://idea.uoregon.edu/~ncite/documents/techrep/tech19.html

Gutiérrez-Clellen, V. F., Simon-Cereijido, G., & Wagner, C. (2008). Bilingual children with language impairment: A comparison with monolingual and second language learners. *Applied Psycholinguistics, 29*, 3–19.

Hall, S. L., & Moats, L. C. (1999). *Straight talk about reading: How parents can make a difference during the early years.* Lincolnwood, IL: NTC/Contemporary Publishing.

Hart, B., & Risley, T. R. (1995). *Meaningful differences in the everyday experience of young American children.* Baltimore: Paul H. Brookes Publishing Co.

Heath, S. B., Branscombe, A., & Thomas, C. (1986). The book as a narrative prop in language acquisition. In B. Schieffelin & P. Gilmore (Eds.), *The acquisition of literacy: Ethnographic perspectives* (pp. 16–34). Norwood, NJ: Ablex.

Hicks, D. (1995). The social origins of essayist writing. *Bulletin Suisse de Linguistique Appliqué, 61*, 61–82.

Hiebert, E. H. (1981). Developmental patterns and interrelationships of preschool children's print awareness. *Reading Research Quarterly, 16*, 236–260

Holdaway, D. (1979). *The foundations of literacy.* Portsmouth, NH: Heinemann.

Huck, C. (1976). *Children's literature in the elementary school* (3rd ed.). New York: Holt, Rinehart & Winston.

Hull, G., & Moje, E. B. (2013). *What is the development of literacy the development of?* Stanford, CA: Stanford University.

Jenkins, R., & Bowen, L. (1994). Facilitating development of preliterate children's phonological abilities. *Topics in Language Disorders, 14*(2), 26–39.

Johnston, M. (2002). Assessment in reading. In R. Barr, M. L. Kamil, & P. Mosenthal (Eds.), *Handbook of Reading Research* (pp. 147–182). Mahwah, NJ: Lawrence Erlbaum Associates.

Johnston, R. S., Anderson, M., & Holligan, C. (1996). Knowledge of the alphabet and explicit awareness of phonemes in prereaders: The nature of the relationship. *Reading and Writing: An Interdisciplinary Journal, 8*, 217–234.

Kameenui, E. J., Carnine, D. W., & Freschi, R. (1982). Effects of text construction and instructional procedures for teaching word meanings on comprehension and recall. *Reading Research Quarterly, 17*, 367–385.

Leung, C. B. (1992). Effects of word-related variables on vocabulary growth repeated read-aloud events. In C. K. Kinzer & D. J. Leu (Eds.), *Literacy research, theory, and practice: Views from many perspectives: 41st yearbook of the National Reading Conference* (pp. 491–498). Chicago, IL: The National Reading Conference.

Lonigan, C. J., Burgess, S. R., & Anthony, J. L. (2000). Development of emergent literacy and early reading skills in preschool children: Evidence from a latent-variable longitudinal study. *Developmental Psychology, 36*, 596–613.

Lonigan, C. J., Burgess, S. R., Anthony, J. L., & Barker, T. A. (1998). Development of phonological sensitivity in 2- to 5-year-old children. *Journal of Educational Psychology, 90*(2), 294–311.

MacLean, M., Bryant, P., & Bradley, L. (1987). Rhymes, nursery rhymes, and reading in early childhood. *Merrill-Palmer Quarterly, 33*, 255–281.

Mason, J. M. (1980). When do children begin to read? An exploration of four-year-old children's letter and word reading competencies. *Reading Research Quarterly, 15*, 203–227.

Mason, J. M. (1992). Reading stories to preliterate children: A proposed connection to reading. In P. B. Gough, L. C. Ehri, & R. Treiman R. (Eds.), *Reading acquisition* (pp. 215–241). Mahwah, NJ: Lawrence Erlbaum Associates.

Mason, J., & Allen, J. B. (1986). A review of emergent literacy with implications for research and practice in reading. *Review of Research in Education, 13*, 3–47.

Mattingly, I. (1984). Reading linguistic awareness, and language acquisition. In J. Downing & R. Caltin (Eds.), *Language awareness and learning to read*. New York: Springer-Verlag.

McCormick, C. E., & Mason, J. M. (1986). Intervention procedures for increasing preschool children's interest in and knowledge about reading. In W. H. Teale & E. Sulzby (Eds.), *Emergent literacy: Writing and reading* (pp. 90–115). Norwood, NJ: Ablex.

McKeon, M. G., Beck, I. L., Omanson, R. C., & Pople, M. T. (1985). Some effects of the nature and frequency of vocabulary instruction on the knowledge and use of words. *Reading Research Quarterly, 20*(5), 522–535.

McGee, L., & Richgels, D. (1996). *Literacy's beginnings: Supporting young readers and writers*. Needham Heights, MA: Allyn and Bacon.

McGee, L. M., Richgels, D., & Charlsworth, R. (1986). Emerging knowledge of written language: Learning to read and write. In S. J. Kilmer (Ed.), *Advances in early education and day care* (Vol. IV)(pp. 67–121). Greenwich, CT: JAI Press.

McGee, L. M., & Schickedanz, J. A. (2007). Repeated interactive read-alouds in preschool and kindergarten. *The Reading Teacher, 60*(8), 742–751.

Moats, L. (1998). *Achieving research-based practice: Replacing romance with reality*. Presentation at Sopris West Summer Institute, A Summit on Literacy, Snowmass, CO.

Morrow, L. M. (1983). Home and school correlates of early interest in literature. *Journal of Educational Research, 76*, 221–230.

Morrow, L. M. (1985). Retelling stories: A strategy for improving children's comprehension, concept of story structure and oral language complexity. *The Elementary School Journal, 85,* 647–661.

Morrow, L. M. (1987). Promoting voluntary reading: The effects of an inner city program in summer day care centers. *The Reading Teacher, 41,* 266–274.

Morrow, L. M. (1990). Preparing the classroom environment to promote literacy during play. *Early Childhood Research Quarterly, 5,* 537–554.

Morrow, L. M. (2001). *Literacy development in the early years: Helping children read and write.* Needham Heights, MA: Allyn and Bacon.

Morrow, L. M., & Gambrell, L. B. (2002). Literature-based instruction in the early years. In S. B. Neuman & D. K. Dickinson (Eds.), *Handbook of early literacy research* (pp. 348–360). New York: Guilford Press.

Morrow, L. M., & Smith, J. K. (1990). The effect of group size on interactive storybook reading. *Reading Research Quarterly, 25,* 213–231.

Morrow, L. M., & Weinstein, C. S. (1982). Increasing children's use of literature through program and physical design changes. *The Elementary School Journal, 83,* 131–137.

Morrow, L. M., & Weinstein, C. S. (1986). Encouraging voluntary reading: The impact of a literature program on children's use of library centers. *Reading Research Quarterly, 21,* 330–346.

Murray, B. A., Stahl, S. A., & Ivey, M. G. (1996). Developing phoneme awareness through alphabet books. *Reading and Writing, 8,* 307–322.

Nagy, W. E., & Anderson, R. C. (1984). How many words are there in printed school English? *Reading Research Quarterly, 19,* 304–330.

Naslund, J. C., & Schneider, W. (1996). Kindergarten letter knowledge, phonological skills, and memory processes: Relative effects on early literacy. *Journal of Experimental Child Psychology, 62,* 30–59.

National Early Literacy Panel. (2004). *A synthesis of research on language and literacy.* Retrieved June 2004, from http://www.famlit.org/ProgramsandInitiatives/ FamilyPartnershipinReading/index.cfm

National Early Literacy Panel. (2008). *Developing early literacy*: Report of the National Early Literacy Panel.

National Institute of Child Health and Human Development. (2000a). *Report of the National Reading Panel: Teaching children to read: An evidence-based assessment of the scientific research literature on reading and its implications for reading instruction* (NIH Publication No. 00-4769). Washington, DC: U.S. Government Printing Office.

National Institute of Child Health and Human Development. (2000b). *Why children succeed or fail at reading: Research from NICHD's program in learning disabilities.* Retrieved June 2004, from http://www.nichd.nih.gov/publications/pubs/readbro.htm.

National Reading Panel. (2000). *Teaching children to read: An evidence-based assessment of the scientific research literature on reading and its implications for reading instruction.* NIH Publication NO. 00-4769. Washington, DC: National Institute of Child Health and Human Development.

Neuman, S. B., Copple, C., & Bredekamp, S. (2000). *Learning to read and write.* Washington, DC: National Association for the Education of Young Children.

Neuman, S. B., & Roskos, K. (1990). Play, print and purpose: Enriching play environments for literacy development. *Reading Teacher, 44*(3), 214–221.

Neuman, S. B., & Roskos, K. (1991). The influence of literacy-enriched play centers on preschoolers' conceptions of the functions of print. In J. Christie (Ed.), *Play and early literacy development* (pp. 167–187). Albany, NY: State University of New York Press.

Neuman, S. B., & Roskos, K. (Eds.). (1998). *Children achieving.* Newark, DE: International Reading Association.

Ninio, A., & Bruner, J. (1978). The achievements and antecedents of labeling. *Journal of Child Language, 5,* 5–15.

Noble, E., & Foster, J. E. (1993). Play centers that encourage literacy development. *Day Care and Early Education, 21*(2), 22–26.

Office of Head Start. (2008). *Dual language learning: What does it take?: Head Start dual language report.* Washington, DC: Administration for Children and Families.

Olfman, S. (Ed.). (2003). *All work and no play…: How educational reforms are harming our preschoolers.* Westport, CT: Praeger.

Owocki, G. (1999). *Literacy through play.* Portsmouth, NH: Heinemann.

Owocki, G. (2001). *Make way for literacy! Teaching the way young children learn.* Portsmouth, NH: Heinemann; Washington, DC: National Association for the Education of Young Children.

Pappas, C. C. (1991). Fostering full access to literacy by including information books. *Language Arts, 68,* 449–462.

Pappas, C., & Brown, E. (1987). Learning to read by reading: Learning how to extend the functional potential of language. *Research in the Teaching of English, 21*(2), 160–184.

Paradis, J., Crago, M., Genesee, F., & Rice, M. (2003). Bilingual children with specific language impairment: How do they compare with their monolingual peers? *Journal of Speech, Language, and Hearing Research, 46,* 1–15.

Pellegrini, A. D., & Galda, L. (1982). The effects of thematic fantasy play training on the development of children's story comprehension. *American Educational Research Journal, 19,* 443–452.

Pickett, L. (1998). Literacy learning during block play. *Journal of Research in Childhood Education, 12*(2), 225–230.

Pikulski, J. J., & Tobin, A. W. (1989). Factors associated with long-term reading achievement of early readers. In S. McCormick, J. Zutell, P. Scharer, & P. O'Keefe (Eds.), *Cognitive and social perspectives for literacy research and instruction* (pp. 123–133). Chicago: National Reading Conference.

Purcell-Gates, V. (1988). Lexical and syntactic knowledge of written narrative held by well-read-to kindergartners and second graders. *Research in the Teaching of English, 22*, 128–160.

Rawson, R. M., & Goetz, E. M. (1983). *Reading-related behavior in preschoolers: Environmental factors and teacher modeling.* Unpublished manuscript.

Read, C. (1971). Preschool children's knowledge of English phonology. *Harvard Educational Review, 41*, 1–34.

Robbins, C., & Ehri, L. C. (1994). Reading storybooks to kindergarteners help them learn new vocabulary words. *Journal of Educational Psychology, 86*(1), 54–64.

Roser, N., & Martinez, M. (1985). Roles adults play in preschoolers' response to literature. *Language Arts, 62*(5), 485–490.

Roser, N. L., & Martinez, M.G. (Eds.). (1995). *Book talk and beyond: Children and teachers respond to literature.* Newark, DE: International Reading Association.

Roskos, K. A., & Christie, J. F. (Eds.). (2000). *Play and literacy in early childhood: Research from multiple perspectives.* Mahwah, NJ: Lawrence Erlbaum.

Sawyer, W. (2004). *Growing up with literature* (4th ed.). Clifton Park, NY: Delmar Learning.

Saltz, E., Dixon, D., & Johnson, J. E. (1997). Training disadvantaged preschoolers on various fantasy activities: Effects on cognitive functioning and impulse control. *Child Development, 48*, 367–380.

Scarborough, H. (1989). Prediction of reading dysfunction from familial and individual differences. *Journal of Educational Psychology, 81*, 101–108.

Schickedanz, J. (1999). *Much more than the ABCs: The early stages of reading and writing.* Washington, DC: National Association for the Education of Young Children.

Sénéchal, M. (1997). The differential effect of storybook reading on preschoolers' acquisition of expressive and receptive vocabulary. *Journal of Child Language, 24*(1), 123–138.

Sénéchal, M., & Cornell, E. H. (1993). Vocabulary acquisition through shared reading experiences. *Reading Research Quarterly, 28*(4), 360–374.

Share, D. L., & Jaffe-Gur, T. (1999). How reading begins: A study of preschoolers' print identification strategies. *Cognition and Instruction, 17*, 177–213.

Share, D. L., Jorm, A. F., MacLean, R., & Mathews, R. (1984). Sources of individual differences in reading acquisition. *Journal of Educational Psychology, 76*, 1309–1324.

Share, D. L., & Silva, P. (1987). Language deficits and specific reading retardation: Cause or effect? *British Journal of Disorders of Communication, 22*, 219–226.

Silvern, S., Williamson, P., & Waters, B. (1983). Play as a mediator of comprehension: An alternative to play training. *Educational Research Quarterly, 7*, 16–21.

Smith, F. (1978). *Understanding reading* (2nd ed.). New York: Holt, Rinehart & Winston.

Snow, C. E., Barnes, W. S., Chandler, J., Goodman, I. F., & Hemphill, L. (1991). *Unfulfilled expectations: Home and school influences on literacy.* Cambridge, MA: Harvard University Press.

Snow, C. E., Burns, M. S., & Griffin, P. (Eds.). (1998). *Preventing reading difficulties in young children.* Washington, DC: National Academy Press.

Snowling, M., & Stackhouse, J. (1996). *Dyslexia speech and language: A practitioner's handbook.* San Diego, CA: Singular Publishing Group.

Snyder, L., & Downey, D. (1997). Developmental differences in the relationship between oral language deficits and reading. *Topics in Language Disorders, 17*(3), 27–40.

Stahl, S. A., & Murray, B. A. (1994). Defining phonological awareness and its relationship to early reading. *Journal of Educational Psychology, 86*, 221–234.

Stanovich, K. E. (1986). Matthew effects in reading: Some consequences of individual differences in the acquisition of literacy. *Reading Research Quarterly, 21*, 360–407.

Stanovich, K. E. (1994). Romance and reality. *The Reading Teacher, 47*(4), 280–291.

Stanovich, K. E. & West, R. F. (1989). Exposure to print and orthographic processing. *Reading Research Quarterly, 24*, 402–433.

Stevenson, H. W., & Newman, R. S. (1986). Long-term prediction of achievement and attitudes in mathematics and reading. *Child Development, 57*, 646–659.

Stewig, J. W., & Sebesta, S. (Eds.). (1978). *Using literature in the elementary classroom.* Urbana, IL: National Council of Teachers of English.

Strickland, D., & Morrow, L. (Eds.). (1989). *Emerging literacy: Young children learn to read and write.* Newark, DE: International Reading Association.

Strickland, D., & Morrow, L. (Eds.). (2000). *Beginning reading and writing.* New York, NY: Teachers College Press.

Sulzby, E. (1985). Children's emergent reading of favorite books: A developmental study. *Reading Research Quarterly, 20*(4), 458–481.

Sulzby, E. & Teale, W. H. (1987). *Young children's storybook reading: Longitudinal study of parent-child interaction and children's independent functioning: Final report to the Spencer Foundation.* Ann Arbor: University of Michigan.

Sulzby, E., & Teale, W. H. (1991). Emergent literacy. In R. Barr, M. Kamil, P. Mosenthal, & P. Pearson (Eds.), *Handbook of Reading Research* (Vol. 2) (pp. 727–757). New York: Longman.

Suskind, D. (2015). *Thirty million words.* New York: Dutton.

Tabors, P. O. (2008). *One child, two languages: A guide for early childhood educators of children learning English as a second language* (2nd ed.). Baltimore: Paul H. Brookes Publishing Co.

Tabors, P. O., & Snow, C. (1994). English as a second language in preschools. In F. Genesee (Ed.), *Educating second language children: The whole child, the whole curriculum, the whole community* (pp. 103–125). New York: Cambridge University Press.

Taylor, D. (1983). *Family literacy*. Exeter, NH: Heinemann.

Teale, W. (1984) Reading to young children: Its significance for literacy development. In H. Goelman, A. Oberg, & F. Smith (Eds.), *Awakening to literacy* (pp.110–121). Portsmouth, NH: Heinemann.

Teale, W., & Yokota, J. (2000). Beginning reading and writing: Perspectives on instruction. In D. S. Strickland & L. M. Morrow (Eds.), *Beginning reading and writing* (pp. 3–21). New York: Teachers College Press.

Torgesen, J. K. (1998, Spring/Summer). Catch them before they fall: Identification and assessment to prevent reading failure in young children. *American Educator, 22*, 32–39.

Treiman, R. (1993). *Beginning to spell*. New York: Oxford University Press.

Vukelich, C. (1990). Where's the paper? Literacy during dramatic play. *Childhood Education, 66*(4), 205–209.

Vukelich, C. (1994). Effects of play interventions on young children's reading of environmental print. *Early Childhood Research Quarterly, 9*, 153–170.

Vygotsky, L. S. (1978). *Mind in society: the development of psychological processes*. Cambridge, MA: Harvard University.

Wagner, R. K., Torgesen, J. K., Laughon, P., Simmons, K., & Rashotte, C. A. (1993). The development of young readers' phonological processing abilities. *Journal of Educational Psychology, 30*, 73–87.

Wagner, R. K., Torgesen, J. K., Rashotte, C. A., Hecht, S. A., Barker, T. A., Burgess, S. R., Donahue, J., & Garon, T. (1997). Changing relations between phonological processing abilities and word-level reading as children develop from beginning to skilled readers: A 5-year longitudinal study. *Developmental Psychology, 33*, 468–479.

Wells, G. (1985). Preschool literacy-related activities and success in school. In D. R. Olance, N. Torrance, & A. Hildyard (Eds.), *Literacy, language and learning* (pp. 229–255). Cambridge, England: Cambridge University Press.

Wells, G. (1986). *The meaning makers: Children learning language and using language to learn*. Portsmouth, NH: Heinemann.

Weitzman, E., & Greenberg, J. (2002). *Learning language and loving it*. Toronto, Ontario: The Hanen Centre.

Whitehurst, G., & Lonigan, C. (1998). Child development and emergent literacy. *Child Development, 69*(3), 848–872.

Whitehurst, G. T., & Lonigan, C. J. (2001). Emergent literacy: Development from prereaders to readers. In S. B. Neuman, & D. K. Dickinson (Eds.), *Handbook of early literacy research* (pp. 11–29). NY: Guilford Press.

Yader, D. (1985). *Preschoolers' spontaneous inquiries about print books.* Paper presented at the annual meeting of the National Reading Conference, San Diego, CA.

Yopp, H. K. (1992). Developing phonemic awareness in young children. *The Reading Teacher, 45*(9), 696–703.

Index

A

Adaptive equipment, 134
Additive model of English acquisition, 50
Address book as dramatic prop, 143
Advanced learners
  language development of, 58
  literacy programs for, 58
Affection, 50
Afternoon activities. *See* Daily schedule
Alliteration, 13, 14, 16
Alphabetic principle, 25
Alphabet/letters and words, 25–28. *See also*
    Literacy skills
  books for learning, 27, 75, 103, 155
  English-language learners and, 26, 28
  magnetic letters, 146
  matching words with printed text, 129
  phonological awareness and, 25–26, 28
  play and, 112
  recognizing written words, 128, 129
  research on, 26
  teacher's role, 27–28
  writing and, 103
Alphabet song, 25, 27
Animals, caring for, 155
Arts
  drama. *See* Dramatic play
  music and movement. *See* Music and
    movement
  objectives, 41
  visual. *See* Visual arts
Assistive devices, 59, 134
Attention, reading aloud, need to capture
    attention of children prior to, 7, 78
Audio materials
  CDs, 127
  listening to with children, 132
Auditory cues and supports, 59
Autobiographies, 35

B

Background knowledge and comprehension,
    30, 31, 32
Bilingualism. *See* English-language learners
    (ELL)
Biographies and autobiographies, 35
Block play
  accessories for, 137–138
  books for, 136
  hollow blocks, 137
  interacting with children, 137–138
  literacy skills and, 135–138
  loose parts in, 138
  materials for, 136
  observing and responding to children, 138
  signs in, 138
  stages of, 137
  unit blocks, 137
Body language, 84, 88
Book Discussion Cards™, 86
Books, 34–37. *See also* Library
  alphabet books, 27, 75, 103, 155
  biographies and autobiographies, 35
  for block play, 136

for children with disabilities, 60
choices by children, 7
comprehension of. *See* Comprehension
on computers, 173
concept books, 35, 75
for cooking, 168–169
for Discovery area, 154–155
for dramatic play, 140–141
engaging with, 36, 128–129
experience with various types of, 34–35, 37
exploring, 128
fairy tales and folktales, 35
fantasy, 35
fiction, 35
informational books, 34, 35, 36, 37,
    154–155
made by children, 7, 37
for music and movement, 35, 163–164
for outdoor play, 179
picture books, 34, 84, 154
play and, 112
poetry, 34, 35
reading aloud. *See* Reading aloud
research on, 36
for sand and water play, 159
selecting for library, 126
songbooks, 35, 164
story retelling. *See* Story retelling
storytelling. *See* Storytelling
teacher's role in promoting, 7–8, 37, 66
for toys and games area, 146
types of, 34–35
for visual arts, 149–150
wordless books, 34, 35
writing. *See* Writing skills

C

Cameras, use of, 174
CDs, 127
Center time. *See* Choice time
Challenging behavior
  in library, 133–134
  writing skills and, 134
Child development and learning
  in advanced learners. *See* Advanced learners
  in children with disabilities. *See* Children
    with disabilities
  cognitive development, 41
  English-language learners. *See* English-
    language learners (ELL)
  language. *See* Language development
  physical development, 41
  social–emotional. *See* Social–emotional
    development
  stages of development. *See* Developmental
    stages
Child-initiated writing, 106
Children with disabilities
  adaptive devices for, 134
  assistive technology. *See* Assistive devices
  auditory cues for, 59
  books for, 60
  classroom space for, 59

language development in, 60
literacy programs for, 59–60
physical and sensory supports for, 60
schedule and routine supports for, 59
tactile cues for, 59
visual cues for, 59
Choice time
  library and, 8
  literacy skills and, 46
Circles, 28
Classroom space
  for children with disabilities, 59
  displaying materials. *See* Displays in
    classroom
  for English-language learners, 54
  for library, 7
  for literacy programs, 43–44, 61
  pets and plants in, 155
  for play incorporating literacy learning, 113
  for story retelling, 99
Clay, 151
Clothesline story props, 88, 98
Cognitive development, objectives of, 41
Collages, 151
Colored pencils, 151
Communication
  by children. *See* Language development
  with children. *See* Interacting with children
  conversations with children, 67
Comprehension, 29–33
  background knowledge and, 30, 31, 32
  defined, 29
  listening comprehension, 30, 32–33, 66,
    84, 128
  play and, 112
  reading aloud and, 31, 33, 84
  research on, 31
  story comprehension, 33
  story retelling and, 33, 97
  storytelling and, 88
  teacher's role, 32–33, 66
Computer play. *See also* Technology
  accessories for, 174
  books on, 173
  word processing programs, 174–175
Concentration games, 146
Concept books, 35, 75
Connecting new learning to prior experience,
    32, 33
Construction toys, 147
Content of curriculum. *See specific curriculum
    areas*
Conversational reading, 86
Conversations with children, 67. *See also*
    Interacting with children
Cooking
  books for, 168–169
  interacting with children, 170–171
  literacy skills and, 166–171
  materials for, 167
  observing and responding to children, 171
  recipes, 170
Coordination, outdoor play and, 180
Costumes, 98–99. *See also* Dress-up clothes
Crayons, 151

The Creative Curriculum®
  interest areas. *See* Interest areas
  literacy, 1–181. *See also* Literacy skills
Cues
  auditory, 59
  tactile, 59
  visual, 59
Culture, English-language learners and, 54

D

Daily schedule
  for literacy programs, 45–48, 61–62
  phonological awareness in, 18
  reading aloud in, 12, 77
Developmental stages
  block play, 137
  writing, 129
Dictation, 106
Digital devices. *See* Technology
Directions
  following, 33
  for routine procedures, 112
  writing, 105
Disabled children. *See* Children with
    disabilities
Discipline. *See* Challenging behavior
Discovery area
  books for, 154–155
  interacting with children, 155–156
  literacy skills and, 153–157
  materials for, 154
  observing and responding to children, 157
  science and, 156
  sensory table or sensory tubs in, 156
  take-aparts in, 156
Displays in classroom
  alphabet, 27
  library, 126
  print at children's eye level, 22
Disruptive behavior. *See* Challenging behavior
Diversity, English-language learners and, 54
DLL (dual-language learners). *See* English-
    language learners (ELL); First languages
Doctor's office play, 144
Dolls in dramatic play, 144
Doughs for molding, 151
Dramatic play
  address book in, 143
  books for, 140–141
  doctor's office play, 144
  dolls in, 144
  dress-up clothes in, 98–99, 143
  food containers in, 143
  interacting with children, 143–144
  literacy skills and, 139–144
  materials and props for. *See* Dramatic props
  message board in, 143
  observing and responding to children, 144
  as outdoor activity, 181
  stuffed animals in, 144
  telephone and telephone book in, 143
  writing skills and, 106–107
Dramatic props
  clothesline story props, 88, 98
  literacy and, 140, 142–144
  picture props, 98
  for story retelling, 98–99
  for storytelling, 95

Drawing, distinguishing writing from, 23
Dress-up clothes, 98–99, 143
Dual-language learners (DLL). *See* English-
    language learners (ELL); First languages

E

English-language learners (ELL), 49–57
  alphabet learning and, 26, 28
  cultural supports for, 54
  developmental sequence of language
    acquisition, 50, 51
  environmental supports for, 54
  family partnership supports for, 57
  individual differences in language
    acquisition among, 50
  instructional strategies for, 52–53
  language supports for, 55
  levels of English language acquisition,
    51–53
  library displays aimed at, 126
  literacy programs for, 49–57
  objectives for, 41
  phonological awareness and, 15
  primary languages. *See* First languages
  pronunciation of, 15
  repetition for, 15
  socio-emotional supports for, 54
  story retelling and, 97
  understanding primary language prior to
    learning English, 9
Environmental print, 19, 21, 22, 143, 146
Environment in classroom. *See* Classroom
    space
Equipment. *See* Materials and equipment
Ethnic diversity, English-language learners
    and, 54
Expressive language, 9
Eye level of children
  alphabet displayed at, 27
  print displayed at, 22

F

Fables, 35
Fairy tales and folktales, 35
Family, reading aloud with, 87
Family partnerships
  English-language learners and, 57
  language development and, 74
  literacy skills and, 8, 63
  phonological awareness and, 18
  tips for. *See* Tips for families
Fantasy books, 35
Fantasy play. *See* Dramatic play
Fiction books, 35
Fingerplay, 12
First languages
  acquisition of language proficiency in, 9
  alphabet learning and, 26, 28
  library books in, 126
  maintaining and promoting, 50
  use in classroom, 12, 51, 52
Fishing. *See* Sand and water play
Flowers
  in Discovery area, 155
  study of, 118–123
Folktales, 35

Food
  containers as dramatic props, 143
  cooking. *See* Cooking
  literacy skills and, 47
Formulaic speech, 51, 53
Friendships, in literacy experiences, 8
Future, concept of, 11, 23

G

Games. *See* Toys and games
Getting attention of children. *See* Attention/
    attention span
Gifted children. *See* Advanced learners
Goals. *See* Objectives
GOLD® assessment system, 42
Gross-motor skills, outdoor play and, 180
Group time
  group games, 180
  literacy skills and, 46

H

Headphones, 127
Hearing impaired children. *See* Children with
    disabilities
Hollow blocks, 137

I

Information, learning to write records of, 105
Informational books, 34, 35, 36, 37, 154–155
Instructions. *See* Directions
Intellectual development, objectives of, 41
Intentional teaching, language development
    and, 9
Intentional Teaching Cards™, 27, 97
Interacting with children. *See also* Teacher's
    role
  block play, 137–138
  cooking, 170–171
  Discovery area, 155–156
  dramatic play, 143–144
  library, 130–132
  literacy skills, 11
  music and movement, 164–165
  outdoor play, 180–181
  play incorporating literacy learning,
    114–117
  sand and water play, 160
  technology, 174–175
  toys and games area, 146–147
  visual arts, 150–151
Interactive storybook programs, 175
Interest areas
  books related to, 12
  literacy skills in, 124–181. *See also* Literacy
    skills

J

Journals, 106

K

Kitchen area. *See* Cooking
Knowledge of print
  defined, 19
  development of, 21
  play and, 112
  reading aloud and, 75
  research on, 21–22
  role of adults, 22
  storytelling and, 88
  teacher's role, 22–24, 66
  writing and, 103

L

Labeling, children helping with, 23
Language, defined, 9
Language delays, 133
Language development. *See also* English-
    language learners (ELL); First languages
  of advanced learners, 58
  in children with disabilities, 60
  environment to promote development of, 68
  examples of supporting oral language
    learning, 69–73
  expressive language, 9
  family involvement, 74
  objectives of, 41–42
  phonological awareness. *See* Phonological
    awareness
  planning oral language experiences, 67–68
  play and, 112
  productive/fluid use of language, 51, 53
  receptive language, 9
  story retelling and, 97
  storytelling and, 88
  supports for, 55
  teacher's role, 11–12, 66
  toys and games and, 12
  writing and, 103
Learning, approaches to, 33
Letters. *See* Alphabet/letters and words;
    Literacy skills
Letter writing, 105
Library. *See also* Books
  book selection, 126
  challenges in, 133–134
  choice time and, 8
  classroom space for, 7
  displaying and caring for materials, 126
  interacting with children, 130–132
  listening to readings and stories in, 132
  literacy skills and, 5, 7, 126–134
  materials for, 126–127
  observing and responding to children,
    128–129
  writing and, 106, 132
Listening materials, 127
Listening skills
  audio recordings, listening to with children,
    132
  comprehension, 30, 32–33, 66, 84, 128
  games for improving, 32
  phonological awareness and, 13, 14
  repeated read-alouds, 84
  responding to adult's tone of voice and
    expression, 7
  Listening vocabulary, 9

List-making, 105
Literacy as source of enjoyment
  development of, 4–5
  play and, 112
  reading aloud and, 75
  story retelling and, 97
  storytelling and, 88
  teacher's role in promoting, 7–8, 66
  writing and, 103
Literacy programs, 38–63
  for advanced learners, 58
  for children with disabilities, 59–60
  daily schedule for, 45–48, 61–62
  for English-language learners, 49–57
  environment for, 43–44, 61
  family involvement in, 57, 63
  guide to implementation, 61–63
  inclusion of all children in, 49–60
  objectives for, 41–42
  overview, 39–40
  tracking progress in, 62
Literacy skills, 1–181. *See also* Reading skills
  arrival and, 45
  block play and, 135–138
  books and. *See* Books
  challenging yet achievable experiences, 5
  choice time and, 46
  components of literacy, 3
  comprehension and. *See* Comprehension
  cooking and, 166–171
  in daily schedule, 45–48, 61–62
  departure and, 48
  Discovery area and, 153–157
  dramatic play and, 139–144
  environment to promote development of,
    6, 43–44
  family involvement, 8, 63
  group time and, 46
  interacting with children, 11
  interest areas and, 44, 125
  language development and. *See* Language
    development
  letters and words. *See* Alphabet/letters and
    words
  library and, 5, 7, 126–134
  modeling, 4, 11
  music and movement and, 12, 68, 161–166
  objectives, 41–42
  offering choices and, 5
  outdoor play and, 48, 177–181
  phonological awareness and. *See*
    Phonological awareness
  play and. *See* Play incorporating literacy
    learning
  print and. *See* Print
  program planning. *See* Literacy programs
  reading aloud and. *See* Reading aloud
  research on, 6, 10
  rest time and, 48
  role of adults in development of, 6
  sand and water play and, 158–161
  small groups and, 46
  snack and mealtime and, 47
  story retelling and. *See* Story retelling
  storytelling and. *See* Storytelling
  teacher's role, 7–8, 11–12, 65
  technology and, 172–176
  toys and games and, 12, 145–147
  transition times and, 48
  visual arts and, 148–152

  vocabulary growth and. *See* Vocabulary
    growth
  writing and. *See* Writing skills
Lotto games, 146

M

Magnetic letters, 146
Markers, 151
Materials and equipment
  adaptive, 134
  assistive, 59, 134
  for block play, 136
  for cooking, 167
  for Discovery area, 154
  displaying and labeling. *See* Displays in
    classroom
  for dramatic play. *See* Dramatic props
  for listening, 127
  for music and movement, 163
  for outdoor play, 178
  for play incorporating literacy learning, 113
  for sand and water play, 159
  for story retelling, 127
  technology, 173
  for toys and games, 146
  for visual arts, *149*
  for writing, 106–107, 127, 132
Mathematics objectives, 41
McGee, L. M., 84
Mealtimes. *See also* Food
  literacy skills and, 47
Message board as dramatic prop, 143
Misbehavior. *See* Challenging behavior
Mobile devices. *See* Technology
Modeling
  language, 11
  literacy skills, 4, 11
  story retelling, 98
  writing skills, 21, 23
Molding materials, 151
Morning activities. *See* Daily schedule
Motor skills. *See* Gross-motor skills
Movement. *See* Music and movement
Musical instruments, 165
Music and movement
  alphabet song, 25, 27
  books for, 35, 163–164
  interacting with children, 164–165
  literacy skills and, 12, 68, 161–166
  materials for, 163
  observing and responding to children, 166
  singing. *See* Singing

N

Name games, 147
Names of children
  children learning to write, 104
  recognition of letters in, 25
Narrative picture books, 34, 84
Narrative talk. *See* Storytelling
Natural environment
  materials and collections, 156
  outdoor play and, 180
Nonverbal period in English language
    acquisition, 51, 52

O

Objectives
arts, 41
cognitive development, 41
English-language learners, 41
language development, 41–42
literacy skills, 41–42
mathematics, 41
physical development, 41
science, 41
social–emotional development, 41
social studies, 41
technology, 41
Observational period in English language acquisition, 51, 52
Observing and responding to children
block play, 138
cooking, 171
Discovery area, 157
dramatic play, 144
library, 128–129
music and movement, 166
outdoor play, 181
play incorporating literacy learning, 114
sand and water play, 161
technology, 176
toys and games, 147
visual arts, 152
Onset and phonological awareness, 13, 14, 16
Open-ended questions. *See also* Interacting with children
literacy skills and, 11
Oral language development. *See* Language development
Outdoor play
books for, 179
dramatic play, 181
games, 180
interacting with children, 180–181
literacy skills and, 48, 177–181
materials for, 178
observing and responding to children, 181
sand and water play. *See* Sand and water play

P

Painting, 150
Parents. *See* Family partnerships
Patience, 11
Peer relationships, in literacy experiences, 8
Pets, caring for, 155
Phonemes
defined, 13
levels of development, 13, 14
research on, 17
Phonemic awareness, 13
Phonics, 15
Phonological awareness, 13–18
alphabet learning and, 25–26, 28
defined, 13
English-language learners and, 15
family participation in, 18
levels of, 13–14
music and movement and, 164
reading aloud and, 75
research on, 16–17
story retelling and, 97
storytelling and, 88
teacher's role, 17–18, 66
writing and, 103

Physical development
objectives of, 41
outdoor play and, 180
Physical science. *See* Science
Picture books, 34, 84, 154
Picture props, 98
Pictures drawn by children. *See* Visual arts
"Picture walk" prior to reading books, 33
Planning
daily schedule. *See* Daily schedule
literacy programs. *See* Literacy programs
oral language experiences, 67–68
Plants in classroom, 155
Play
block play. *See* Block play
computer play. *See* Computer play
dramatic play. *See* Dramatic play
literacy skills and. *See* Play incorporating literacy learning
outdoor. *See* Outdoor play
print and, 24
sand and water. *See* Sand and water play
Play incorporating literacy learning, 112–117
benefits of, 112
factors for consideration, 5
getting started, 113
interactions with children during, 114–117
materials for, 113
opportunities for, 37
physical environment for, 113
teacher's role, 114–117
tips for families, 117
Poetry, 34, 35
Postings in classroom. *See* Displays in classroom
Pretend play. *See* Dramatic play
Print, 19–24. *See also* Literacy skills
conventions of, 20–21, 23
environmental, 19, 21, 22, 143, 146
forms of, 20
functions and value of, 19
knowledge of. *See* Knowledge of print
in literacy-rich environment, 43, 44
matching words with, 129
research on, 21–22
Printmaking, 151
Pronunciation, 15
Props. *See* Dramatic props; Materials and equipment
Puppets, 99
Puzzles. *See also* Toys and games
literacy skills and, 146

Q

Questioning. *See also* Interacting with children
encouraging children to ask questions, 32, 33
open-ended questions, 11

R

Reading aloud, 75–87. *See also* Storytelling
book selection for, 76
capturing attention of children prior to, 7, 78
comprehension and, 31, 33, 84
in daily schedule, 12, 77
effective methods for, 78–79
example of, 80–83

follow-up activities, 79
to groups of children, 23
knowledge of print and, 75
in library, 130–131
locations for, 78
to one child, 131
phonological awareness and, 75
"picture walk" prior to, 33
planning for groups and individuals, 77
practicing prior to, 78
repeated read-alouds, 84–86, 128, 131
research on, 10, 36
time allowed for, 77
tips for families, 87
tips for teachers, 78–79
vocabulary growth and, 75, 84
Reading skills. *See also* Books; Literacy skills
conversational, 86
pretending to read, 128
research on, 10
Reading vocabulary, 9
Receptive language, 9
Recipes, 170
Repeated read-alouds, 84–86, 128, 131
Repetition
for English-language learners, 15
rereading. *See* Reading aloud
story retelling. *See* Story retelling
vocabulary growth and, 11
Rephrasing, 32
Research. *See* Theory and research
Responding to children. *See* Interacting with children; Observing and responding to children
Rest time, literacy skills and, 48
Retelling stories. *See* Story retelling
Rhyming, 13, 14, 16, 68
Rime and phonological awareness, 13, 14, 16
Routines offering support to children with disabilities, 59
Rules, games with, 33

S

Sand and water play
books for, 159
interacting with children, 160
literacy skills and, 158–161
materials for, 159
observing and responding to children in, 161
Scheduling. *See* Daily schedule
Schickedanz, J. A., 84
Science
Discovery area and, 156
objectives, 41
Second-language learning. *See* English-language learners (ELL)
"See, show, say" (3S) strategy, 86
Sensory learning, 28
Sensory table or sensory tubs, 156
Sentence construction, 14
Sequence cards, 147
Shapes and patterns, 28
Showing while telling, 86
Sight vocabulary, 129
Signs, in block play, 138. *See also* Displays in classroom
Singing, 66, 68, 164–165. *See also* Music and movement

Small groups
  literacy skills for, 46
  reading groups in Library area, 130–131
Snack time. *See also* Food
  literacy skills and, 47
Social–emotional development
  English-language learners and, 54
  objectives of, 41
Social studies objectives, 41
Sociodramatic play. *See also* Dramatic play
  language development and, 112
Songbooks, 35, 164
Songs. *See* Music and movement; Singing
Sounds, connecting written symbols with, 128.
  See also Phonological awareness
Speaking skills. *See* Language development
Speaking vocabulary, 9
Special needs children. *See* Advanced learners;
  Children with disabilities
Stages of play. *See* Developmental stages
Start of day. *See* Daily schedule
Storybooks. *See* Books
Story comprehension, 33
Story retelling, 97–102
  benefits of, 97
  classroom space for, 99
  comprehension and, 33, 97
  example of, 99–102
  facilitating, 33
  getting started, 97–99
  materials for, 127
  modeling ways to retell stories, 98
  props for, 98–99
  selecting appropriate stories for, 98
  support for, 99
  teacher's role, 132
  tips for families, 102
Story structure, 88, 97, 128
Storytelling, 88–96. *See also* Reading aloud
  active participation during, 7
  benefits of, 88
  example of, 91–95
  making pleasurable, 7
  oral, 90
  preparing for, 89–90
  props and visual aids used with, 95
  selecting appropriate stories for, 89–90
  thinking of yourself as storyteller, 89
  tips for families, 96
  tips for teachers, 90
Story time, 7. *See also* Library; Storytelling
Studies and projects in literacy to learn (study
  of flowers), 118–123
Stuffed animals in dramatic play, 144
Subtractive model of English acquisition, 50
Syllables, identification of, 13, 14, 16

T

Tablets. *See* Technology
Tactile cues and supports, 59
Take-aparts, 156
Teacher–child relationships
  challenging behavior. *See* Challenging
    behavior
  children with disabilities. *See* Children with
    disabilities
  cultural differences of English-language
    learners, 54
  interactions. *See* Interacting with children
Teacher's role

alphabet, learning of, 27–28
books, 7–8, 37, 66
comprehension skills, 32–33, 66
English-language learners. *See* English-
  language learners (ELL)
interacting with children. *See* Interacting
  with children
knowledge of print, 22–24, 66
language development, 11–12, 66
literacy skills, 7–8, 11–12, 65
modeling. *See* Modeling
observing. *See* Observing and responding
  to children
phonological awareness, 17–18, 66
play incorporating literacy learning,
  114–117
story retelling, 132
vocabulary development, 11–12, 66
Technology. *See also* Computer play
  assistive. *See* Assistive devices
  books related to, 173
  interacting with children, 174–175
  literacy skills and, 172–176
  materials, 173
  objectives, 41
  observing and responding to children, 176
Telegraphic speech, 51, 53
Telephone and telephone book as dramatic
  prop, 143
Theory and research
  alphabet, 26
  books, 36
  comprehension, 31
  knowledge of print, 21–22
  literacy skills, 6, 10
  phonological awareness, 16–17
  reading aloud, 10, 36
  reading development, 10
  vocabulary development, 10
Three-dimensional art, 151
Time during day. *See* Daily schedule
Tips for families
  play incorporating literacy learning, 117
  reading aloud, 87
  story retelling, 102
  storytelling, 96
  writing skills, 111
Tools. *See* Materials and equipment
Toys and games
  books for, 146
  concentration games, 146
  construction toys, 147
  group games, 180
  interacting with children, 146–147
  language development and, 12
  listening games, 32
  literacy skills and, 12, 145–147
  lotto games, 146
  materials for, 146
  name games, 147
  observing and responding to children, 147
  outdoor activities, 180
  rules for, 33
  with storybook or nursery rhyme characters,
    147
Transition times, literacy skills and, 48

U

Unit blocks, 137
Utensils. *See* Materials and equipment

V

Vision impairment. *See* Children with
  disabilities
Visual arts
  books for, 149–150
  interacting with children, 150–151
  literacy skills and, 148–152
  materials for, *149*
  molding materials (clay and dough), 151
  observing and responding to children, 152
  painting, 150
  three-dimensional art, 151
  woodworking, 151
Visual cues and supports, 59
Vocabulary growth. *See also* Language
  development; Literacy skills
  comprehension and, 32
  personal word collections and, 28
  play and, 112
  reading aloud and, 75, 84
  repetition to reinforce, 11
  research on, 10
  sight vocabulary, 129
  story retelling and, 97
  storytelling and, 88
  teacher's role, 11–12, 66
  types of, 9
  writing and, 103

W

Water play. *See* Sand and water play
Wheelchair accessibility, 59
Woodworking, 151
Wordless books, 34, 35
Word processing programs, 174–175
Words. *See also* Alphabet/letters and words;
  Literacy skills; Phonological awareness
  learning about, 129
  matching with print, 129
  personal word collections, 28
Work time. *See* Choice time
Writing materials, 106–107, 127, 132
Writing skills, 103–111. *See also* Literacy skills
  benefits of, 103
  challenging behavior and, 134
  developmental levels of writing, 129
  distinguishing writing from drawing, 23
  dramatic play and, 106–107
  example of supporting children's writing,
    107–111
  getting started, 104–107
  library and, 106, 132
  materials and opportunities for, 106–107,
    127, 132
  modeling of, 21, 23
  planning writing experiences, 104–106
  promoting, 22–24
  strengths, needs, and interests of children,
    104
  tips for families, 111
Writing vocabulary, 9